To

The Members of '73 Squad'

wherever they may be

Their names do not appear in this book,
but they are here in spirit.
So – also in spirit – are all the people
who tried, with varying degrees of success,
to turn us into soldiers.

3

NATIONAL SERVICE: EARNING THE PIPS

REFLECTIONS ON OFFICER SELECTION 1947-1963

Berwick Coates

Published by Berwick Coates

© Berwick Coates 2021

ISBN 978-1-78222-853-0

Internal photographs by the author.

Book design, layout and production management by Into Print
www.intoprint.net
01604 832149

Acknowledgments

No book gets born all by itself, and the author is not the only midwife. I owe a debt, as before, to Yvonne Reed, who was involved from the very first pangs as Head of Accuracy, Correctness, and Style; to Mark Webb, of Paragon Publishing, who does the technical stuff with paper, print, promotion on the internet, and all other matters mechanical; and to my son Stephen, who is strong on ideas, research, sideways thinking, patience with a parent, and general filial devotion.

Contents

1   20p. a day

I DON'T RECKON NATIONAL SERVICE was all that bad – not really. Looking back. I shall probably attract more abuse for that statement than I ever received in two full years in the Army. Rather like the chap who said that he thought the fuss made over Princess Diana's funeral was a mite over the top – and look what happened to him. Or the High Court Judge who asked who the Spice Girls were.

Going against the tide, you see. Risky.

I mean, consider what happens when they ask famous people about their memories of National Service. Talk about a chronicle of woe and a diatribe of recrimination. All about mindlessness and boorishness and endless repetition and stupid rules; about degradation and humiliation and abuse; about interruption of promising careers and warping of delicate aesthetic tastes.

As if the Armed Forces had a monopoly on mindlessness and stupid rules. Have they never heard of the Civil Service? Or committee meetings? Or Question Time in the House of Commons? Why single out the Army for its apparent absence of cerebration? As for endless repetition, anybody who has had anything to do with the art of instruction will tell you that the oldest, safest, most proven and most permanent way to get something into someone's head is to repeat it – endlessly. In one form or another – it doesn't have to be the same way. Mindbenders from Confucius to Hitler have subscribed to that idea. Look at all the advertising jingles we learn from the box – and we're not even listening. Speaking as one who has been on the receiving or the giving end of education for most of his life, I have often been struck by the Forces' excellent record in this field. When they teach you something – firstly they teach you all about it, from A to Z; secondly, they teach you systematically and logically (it may be tied hand and foot to the training pamphlet, but the training pamphlet does contain all the relevant knowledge – it is a sort of expert); and thirdly, when they have finished teaching you, you generally stay taught. Interestingly, the most carping critics among those intellectuals I spoke about could all remember their Army (or Navy or Air Force) numbers.

Degradation? Humiliation? Abuse? Well, of course, there must have been some. But is the office or the factory floor free from it? Or the public school changing room? Or the football terrace? Or the council estate? If the Army really was as mindless as its reminiscent critics would have us believe, how come it showed the imagination and creativity to evolve degrading, humiliating, or abusive practices which took such arts into fresh and more rarefied – nay – unique realms of misery-infliction?

And, while we're on the subject, and supposing for a minute that the moaners were right, how come the British fighting soldier in the 1950's (the high-water mark of National Service) was still, ten years after the War, reckoned to be the most reliable and adaptable human combat unit in the world? Not all the fighting was being done by the Regular Army. I was at college with someone who had lost a leg in Korea, and I did not detect a trace of bitterness in his make-up or in his speech.

Which brings us to the interruption of promising careers – you know, two years of roughing it with unsavoury, common people; accommodation which would have made a Spartan wince; nasty, dirty jobs to do in nasty, dirty parts of the world; the trauma of separation from the balmy groves of Academe. Have you noticed the ambition of increasing numbers of school-leavers these days? There they all are, with their bunches of 'A' Levels and their Prefects' badges and their First Eleven Colours, and their places at university assured, and they can't wait to take 'time out'. Doing what? Cadging lifts on trans-globe hikes in bone-shaking lorries full of dark-jowled Kurdish freedom-fighters; bottle-feeding starving infants in Rwanda; horse-breaking in the outback; kipping fifty to a room in a long-house in Borneo; avoiding requests in Caracas Airport from Colombian drug-pushers to hold their bags for a minute. The rougher, the dirtier, the dodgier the better. And they fully expect the experience to prove an enhancement of their university and future career.

So where does that leave us? It leaves us with a possibility – two possibilities actually. Firstly, that those vociferous, intellectual critics might be wrong. Secondly, that the abiding impression about National Service that has reached us has been conditioned, even totally shaped, by the memories of those very critics, for the simple reason that they were the ones who got into print, into the newspapers, on the radio, and on to the box.

Far from their careers being blighted by two years in uniform, some of them craftily built their careers *out* of it. Plays about the ubiquity of deep-fried chipped potatoes and the varying height of young soldiers in the tropical jungle, I venture to suppose, did nothing bad for the respective authors' self-esteem or bank balances.

Now – suppose the silent majority were to speak up. It might tell us what it was really like for that majority. For example, we know next to nothing about what life was like for a medieval peasant because your average medieval peasant could neither read nor write, and even if he could have, he would have had little time in a busy day to record his experiences and his thoughts. We have to deduce a life for him, from the pitiful and scanty remains of artefacts and field systems, and from the pious remarks of his superiors who generally thought it was good for a peasant to be a peasant because it was God's Scheme for everything. Suppose those peasants had been able to speak. . . .

Now, I wasn't a particularly brilliant undergraduate or games player, nor a dazzling intellectual, nor a gifted writer – not that much of a soldier either, if the truth be known. Yes, I know, the fact that I admit to 'undergraduate' marks me at once. But I was pretty ordinary for what I was, that is the point. So I feel admirably placed to give the humdrum view, to show what it was probably like for the general run of us.

It is about time to suggest that, for many of us, National Service was not necessarily the awful combination of Dotheboys Hall and Changi Jail that our more articulate and literary survivors would impose upon a credulous world. It was no Butlin's holiday camp either. It was like every other slice of our lives – a bit of good and a bit of bad and a large chunk of ordinary. Oh – and perhaps a bit of funny too. And seeing it like that – good, bad, indifferent, funny – isn't that what gets us through everything?

We need reminding of this from time to time. We need alternative voices to those literary 'forces' which have a distressing propensity to focus on the bad parts. War may have been hell, and still is, but I should like to put it to the jury that National Service was not. Not for most of us.

It began, for all of us – intellectual and otherwise, budding playwrights and ploughboys, rebels and conformists – with a buff letter 'On Her Majesty's Service'. 'You are required to report. . . . ' Where to go. When to arrive. No more. No words wasted. But there was one charming little addition. A postal order. Your first day's pay in advance – how considerate of them. Four shillings. 20p. I kid you not. 20p. But even that was a rise on what soldiers had been paid during the War, which had finished only ten years before. My father told me that, when he joined up in 1939, his first week's pay had been five shillings – 25p. For a week. So you see? It was all relative.

To be strictly accurate, this letter was not my first brush with the military machine. I was twenty-one, with a three-year university course behind me. National Service normally began at eighteen. One of the great debates that raged – at any rate among the youth of the nation who hoped to go on to university – was, which should come first? Army or University? (From now on in this chapter I use the word 'Army' as a means of referring to the Armed Forces generally, although, as you will have gathered if you have been following me closely, it was the Army for which I was destined. I should imagine that there were many factors common to all three services.)

Yes – Army or University? We were given to understand that

there was a choice. Boys in their final year in hundreds of sixth forms up and down the country furrowed their pink brows and pondered the mighty question of whether a couple of years in uniform first would make them 'more mature' – as if they could have any idea at that age. Or would the 'sophistication' of a university equip them better to deal with service life? Ha! When, to many a prognathous corporal, anything beyond the eleven plus represented 'brains' and was therefore suspect. And ripe for cutting down to size. (Incidentally, another great debate was whether membership of one's school cadet force enabled one the more easily to obtain a commission. Ha! again. I don't remember anyone ever asking me whether I had been in my school cadet force. My impression, then and since, is that the War Office couldn't have cared less whether we had, as fifteen-year-olds, clambered over some distant heath in oversized, bulgy khaki uniforms, or daubed our downy cheeks with blacking and crawled through soaking bracken on night patrols in the local park. More of this 'commission' business later.)

Oh, and I hadn't. Been in the school cadet force.

So – once again – Army or University?

No shortage of advice. Parents. Neighbours. Relations. You expect that. Most of it well-intentioned and ill-informed. At least they only *think* they know best. Worse – far worse – were those who *knew* they knew best.

Everybody has a family acquaintance like Mrs. Titchmarsh. On all the committees. Knows everybody. Brow and jawline like Mount Rushmore. Never had a doubt in her life. Fixes you with her eye and says, 'I see. And into which regiment are you going to be commissioned?'

It's one of those 'When-did-you-stop-beating-your-wife?' questions, isn't it? Unluckily, this wasn't the new millennium, when you might have been tempted to tell the silly old bat that she was living in the wrong century. It was the 1950's. A respectable suburban house. No teenage purchasing power. No Top of the Pops. No school counsellors pushing stuff into your head about 'talking things through'. No politicians droning on about a children's charter. No media hype, no dropping out, no communes, no four-letter words in print, no live-in lovers, no partners, no drugs, condom machines, porn videos, earrings for men, studs in noses, or zips in trousers. Imagine – no Eurovision Song Contest. 'Mainline' was still the 6.45 to Waterloo; 'rock' was what you bought at the seaside; a 'trip' was a fourpenny bus ride on Sunday afternoon; 'hardcore' was the inside of a cricket ball. 'Young people' didn't exist. The world had barely got used to the term 'teenager'. A decade out of the War, we were unbelievably obedient, tightly-mannered, and conformist.

'Into which regiment are you going to be commissioned?'

What could you do? How could you begin? You simply fiddled with the frayed hem of your knitting pattern pullover and mumbled something about not being too sure yet.

Which would provoke a raised eyebrow or two, and some heavily sententious remarks to the effect that one never got anywhere unless one showed decisiveness and determination. These were coupled with a comparison between us and the keen-eyed, tense-jawed previous generation which had known exactly where it was going and exactly what it wanted. (The one which caused the Second World War.)

How enviable certainty is! Especially when you don't have any. When you are too young to realise, as Peter Ustinov has pointed out, that it is the certainties in this world that have divided people, the uncertainties that have united them. It is only later that you understand that certainty is, on the contrary, slightly frightening.

I once saw a documentary about young boys in private preparatory schools. Well scrubbed and frightfully well spoken – though that is of course no crime. What was impressive about them was the awful – perhaps I should have said 'awe-inspiring' – certainty with which they outlined their future careers. 'Oh, yes,' said one plummy little goblin, 'when I am thirteen I shall go to Winchester. And after that I shall go to Trinity Hall.' (He pronounced it 'Hawl'.)

Note. He did not *hope* to go to public school. He *knew* he was going there, and he knew which one. He did not wonder whether he would reach the required standard for any university; he *knew* he was going. He knew which one – Cambridge. And he even knew which college in Cambridge. He was seven. I believe there was a later documentary which vindicated his forecasts.

The other species of expert is the one who has done everything – or says he has. Ever met the Major Burleigh type? Sort of professional guest. 'Retired', of course, though the 'Major' nomenclature was much in evidence. Fond of reminiscence; fond too of pretty well anything alcoholic. The outpouring of the former varied in exact proportion to the intake of the latter. His regular accounts of his wartime experiences became progressively harder to unravel and relate to each other, much less believe, as his elbow became more lubricated.

He claimed acquaintance with every military theatre of war between 1939 and 1945 except the Russian Front. He had been 'attached to the staff' of every Allied general from Eisenhower and de Gaulle to 'Vinegar Joe' Stilwell and Chiang-Kai-Shek. He had been involved in 'jolly queer shows' in Crete, Norway, Borneo, and Abyssinia. He had ventured 'behind the lines' in the Apennines, the Ardennes, the Western Desert, and the Burmese jungle. He had served 'on special detachment' in liaison groups, intelligence groups, partisan groups, demolition groups, rearguard groups, advance groups, and back-up groups. He had been 'one of the last five men' off the beaches of Dunkirk. It had been his white handkerchief which had been tied to the flag of surrender at Tobruk. 'Always kept a clean one. Tucked away just in case. Lifelong habit.' (He escaped later, of course – with Douglas Bader. Bader got recaptured two days later, poor chap. 'Tin legs, you see.') He had helped to get the lifts going again on the Eiffel Tower after the Liberation. And he was the interrogating officer who had tried to prise the cyanide capsule from between the teeth of the captured Himmler. 'Grubby little beggar. Shocking fingernails.'

It was hardly surprising that he maintained the 'Major' rank into civilian life. The wonder was that he had not bumped it up to Brigadier. Perhaps he had thought about it – even tried it out on the back of an envelope. Decided that the jarring alliterative juxtaposition might have raised suspicions.

He ticked over on small stipends from a string of sports clubs and charity organisations for which he performed nominal fund-raising tasks. It kept him in tweed jackets and printed notepaper, and was enough to satisfy a purse-lipped landlady. The required visits and socialising ensured that he rarely put his hand in his pocket for meals, cigarettes, or drinks. It was a perfect arrangement.

The Major's reaction to the news of any young man's imminent entry into Her Majesty's Forces was predictable and mind-numbing in its unhelpfulness.

'Teach you a thing or two, m'lad. Wish I had it to do all over again. Reminds me of a young feller I came across with the Resistance in Brittany. Very fair hair. I particularly remember his hair. . . . '

So much for family and the experts.

Friends were not much better.

'The bulling is something awful. Their idea is to make life absolute hell for the first fortnight, just for the sake of it.' ['Bulling' ? If you don't know, see Chapter 8.]

'Friend of mine said he cried himself to sleep for a week.'

'It ruins you for study afterwards. Blokes at university are bags of nerves, can't concentrate, fluff their exams, get sent down.'

'Chap I know had a nervous breakdown. Jealous of his degree. They broke him. Just like a dry stick. Broke him.'

You try to throw up a feeble *laager* of resistance, if only for your own peace of mind.

'Surely some must survive?'

They're ready for that one too.

'Good Lord, yes. I knew a chap who had a degree in Maths. He got a posting as paymaster in some regiment, with captain's rank and pay.'

'My brother-in-law's cousin knew a general who wangled him a job in the War Office. Just like any City businessman, he was. Never even wore uniform.'

'My friend went on the Army Russian course. Spent two years in Cambridge. Then he came out and went to Oxford to read Modern Languages. Neat, eh?'

'A bloke from our school went to live in Guernsey, and never got called up at all. You only have to stay there till you're twenty-six.'

'And you can always be a conscientious objector. They make you clean lavatories instead.'

Which got you no nearer to resolving the Army-or-University-first problem. It got you no nearer any useful conclusion at all. As you had no degree in Maths, no relative on the Imperial General Staff, no natural propensity for Slavonic languages, no burning desire to spend several years in the Channel Islands, and no obsession with indoor plumbing, you were faced with the prospect of a period of inhuman privation and mental torture which had every likelihood of reducing you to a gibbering wreck within a month.

At least it had the merit of forcing you back on yourself. It would have to be your own decision, for better or worse. Ignorance, immaturity, wrong priorities and all.

So – Army, Navy, or Air Force? Not that a wayward selection officer would necessarily give you what you asked for, but one could always hope. It was as well to have an answer ready just in case you were to be given a choice. Not much trouble there. Army, without question. Family tradition? Hardly. My father's father had been a stationery buyer for a grocery chain all his working life, and my maternal grandfather had been a horse-bus driver. My father had volunteered in 1939 because I fancy he thought it would be fun. He always maintained afterwards that his veterinary practice had half-died because so many people had had their pets put down for fear of the air raids. My mother gave a short derisive laugh and made reference to a fat file of unpaid bills that would, Father hoped, not pursue him into khaki. (It would seem, correctly.) There was also the fact that the vast majority of young men were sent, when their time came, into the Army. It was far and away the biggest of the three arms. So, statistically, I had a greater chance of having my request fulfilled.

More to the point, I preferred the sober security of the Army. You could get shot at in the Army, probably more than in the Navy or the RAF. But I didn't fancy getting shot at on the water; even if you survived the shooting, there was still all that wet. And in the Air Force, all that air. I could, at a pinch, swim a bit, but, as the man said, I couldn't fly an inch. No – if I was going to risk life and limb, I wanted solid earth under me. No Senior Service noble tradition for me. And as for the wide blue yonder, you could keep it.

Now – University first? Or National Service? There usually was a genuine choice here. If you wanted to go straight on to college, you simply filled in a form, and that was, so far as I remember, that. Well, I had enjoyed my school life, and I was very fond of History, my chosen subject. At the time, I could think of nothing I wanted to do more than three years of History – to say nothing of three years of hockey and cricket. If something unattractive like National Service could be put off for three years, that was fine. The Government might have changed its mind by then – who knew?

And the clincher was the bird-in-the-hand argument. At the end of that three years at college, I hoped to get a degree. Now, remember these were the days before the great opening up of university education, before they built all those new universities in places where they'd only had cricket grounds before. I was a boy from a very ordinary home. My mother and father had separated, and my mother had brought me up single-handed, on a shoe-string. I was on free school meals and free milk and free bus fares and free scholarship. To be 'going to university', then, for a lad like me, was quite something. Only one member of my father's family had ever done it (a distant cleric), and nobody at all on my mother's side. Not all that many pupils from grammar schools went anyway. Not then.

So, having got this far, and having, though I say so myself, worked rather hard to get there, I was going to do nothing to jeopardise it. Two years' extra maturity after the Army? You could keep it. What did it mean anyway? Thicker sideburns and a richer vocabulary of swearwords. Big deal! No. Get a degree – that became what I later discovered in the Army was called 'the overall strategic objective'. Whatever happened afterwards – whether I became a brilliant officer, a humble corporal, a mind-broken zombie, or a dehumanised killing machine – I would be able to put 'B.A.' after my name. Nobody – not even God – barring miracles or Armageddon – would be able to take that away from me.

So I filled in my deferment form and went off to college.

2   Health Grade 'A'

THE LONG ARM OF OHMS reached out for me near the end of my third year at college, a few weeks before my finals. The plain buff envelope contained something much less interesting than a naughty book (about the only way you could get them in those days – no full frontals in newsagents, much less soap-opera required lesbians on the telly), but it concentrated the thoughts far more than any forbidden magazine.

It informed me that a centre for medical examination was about to be set up in my university city, for the purposes of ascertaining whether the young men due to enter HM's Forces in the coming autumn had all their limbs sewn on at the right corners, and that I was required to present myself on the date indicated in section whatever-it-was. If nothing else, it took my mind off worrying about the coming exams.

I don't think I'd ever had a 'medical' before. Not a full, proper, thorough, clothes-off, one-hundred-per-cent going-over. The usual coughs and colds as an infant. 'Put him to bed for a couple of days and give him this medicine.' That sort of thing. The most painful complaint I had had was sinus trouble. Terrible headaches – well, terrible for a nine-year-old. The doctor looked at my face, prodded my cheeks, and asked me where it hurt. I told him 'just over the eye'.

'Ah,' he said, and began tapping the spot indicated, with fingertips like hammers. He carried on tapping absently as he turned and explained the machinery of the sinuses to my mother.

'Recurring pain, probably at the same time every day. Am I right?' Still tapping.

'Yes,' said my mother. 'What can you do about it?'

'Not a great deal. I can give you some inhalant; that might give some relief. Time, probably, will do the trick.'

Tap, tap, tap.

'It might come over one eye; it might come over the other. No telling.'

At this point the patient reminded the company of his existence by slumping forward and nearly being sick.

Neither my mother nor I forgave him for that. We never went to him again.

Then there was dear Doctor Malvern. A busy, tablets-and-medicine-bottle GP. They didn't call them pills. (When did 'tablets' become 'pills'?) He looked after my mother and me for years. Saw her through a couple of stays in hospital, and saw me through the usual spots and allergies of adolescence. But I don't think I ever had to remove – not completely – a single item of clothing in his presence. You simply pushed things down or lifted things up.

I liked Doctor Malvern. He was usually in a hurry, true. But he spoke clearly, he looked at you when he spoke, and he spoke English. You know – a collar-bone was a collar-bone, not a clavicle. When he didn't know, he said he didn't know. And if he was guessing, he took the responsibility for his guesswork. You weren't sent off every other time to distant addresses for ghastly 'tests'. Probably for the simple reason that there weren't all that many tests available. You were on the doctor's 'panel', and you went to see him when you were ill. If you were very ill, you were sent into hospital, where, as Richard Gordon said in *Doctor in the House*, you got better or you died according to your luck.

Come to think of it – pretty much like today. The whole business is hedged around with many more clinics and specialists and referrals and waiting lists and tests (always tests), but it comes down in the end to genes, guesswork, and luck, plus a bit of medical skill if it is applicable.

To be fair, I was never particularly ill. Neither were my father or my mother. Genes, you see? As I said. But it was the War too. That was the lucky bit.

Yes. The War. Food rationing. Now I know, if you laid out the complete food ration for one person for a week, it wouldn't look much. The colour supplements are doing it all the time, and eager primary school teachers cut out the photographs for classroom projects on 'What it was like in the War'. It misses the point. It misses two points. First, obviously, a person couldn't live on it, and wasn't expected to. There were many items that were not on ration that were available in unlimited quantity.

The second point, and the one more frequently missed, is that the rations, for all their sparseness, were soundly based on the principle of a healthy, balanced diet. I read an article not long ago, about one of the scientists who were employed by the Government to draw up guidelines for a healthy, wartime diet for the nation. She was still sprightly at over ninety – living proof of the value of her work. What you got was good for you, and you got enough of everything that was vital. And so many of the things that were bad for you – like sweets – were also rationed, so you couldn't ruin your constitution and your teeth even if you wanted to.

Many oily, fatty, stuffy foods were virtually unknown. Olive oil was something you drank a small thimbleful of if you had a duodenal ulcer, or your grandmother poured into your ear to cure the earache. Chips were served only in fried fish shops. If you had asked anyone what he thought a pizza was, he would probably have guessed that it was the latest faulty Italian anti-tank rocket. A bistro would have been translated as a new kind of gravy browning. Indian, Greek, Danish, and a host of 'ethnic' eating houses were totally absent from suburbs and country towns. The very country Vietnam did not exist, never mind its cooking. Caffeine poisoning was impossible because ninety-five per cent of the population only drank 'coffee' out of a bottle called 'Camp'. Percolators and filters would be presumed to live under the bonnet of a car. The generation that was raised on wartime rationing may have been an ignorant and an unsophisticated one, but it grew up to be a healthy generation.

I went through eight years of grammar school without a single day's absence. Felt rotten, naturally, several times, but never enough to warrant staying away. So Doctor Malvern never really had an excuse for asking me to take my clothes off.

At school they weighed and measured us, and cannily did it during PE lessons, when we already had our clothes off. So my mother, after she had read my termly report to see if I was top in Latin or bottom in Divinity, could glance at a little box at the bottom, which informed her that I was now four feet eleven and a half inches tall and weighed seven stone nine pounds, and my chest expansion was two and three-quarter inches.

My dental health care had been even more scrappy. I remember only three brushes with the dental profession before my nineteenth birthday. Brushes – sorry about the pun. Quite unintentional.

The first was with a man in Holborn. Between my jaws he shoved a gag which tasted of a paving stone that had been scrubbed with carbolic (about the same size too). After whatever he had done to my teeth he gave me a stick of barley sugar that was twisted like a chairleg. It may have been philanthropy on his part, but it is difficult not to suspect that it was a useful insurance policy as well. If I had sucked enough of those, I should guess, my teeth would have absorbed enough sugar to ensure sufficient decay to make further visits to him unavoidable.

The second occurred when I was seven. Like thousands of other children in and around London, I was evacuated to escape the Blitz. I fetched up in a West Country village school. One day some hatchet man descended upon the hapless inmates, and whipped out about seventy-nine pairs of front teeth in an hour and a half. Well, that's what it seemed like. The speed and shock of it remained with me for years. The irruption into the body. It begins to give to a male a glimmering of the trauma of rape.

The third incident was not much better. I was taken to our local suburban clinic (I had been brought back from evacuation), where I had one or two molars removed. I was given a general anaesthetic, or, as they said, 'gas'. I suppose, once again, as they had a lot of patients, they had to move quickly, and they didn't want ex-patients lolling about in much-needed chairs after the extractions. So the exact amount of 'gas' was churlishly rationed. That meant that there must have been the risk of the patient not being totally inert, as you might say. At any rate, I was ert enough to retain a memory of the teeth coming out, and it can only have come from some level of consciousness. That was a shock too.

One way and another, I didn't like dentists, and never went near one again for the next nine or ten years. Miraculously, I never had toothache in all that time. Cowardice on my part, and a certain amount of oversight by my mother, I admit. But she was a working woman – out of the house at a quarter past eight, and back at about six. For three or four years she did an evening job too. Meals on the table were more important than shine on the teeth. She knew how I had been upset over that short ration of gas, and she didn't want to distress me. Over-fond? Maybe. But that was how it was. That was how it was.

It caught up with me during my first term at university. I felt pain, and I had to go. I was terrified. Nearly passed out before he had touched me – and he only had a mirror in his hand. He needed it; the inside of my mouth looked like a bomb site. During the next two years or so, I had three out and five or six filled. Taught me a lesson. Always been regularly since.

I didn't expect the medical men at the university examination centre to be over-concerned with my teeth, but I was at last ready for them. The bomb site between my jaws had been rehabilitated.

I don't know what I did expect really. Something thorough. Well, this was the Army, and I had seen enough 'Gung-Ho' American films to know that one had to be pretty robust. In fact one of those films had actually been called *Gung-Ho*. Talk about tough! They flung the pins and spat out the hand grenades.

It was difficult to reconcile the inference about toughness with the clear knowledge that the Army had accepted my father with alacrity, and he wore glasses. And was practically blind in one eye. Wartime too. Perhaps it didn't count in the Royal Army Medical

Corps (where he was placed). You had to have perfect eyesight only to go to some place where you got shot at; you didn't need it to extract bullets from soldiers who had been shot.

It was more difficult to reconcile it with the stories that ran around. About huge needles, and Tarzan-proof obstacle courses, and intelligence tests that would not have imposed upon your average orang-utan. All mixed up with a garbled montage of half-remembered film images and jokes that curdled together in the mind's eye to produce a jumbled tableau of muscular orderlies in short sleeves, white suits with jackets buttoned like Prussian greatcoats, steel name tabs on neck strings, fainting recruits, decorously-placed white towels, hairy nipples, and urine samples.

Music-hall comedians still did a brisk trade in joining-up jokes. As old as the War. Probably as old as the First War.

About the terrified recruit who was told to strip and go and sit in a cubicle. When he got there he found another naked, frightened inmate.

'You joining up too?' he said, to break the ice.

'No. I'm only the postman come to deliver a letter.'

Or the one about the question they ask everybody who pretends to be crazy.

'Which would you rather have – a shilling or a sixpence?'

If you try to act stupid and take the sixpence, they take you in and you spend the first six months in an Army school for the illiterate. If you take the shilling, they reckon you aren't so stupid, so they drag you in anyway.

Or the second oldest joke in the book, which must go back to Trafalgar, I should think:

'I want to join the Navy.'

'Can you swim?'

'Why? Haven't you got any ships?'

Now, all this may sound pretty feeble, and totally unreliable. And it is. But it was about all we had to go on.

The ground floor of the building – some kind of a drill hall

– where I finally presented myself, and my buff envelope with 'OHMS' on it, had been divided into sections by plywood partitions. They helped to cut off the wicked draughts that swept in through crevices in window frames and door jambs, and they helped the team of doctors to perform their respective duties without getting in each others' way. And they provided a little primitive privacy for the embarrassed examinees when they were called upon to perform that biological function the product of which is always of such absorbing interest to the medical profession.

By the first of many ironies I subsequently discovered about soldiering, there was only one military doctor present, and he was tucked away in one of the cubicles, behind a desk piled high with forms, paper-clips, rubber stamps, medical reports, cigarette-ends, and empty teacups. He had not even a stethoscope round his neck to proclaim his calling, and only the 'R.A.M.C.' flashes on his shoulders indicated it to the well-informed. (That was me. Well-informed. Remember? My Dad had been in the Medical Corps. I still had his cap badge, preserved in a large tin at home, along with my Dinky cars and stale conkers.)

The actual examining, such as it was, was carried out, as briefly and impersonally as possible, by a group of civilian general practitioners, who, judging by their attitudes of sullen resignation, had been dragged there from profitable private patients in order to decide, by a few elementary experiments, whether the representatives of the youth of Britain paraded before them would still be breathing after two years in battledress.

Waiting for a long time, on a hard wooden bench, in one's underclothes, when one has no idea what is coming, is rarely conducive to peace of mind or self-confidence. When I was finally summoned and stood up, I began to sympathise with James Cagney in his gangster films, when he had to make those last walks to the chair in Alcatraz.

The first doctor, who was sitting at a desk, looked up at me ill-humouredly, and pulled a large form off one of the piles in front of him. He reached for his glasses with one hand and his pen with the other, and bent over the table.

'Name,' he said without looking up.

'Coates,' I said, and added, for good measure, 'sir.'

Well, it was an Army medical, and I didn't want to get off on the wrong foot. I spelt it, because a lot people leave out the 'e', and most of us are particular about our names.

He sniffed.

'Christian names?'

Second snag. A wayward mother and a proud father had imposed upon their helpless infant son a pair of names so unusual that I would take money from anyone that they do not appear, together, as the Christian names of any single person, in any telephone directory in the world.

The first one is Berwick. That's right – as in 'Berwick-upon-Tweed'. Long story. Years before I was born, my mother had once known a man whose nephew was called Berwick. She had been taken with the name, but time had passed, and she had forgotten about it. When she was recovering from the birth, and she was told that it was a boy, the first name that surfaced from her subconscious was 'Berwick'. The nurse said later, when she was feeling better, 'Oh, Mrs. Coates, you said "Berwick", but of course you meant "Derek".'

My mother rose instantly to the challenge, post-natal fever and all, and denied any such implication. So 'Berwick' it remained.

Very few people know what to do with the sound 'Berwick', so they translate it into something with which they are familiar. At various times in my life, I have been addressed, after some hesitation, as Derek, Eric, Barry, Garry, Warwick, and so on. So you always have to spell it.

I spelt it now. The doctor stiffened slightly, and made a correction in his writing.

'Do you have a second name?'

'Yes, sir.'

Deep breath.

He, having learned his lesson, kept his pen poised over the square in the form.

Best to let him have it with both barrels. Get it over. Surgeon's knife, and all that.

'Manchee, sir. M-a-n-c-h-e-e.'

I have to hand it to him. He kept his head down, and showed no sign of stress at all. However, so used am I to startled or amused reactions to the imparting of this news that I have always felt impelled to offer some kind of limp excuse.

'Family name, sir.'

As if that would somehow make him think better of me. It didn't. His rhythm was not interrupted at all. Nor did he look up.

With his pen hovering over another square on the form, he shot his next question.

'Regular, or National Service?'

I had not been able to upset his *sang froid*, but this query upset mine.

I had never been so scandalised in my life. God knows, two years out of one's life was surely enough. To think that anyone, even an Army-sponsored doctor, might entertain the idea for a minute that one might be willing to sign on for three, six, or nine years with the Colours was enough almost to rob one of the power of speech. Could he not see? Did he not know that he was dealing with under-graduates? Young men who were shortly going to get a degree (God and the examiners willing).

The very idea!

I pulled together the shreds of my composure.

'National Service.' No 'sir' this time. I wanted him to see that I was deeply moved.

It made no impression.

'Can you read those?'

He jerked a thumb behind him to a large placard on the wall, bearing the usual letters of varying size, descending to the last line of tiny consonants that, according to Michael Bentine, can not only be read by Polish servicemen, but pronounced as well.

When I had satisfied the top of his head that I could read enough of them, he actually glanced up for a moment, then bent and scribbled some more.

'Take that with you to the next cubicle.'

As I made my way there, I glanced at the form I had been given. I was surprised to discover that from my first interview it had been deduced that I had a fresh complexion, and that my weight was average for my height.

The second doctor multiplied my already numerous goose pimples by dabbing a freezing stethoscope all over my chest and back, before adding his own comments to the form. As I moved to MD number three, I noticed that my emotional stability had been assessed as 'normal'. Nice to know. Especially as, at the time, I felt anything but placid.

The third GP looked into my ears and down my throat, and recorded on my form that I did not suffer from curvature of the spine. A fourth peered at my hands like a student palmist and asked me without preamble whether I suffered from ingrowing toenails.

I remember satisfying a fifth that I was not colour blind, and a sixth that I was given neither to coughing blood nor to bedwetting.

Finally, I reached the booth of a much more cheerful man who actually wished me good morning. He looked at my form, now fairly crammed with brilliant diagnoses which exhibited a level of observation and inference that would have made Sherlock Holmes look a novice. He nodded sagely, and asked me to remove my pants.

He misinterpreted my grimace of surprise and said, 'Sorry, old chap. Can't be helped. Draughts get in everywhere, don't they?'

He got up and walked round his desk, peering down at what I had on offer as if it were some prize bloom in a flower show.

'Cough,' he said suddenly.

Stripped of clothes, dignity, and initiative, I obeyed, the crazy query racing across my mind – whether this little experiment was intended to determine whether you could or you couldn't or whether you had or you hadn't.

The doctor's face cleared, and he flashed a beaming smile.

'That's fine, old boy. Now, there's just one more thing.' He nodded towards the next cubicle. 'Leave us a sample of your water in there, will you?'

He might have been the proprietor of a hotel asking a satisfied guest to drop a few coppers in the staff Christmas Fund box.

I walked into the booth which he had indicated, taking care to shut the door behind me. The only furniture was a small table, dotted with a collection of glass jars of varying capacities – one of the Army's rare departures from uniformity. Presumably some military administrator or other had, with a flash of imaginative genius, recognised the anatomical fact that chilly patients could not all be expected, at the drop of – well, shall we say? – a hat, to produce exactly the same number of uric millilitres. Each arrival was therefore afforded a tantalising choice of receptacle. All he had to do was assess the room temperature, the state of his own nerves, the number of hours since he had last urinated, and the amount of liquid he had consumed since that time, and he would be in a position to make an accurate and felicitous choice of glass vessel.

After I had fulfilled Nature's needs, and the Army's requirements, I carried my jar, now duly primed, to yet another desk, to be handed over for analysis. Unfortunately, the analyst had just popped out for a cup of tea (or to go to the toilet), so a small queue had formed. Chairs had thoughtfully been provided.

Now, I don't know whether you have ever sat in a row of chairs, clad only in your lower underclothes, holding a jar of your own urine, amid a group of other young men similarly equipped, but I can tell you it is not particularly conducive to conversation. Since the only thing that distinguished us from one another was the colour and cubic capacity of what we were holding in the jars, each of us could do little to prevent his eyes being morbidly drawn in the direction of these offerings.

I finally reached the last cubicle of all, where the tired RAMC officer took my form away from me (I had been getting quite attached to it; it had become a mine of information). He scribbled on it, and dumped it into a tray.

From a small pile at his elbow he drew a white card, wrote on it, signed it, and passed it across the table, indicating with a wave of his hand that I could get dressed and leave.

The card declared that, as a result of a full medical examination by authorities approved by the Army Council, Berwick Manchee Coates was pronounced to be in Health Grade 'A'.

3   Sign here

THE REGIMENTAL DEPOT WAS BARELY a mile from where I had gone to school. It bordered the road along which we had walked a thousand times to the school playing field. As the old novelists would have had it, 'little did I think', as I passed it on all those afternoons, that I would one day be immured behind the tall, forbidding, red-brick walls that surrounded it. It looked not unlike a county prison.

So I was going to have no trouble finding it. And there was a trolleybus stop right outside.

That dates it, doesn't it? Trolleybuses. Those scarlet, hissing, hiccuping giants were thick on the ground in my part of the world. You could go anywhere on them from Wimbledon to Hampton Court, with digressions to Tolworth, Twickenham, Thames Ditton, and other shearing stations in the North Surrey outback. Rumour had it that you could reach out as far as exotic locations like Sheen, Barnes, Hounslow, and Isleworth – as long as you possessed an up-to-date visa.

Those of you who are connoisseurs will be delighted to know that, if one went to Southend-on-Sea, one could witness, in action, *blue* trolleybuses. Rare as the osprey and the peregrine falcon. We used to visit Southend regularly, if not frequently, when I was young, to see my grandparents. For me the trip held out the prospect of three pleasures – having home-made gooseberry jam for tea at Grandpa's bungalow; throwing flat pebbles to bounce over the water at the seaside; and travelling in a blue trolleybus.

There was a distinct lack of eager anticipation as I got off this particular red trolleybus towards the end of September, 1955.

The gateway was enormous when you actually got up to it. Like going close to the landing wheels of a Lancaster bomber.

Just inside was a huge corporal. I knew he was a corporal because

31

Sign here

I had been one of those tiresome little boys who collected useless information. There was a time when I could have told you where the longest railway platform in the world was, and who won the Grand National in 1899. Mercifully, I can't now.

So I knew how many stripes you had to have. But I had never seen a corporal for real, as you might say, in the flesh, face to face. To talk to.

Not that he talked much. This corporal was barely human. He was not so much dressed as encased in a battledress, seamed with knife-like creases. He moved as if he dared not bend his limbs for fear of disturbing them. He wore a belt and cross-strap of a whiteness that would have attracted the attention of a detergent advertiser. I think his gaiters were white too, which naturally contrasted vividly with the Bentley headlight dazzle of his toecaps.

When he saw that I was approaching, his upper lip rippled with distaste.

'New intake?'

'Yes.'

'Over there. Documentation.'

He waved an arm towards a long, wooden hut about thirty yards distant, and then turned away, stalking stiffly out into the sunshine on the pavement, as if even this brief interchange had seriously impaired his social prestige.

A large array of red brick buildings surrounded the parade ground, but there was not a single human being in sight. Odd. Still, the wooden hut was clear enough, so I did what the loquacious corporal had suggested.

Inside was a sort of reception committee of half a dozen or so. Private soldiers all of them. All about my age, or younger. They were sprawled on chairs behind a long line of trestle tables, on each of which were the inevitable ramparts of forms, pamphlets, stamps, and paper-clips.

'Over 'ere!'

The welcoming, informal touch.

You started at the left-hand end of the line of tables, and progressed along, in the manner of a customer in a self-service restaurant. Instead of helping yourself to buns and beans and apple pie, you found Army forms pushed forward with one hand and a topless cheap biro with the other. It was up to you to decipher the form enough to determine exactly where you were required to sign your name. God knows what we were signing away.

Refusal was quite out of the question. The slightest hesitation was resolved by the stubbing of a grubby forefinger into the necessary place on the form. We were not human beings at all; we were disembodied hands which hovered before their eyes for a few seconds.

Perhaps that is uncharitable.

Yes, they did take notice of us, because they were taking such pains to create an impression of long service: exaggerated indolence, sitting practically on their shoulders, berets hung carelessly on the bits that stick up on the backs of cheap folding chairs, cigarettes brandished all over the place, or clamped between lips which looked as if they saw a razor only twice a week.

I hadn't been in the Army five minutes, and I would have been the last to call myself a man of the world, but I did know when I was being given the treatment, and I was certainly getting a hefty dollop of it now.

In an effort to bring a dimension of humanity into the proceedings, I paused at the last table. Taking slightly longer than usual to sign my name, I said casually, 'How long have you been in then?'

A gleam of triumph came into the young soldier's eye, as if that were the one question he had been waiting for all day. He leaned managerially back in his chair, glanced smugly at his companions, looked back at me, took a huge draw on his cigarette, exhaled, and, with something of the complacency of a centenarian discussing his age with the Queen, said, 'Twelve weeks.'

A week, as Harold Wilson famously observed, can be a long time in politics; it can be a positive lifetime in the Services. I was to discover the truth of this within two or three days, by which time it was to seem as if I had been in for a month. The ten weeks of our basic training loomed ahead like a life sentence. When we completed six weeks of it and witnessed another intake come in, we felt like veterans of Napoleon's Imperial Guard. Small wonder these nicotine-stained young men were pleased with themselves with twelve whole weeks of service under their belt. I didn't enjoy their attitude of superiority, but I could understand it.

I was directed to the barrack room that was to house the 'new intake'. It was half of the lower half of a large brick block on the right of the parade ground as you looked at it from the main gate. The other half (of the lower half) housed the seasoned troops who were half way through their basic training, with five or six weeks of service behind them – the Imperial Guard I was talking about.

The upper half of this brick block was soon to produce a great awakening for me. When the earth moved. Rather like the one Charles Darwin experienced on the Galapagos Islands. A bewildering, breathtaking, jaw-dropping new species. Not of animals. Of human beings. I speak of the Depot Permanent Staff.

Despite the word 'permanent' attached to their classification, by no means all of them were regular soldiers. Indeed, the opposite was probably the case. This needs some explanation.

The Army, in my time, was made up, naturally, of 'Regular Soldiers' and 'National Servicemen'. (I shall not bother to use inverted commas any more to indicate the official difference.) The Regulars signed up usually for multiples of three years with the Colours. A National Serviceman had to serve for two, with the option of converting his contract to a regular one at the end if he wished. Incredibly, quite a few did. Perhaps not so incredibly, on second thoughts, but that is another story.

I have no figures for the respective percentages of each type, but, as I said, the Regulars were pretty comprehensibly outnumbered. Now, I was in the infantry. Most infantry regiments were based on a county, and therefore tended to have a regimental depot in the county town, or at least in some important urban area in the county.

Was the regiment housed in the Depot? By no means. The Depot was only the administrative and training headquarters of the regiment. What happened when a soldier had survived his first ten weeks? When he was officially classified as 'trained'? He was usually packed off to 'the battalion' – to wherever the rest of the regiment was stationed. In normal peacetime conditions, it was usually single battalion strength, just under a thousand. Perhaps two battalions at most. In wartime, with conscription, a regiment could have several. The usual posting in the 1950's was Western Germany, part of NATO defences against the wicked Russians. If your luck ran out, you found yourself en route to Malaya, to chase terrorists through the jungle, or to East Africa, to try and follow the Mau Mau through the forest. And don't forget that the Korean War was only recently over, and many a regiment had fought a flat-out campaign there – and, incidentally, won medals and battle honours – National Servicemen and all.

I presume then that National Servicemen outnumbered Regulars in the battalion to roughly the same extent, except that more Regulars were needed to continue the advanced training. It could be to teach these newly-'trained' soldiers to handle more complex weapons like three-inch mortars, anti-tank guns, or rockets. Or to acclimatise them to more daunting weather. Or it might be manoeuvres involving much larger units of men – brigades, divisions, corps, army groups, and so on. Hundreds of things.

Remember, a fresh intake of young men passed out of the Depot every six weeks or so, and normally made its way to 'the battalion'. By a natural process, every six weeks an intake of young men came to the end of their National Service, and were duly demobbed. So there was a touch of the conveyor belt about it. Perhaps one reason why National Servicemen were not, so I am given to understand, popular with Regulars. Most of them didn't want to come in, they didn't like it when they were in, and they counted their days until they could get out. Hardly good company.

It's all right, I haven't forgotten about the Permanent Staff. In fact I was just coming to them. If you have been following me closely, you may know what I am going to say next. In any large organisation, there must always be a group who don't move, who keep the wheels turning, who mind the shop, who peel potatoes on Christmas Eve. Now, just as National Servicemen outnumbered Regulars in the battalion, so they outnumbered them among the Permanent Staff.

Who were the Permanent Staff? Clerks, officers' batmen, tailors, cooks, Sergeants' Mess barmen, storemen, drivers, regimental police, that's who. Plus a large, amorphous group of odd-job men who performed 'General Duties'. These students of Machiavelli were possibly the most resourceful of all. Any General Duties man worth his salt could have written a Doctor of Philosophy thesis on the art of the avoidance of such duties. Logical, when you think about it. But allow me to illustrate.

Attendance on morning muster parade was rarely necessary more than three times a week, as a word in the right quarter with the relevant quartermaster's orderly (another member of the club – a lot of mutual help here) served to ensure that one's name appeared on the list of men required for the Depot ration truck. Trucks had work tickets – a sort of motorised diary which detailed by the hour where the vehicle was supposed to be at any time of the day or night. Skilful entries on the work ticket, in collusion with the driver (also in the club), produced a leisurely morning's ramble, starting at about nine-thirty and punctuated with well-earned visits to local cafes and hostelries, while at the same time providing documentary proof of a frantic six-hour rush commencing at crack of dawn.

As for the rest of the day – a doddle. You followed simple rules. Never leave the barrack block at the same time as the Company Sergeant-Major left his office for his mid-morning or mid-afternoon tea breaks. Never be seen out of doors without a tool or a piece of paper in the hand, or, better still, a clip board under the arm. Never play cards except in the inner office of the Arms Storeman, because there was ample warning of approach by the slamming of three intermediate doors. Never go near the Orderly Room. Never be seen talking to recruits, in case of being roped in by training staff as Firing Point Assistants on the miniature range. And always regard the gymnasium as the epicentre of an outbreak of yellow fever.

Although one avoided the Orderly Room (because of the proximity of three offices of sinister repute – that of the Adjutant, the ORQMS, and, worst of all, that of the Regimental Sergeant-Major) whenever possible, it was nevertheless vital to cultivate the good offices of the Orderly Room Clerk. Leave passes went through his hands. He it was who ensured that his friends' leave passes found their way into the 'IN' tray of the Orderly Officer. This young man was usually a National Service subaltern, and so signed exactly what his sergeant-major or chief clerk put in front of him as a matter of course. If he bothered to read the documents, they were couched in such initial-ridden jargon that he couldn't understand them. Permanent Staff rarely had any trouble with weekend thirty-six-hour passes – unless the subaltern himself had left too soon on a weekend of his own immediately after his tour of duty.

If the Orderly Room Clerk turned nasty, one's name crept mysteriously to the top of the list of men available for weekend guard. If the whole world turned upside down, an unfortunate Permanent Staff veteran could find himself sweeping up autumn leaves with a loose-headed broom in a gale, or delivering coal to the Married Quarters with a broken wheelbarrow and a rusty bucket.

It was a mercy that the really objectionable jobs, like scraping the grease out of the cookhouse's mammoth baking tins, or swabbing the floor of the Sergeants' Mess after one of their 'social evenings', were reserved for ignorant recruits who turned left when they should have turned right, or who pointed a loaded rifle at an instructor and complained that the magazine seemed to be blocked.

You would have thought that the nastiest job of all would be toilet-cleaning, and that this was reserved for the worst, most hopeless loser in the place. Not so. True, each barrack block had its own toilet 'suite', and each member of each barrack room had to take his turn cleaning it. But there were many more toilets about the place, and these were the regular responsibility of a Depot Sanitary Orderly – a fully-fledged member of the Permanent Staff. Incredibly, he didn't seem to mind. He had a couple of misbehaved recruits to do the nasty business with the trowel and lavatory brush. It was his own little empire, and nobody, understandably, interfered with him. A philosopher, he tolerated the inevitable nicknames – mostly variations of the banal – Craphouse Dan, Flush Harry, Chain-Gang Charlie. Odie (Cologne understood) was a step up. His was a familiar figure, especially in winter, when he could be seen wheeling around home-made braziers to stop the pipes freezing, bringing warmth and good cheer to the outside ablutions.

I am not qualified to pontificate upon the deepest thoughts and aspirations, much less the motives, of Regular soldiers, but I can suggest possible explanations of the mentality of those of the Permanent Staff who were National Servicemen. It must be repeated that ninety-nine out of a hundred of young men who were conscripted by Act of Parliament into the Armed Forces for two years did not want to be there. Of course they had no choice, and basic training kept them so busy for their first ten weeks that they had no time to think much. Grumble, yes, but not think. If, after their basic training, they were posted to an area where there was some military action, once again, they had little time to think. Once again, time to grumble, yes. Time to be afraid. True. Now and again, time to be brave and win medals.

But far and away the majority were posted to an area where, mercifully, there was no war going on. Somehow or other, the authorities had to think of ways to keep these hundreds of thousands of National Servicemen occupied for the next twenty-one and a half months, until their demobilisation. In Germany, NATO laid on manoeuvres and exercises and simulations of war and so on, but I doubt if such make-believe war produced any sense of urgency or fulfilment.

So there was plenty of scope for boredom. At home, at a regimental depot, there was even more. I don't know if the Armed Forces invented the word 'skiving', but National Servicemen were the ones who raised the practice to a fine art. Because you had so little to do that was vital or interesting or valuable, you devoted your entire resources to the avoidance of the few duties that were required of you. It probably made you far more inventive than you would have been if you had been in the front line.

Once basic training was over, the thing to do, it seemed, was to move Heaven and earth to obtain a 'soft number', a sinecure that demanded the least of activity and the minimum of responsibility. This, sadly, was the fate that many National Servicemen devised for themselves. In the same way, we are told that soldiers in the trenches on the Western Front during the First War, during the unbearable longueurs between artillery barrages or frontal attacks, used to have earwig races.

Nothing so energetic for your National Service skiver, who, if he was sharp and lucky enough, found his way into the Depot Permanent Staff. Once there, he was a member of an exclusive club that looked after its own, kept to itself, and divided the remainder of military personnel into varying inferior forms of animal life. Officers were fools and idiots, fit only for outwitting – and that was not difficult. Sergeants and corporals understood you better, swore as bitterly as you did, and were harder to deceive. Not that that stopped you trying. They were not such frequent fools, but their parentage was, naturally, in question.

But far and away the lowest form of animate existence was the trainee National Serviceman, for whom no colloquial epithet, however vernacular or vicious, was inappropriate.

Who did these 'erks', these 'sprogs', these – fill in any four-letter vulgarism that comes to mind – think they were? Hadn't been in the Army five minutes. When you had polished up the brass lettering on the plate outside the Officers' Mess no fewer than three hundred and seventy-four times; or when you had applied so much 'Brasso' to your cap badge that the regimental motto had become illegible; or when you estimated your length of service not by how much you had done, but by how much you had left to do – well, then, the Permanent Staff grudgingly admitted, and only then, you could reckon you had done some soldiering.

This superior attitude, this military sophistication, this Napoleonic savoir-faire, was conveyed to the outside world by certain fads of dress, or rather undress. For instance, they never wore belts unless it was absolutely vital. When they wore berets, it was in the recognised 'Permanent Staff' manner – shrunken and faded, laying right on the eyebrows with the badge dead centre instead of above the eye, and so hardened by the combined long-term action of rain, sweat, and hair-oil that it could be picked up in one hand and donned like a trilby. One could usually tell an Officers' Mess steward by his seemingly inexhaustible supply of cigarettes, and by breath that smelt not infrequently of malt whisky. A clerk proclaimed his occupation by biro inkstains on his battledress blouse pockets, and an untidy shambler with threadbare trousers was more often than not a driver. Clothing storemen were usually better dressed.

These Beau Brummels of the infantry, these bucks of the line, had occupied the upper storey of the barrack block for so long that they had taken to regarding it almost as private property. Visits from an outsider, any outsider, were an intrusion on their monastic privacy.

Certain visits, of course, were unavoidable, and had to be tolerated. Those, for instance, of the Regimental Sergeant-Major, on his periodic inspections. After all, he had been a member of the Permanent Staff once (probably during the Crimean War), and was fully aware of what its members could do – and what they could neglect. He would use his pace stick rather pointedly to disturb the layer of dust on the surface of the water in the fire buckets, or run his finger along the top of the door and push the blackened tip of it under the nose of the nearest stiff-backed soldier.

But if any National Service trainee, especially a new recruit, dared to show his face upstairs on the most innocent of errands, he would be received as if he were a drunken cavalier gate-crashing a Puritan prayer meeting. So far beneath their dignity did they consider recruits that they refrained from the jeers and complacent smirks which came from everyone who knew what the new arrivals were in for. Expressions of disdain were confined to a long-suffering raising of the eyes Heavenwards whenever it was their misfortune to pass within speaking distance.

Most of the sniggers and cheap jokes came from those members of the Imperial Guard who were half way through their ten weeks. At least that had been the case until quite recently. But, as we later found out, so much barrack room damage had been caused when a batch of newcomers from college, factory, shop, pit, and palais, exasperated beyond words by the unremitting malicious jibes, temporarily set aside their cultural differences in common urge to teach a few lessons in courtesy to the aforementioned veterans, that the Commanding Officer had decreed that, in future, on the day that the new intake arrived, all other recruits were to train miles away on the rifle range, and moreover were to train so hard and so long that they would have no energy left for anything else in the evening except cleaning their rifles.

No wonder the barracks looked empty. It looked empty for the very simple reason that it was.

4   Eddie the Gunge

So I WAS LEFT VERY much to myself.

I found the right room in the barrack block. A handful of baffled civilians had already arrived before me. As we exchanged names, home towns, and so on, more and more drifted in.

We each found a vacant bed, threw our bags into adjacent lockers, tested the taps in the wash-house to see if there was any hot water (and were disappointed), and speculated upon the likelihood of any of the Depot authorities being aware of our arrival. Well, of course they were aware *of* our arrival – witness the biro-smudge brigade on the reception committee. But nobody in real authority seemed to be doing anything *about* our arrival.

So we sat about and talked. The initial ice-breaking was not as bad as it might have been, because an immediate corporate feeling sprang up between us by virtue of the common cross that we had all been called upon to bear. There were murmurs of sympathy as each one of the growing company gave heartrending details of the promising studies or plum job or brilliant career from which he had been wrenched in order to give the Government an excuse for maintaining the Army estimates at their accustomed astronomical level.

On the bed next to me was Jack Gatewood, who had just completed a diploma course at an agricultural college. All he wanted out of life was a job as a farm manager and the chance to marry his girl friend. So the Army was a bit of a nuisance. But he was sensible enough to see that it had to be survived, and he had enough sense of humour to get him through it.

Next to him was a pale-faced chap with a fine moustache. Turned out he was a good deal older than the rest of us – twenty-six, to be precise. Now twenty-six, as I explained earlier, was the cut-off age.

Make it to twenty-six without having been called up, and you were in the clear. Apparently Bill Glover had kept himself out of military clutches by pursuing degree courses in a succession of foreign universities since he was eighteen. God knows how many letters he had after his name. His last posting, I remember, was somewhere in Africa. He had come home to set up another one, see his family, and so on, and 'they' had got him – just before his twenty-sixth birthday.

It was to his credit that he was philosophical about it. At least he was by the time he met us; perhaps he had already done his share of swearing and self-sympathising. Anyway, there he was – pipe, moustache, spectacles and all – hoping, after his basic training, to win a posting in the Education Corps. Practical. Sensible, too, because there were few less military-looking young men in the whole Army. He was not strong; he was not athletic. His eyesight was suspect. And his physique was anything but Tarzanesque. How he had passed the medical we never knew.

Perhaps the garland for unfitness, though, should go to Martin Forrest. I should think running for president of his university drama society had been all the exercise he had taken since leaving school. He really had no puff at all. Possibly not unconnected with a regular consumption of cigarettes. He had artistic pretensions, and no military aspirations whatever. Details of Martin's post-school career were shadowy, but he looked the sort of narrow rake who had spent his time since the sixth form in a succession of vague artistic courses in vague southern European universities. In the vacations, he might have raised the wind by persuading a string of rich business men that he was eminently qualified to give private coaching in English or Latin to their nubile daughters. It was an enjoyable line of speculation to wonder how far he would have been prepared to go in order to teach them the difference between the Active Mood and the Passive. He was another candidate for the Education Corps.

So was Dai Davies, a diminutive son of the Principality, whose lack of inches was made up for by his extrovert personality, and by his appetite. He also had a fine baritone voice. Graduate. A third potential teacher.

Now you may think I am descending into improbable cliché by providing the narrative with a Welshman, and moreover a Welshman with a baritone voice. It is true that I have changed people's names, but the types, the characters are real enough. I can assure you that we really did have a Welshman among us, and that he was a baritone. Heaven knows what he was doing joining up in the Home Counties. He lived in Wales. And you are not going to believe it, but we had a Scot too (from Scotland), and several Londoners, and a Yorkshireman. No – I tell a lie – two Yorkshiremen. If a scriptwriter had put in all these apparently stock characters, no editor would have accepted it. But I swear we really did have them – all in our squad. I repeat – I have changed only the names.

There were one or two others – sort of ordinary locals like me – with a university degree, and the rest were straight out of school. And public school at that, many of them. Some illustrious names were represented. Again, no editor would have swallowed it, but I swear (again) that schools like Charterhouse, Radley, Lancing, Westminster, and Haileybury had their old pupils among us. And those are only the ones I happen to remember.

Was our squad typical then? No. It would be foolish to suggest that every National Service batch of recruits could boast half a dozen or more old pupils of public schools, to say nothing of a dozen or so university degrees. So how can I maintain, as I hinted in the first chapter, that I am going to give the humdrum view of the Army, the voice of the majority?

Because, degrees or no degrees, public school or no public school, we were all in the same Army, and the Army is nothing if not democratic. We all had to wear the same uniforms, learn the same rules, bash the same square, practise the same rifle drill, eat the same food, go on the same marches, suffer from the same blisters, and live in the same barracks. Because we, whether fresh from school or basking in the afterglow of our degrees, were as ignorant, as unaware, as unworldly, as wet behind the ears, as anybody else. If the truth be told, probably more so.

If anything, we were at a slight *dis*advantage compared with the average training platoon. We had not roughed it in tenements and back streets and village squares. We were far less acquainted with irate neighbours, constables, magistrates, and probation officers. We were positively pink in our innocence. And the Army, as we were to discover, was the university of survival, not of degrees.

Again, we were much more of a sitting target for the spleen and sarcasm of our corporals (not so much the sergeants) by very virtue of our generally higher level of education. We were 'brains', so we must be superior, toffee-nosed, so it followed that we deserved to be cut down to size. Sheer logic. Any Regular NCO could see that. Quite a lot of National Service NCO's too – they were usually worse.

It followed too that we were keen. Not keen to be in the Army – perish the thought! But, now that we were actually 'in', we were anxious to show that our relatively sheltered existence would not prevent us from performing whatever drill, exercise, or test that our cynical superiors might place before us. If they were waiting for us 'brains' to make fools of ourselves, well, we would bloody well show them.

So – we might laugh at the Army, sneer at its stupid rules, snigger behind their backs at its officious corporals, and generally refuse to take it seriously – but, when we were out there, on the parade ground, or on the range, or in the gym, or halfway round the assault course, none of us wanted to be shown up as 'not up to it'. Curiously, the easier, the more elementary, the greater the insult to the intelligence the problem was, the harder we tried to make sure that we didn't make a stupid mess of it. It didn't always save us from doing so, but we did try.

Oh, yes, we were humdrum all right. We were typical young men unsure of ourselves – for whatever reason does not matter – discovering all sorts of things about life, and about ourselves, for the first time.

On consideration, perhaps there was one advantage for those public schoolboys. Many of them had survived such Spartan privation in their boarding accommodation for five, six, eight, ten, or more years that the Army, coming straight afterwards, was, in living standards, a doddle. If anything, an improvement.

One more thing. We didn't know it at the time, but there was one piece of history in our favour that helped us all to get through. Something that was to be denied to the generation that came after us. The War. We had all been at primary school for most of it. So we knew about rationing, and air raids, and millions of uniforms all over the place. Many of us had slept in shelters in the garden; we had played on bomb sites; we had collected shrapnel from the gutters; we had suffered the pain and separation of evacuation; we had missed a father away on active duty; some no doubt had had the misery of an elder brother taken prisoner or missing or killed.

We had coped, one way or another. So I imagine it might have made us better able to cope now. I have noticed this with our generation ever since. Those of us who went through the War, whether as child or as adult, endured a unique experience. No doubt it has often made us uniquely boring too, to those young unfortunates condemned to listen to our reminiscences. But the War gave us a yardstick. All future alarms and difficulties could be measured against it. We had been given a truly remarkable sense of perspective.

We would not repeat the experience – not for a king's ransom – but I have yet to meet anyone who lived through the War who said that he or she would rather not have done so.

Of course, at eighteen or twenty-one, we were not aware of any of this. To all of us, the Army was something pretty awful that had to be got through, and we had no idea, at the time, of how well we were going to cope. But cope we did.

All except Hamilton. Well, I shall call him Hamilton. Very clever, Hamilton. Spoke I don't know how many languages. Sociable. Nice chap. Perfectly willing to do his bit.

The trouble was that he was quite the most inept, inefficient, ham-fisted bungler who ever graced a barrack room. It was quite unfathomable how much time he could use up doing practically nothing, and yet at the same time appearing to be fully occupied. We soon discovered that we had to get up at six o'clock. Well, OK, it was the Army. We also discovered that, in addition to the normal business with wash-basin and toilet, we had to attend to the making of our beds and to an individual duty connected with the cleanliness of our barrack room.

This was all fair enough. We naturally found the early rising and early activity rather tiresome, but, equally naturally, we soon became used to it. And, to give the Army its due, they had in fact allocated us plenty of time. We were awakened at six, and we didn't have to be on parade until half-past eight. Two and a half hours, and the only other thing we had to do was eat breakfast. Long before our ten weeks were over, most of us found time for a gossip, a smoke, or a casual skip through the morning paper as well.

Hamilton found this quite beyond him. The most he could manage was to get himself up, washed, and dressed. Before two or three days had gone by, we learned that to chase, nag, or bully him only made him worse. It became much easier for us to put away his kit from the day before in his locker, make his bed, clean under it, and do his barrack room duty for him.

It took all sorts to make a world, and you saw them all in the Army. The very antithesis, the complete opposite, to Hamilton, was Eddie. Hamilton, I hope I have been able to explain, could not cope. Eddie could. If ever there was a coper supreme, it was Eddie. A sort of cross between Robinson Crusoe, the Admirable Crichton, and the Artful Dodger.

I never found out what his surname was. I don't think Eddie was his Christian name either, but somehow he got christened Eddie. It suited him, and it stuck. It was Eddie who introduced us to the splendid military adjective 'gungy', which had a devastatingly wide applicability. Everything was 'gungy' – the weather, the rules, unpleasant corporals, food, an object with the suspicion of dirt on

47

it, in fact practically anything that was in any way, for any reason, not totally acceptable. So Eddie, having acquired one nickname, was accorded a sort of extra sobriquet – he became for all of us 'Eddie the Gunge'.

Eddie, it turned out, was not in our platoon. It was not clear where he did belong. He was a National Serviceman, certainly. I can only guess that he belonged to the squad that was next 'up' from us, the squad that had already done the first half of its basic training. Why he was not out on the range with his fellows on the day we arrived was another minor mystery. But then, as we soon found out, Eddie was expert at 'skiving' – like the Permanent Staff. If the Army hadn't invented the word, it should have done. Eddie could have filled a whole training pamphlet with 'good skives'.

Eddie was a curious phenomenon. We saw him frequently. He was always dropping in, but we never knew where he came from, or how he found the time. Nobody ever accompanied him back to his own barrack room. You never saw him actually arrive. You just looked up and there he was. He manifested himself, like Jeeves. Floated in like some sort of gas. Before you were fully aware of it, he was, to borrow another phrase from P.G. Wodehouse, in your midst.

He was so full of news, gossip, lowdown, smart lines, and general *savoir-faire* that it never occurred to any of us to ask him anything about himself. We were so anxious, in our first days, to pick up whatever useful scraps of information that were going, and Eddie was so good at supplying them, that the traffic always seemed to go one way. He was so endlessly resourceful, so knowledgeable, so totally unputdownable that we took heart from him. He did not sneer about the superiority of his extra experience; he was willing to share whatever he had in the way of military intelligence. Before forty-eight hours had elapsed, we were willing to accord his every utterance the force of Holy Writ. We hung on his every word. We pondered deeply every titbit of advice.

He must have enjoyed it. I don't think for one minute that this son of the south London suburbs found an instinctive affinity with a roomful of university graduates and ex-sixth-formers. No. What he liked was the audience. Never in his whole life had he had such a gaping cluster of pink-faced, believe-everything innocents surrounding him. It was sheer Heaven. Any time life was getting you down, buzz along to the recruits' barrack room, cadge a few cigarettes, open your mouth, and they'll treat you like God. Great for the morale.

It was Eddie who suggested that we stop hanging around doing nothing and go and get some lunch. We had no idea where the cookhouse was, but of course Eddie did. Not only that; he procured us cutlery – a minor miracle. That is not to suggest that most Army personnel ate with their fingers. Oh no. The Army had its standards. They didn't run to tablecloths and finger-bowls and wine lists, but they did embrace basic crockery and cutlery.

Trouble was, each soldier was issued by the Quartermaster with his own mug, knife, fork, and spoon. They became a permanent part of his kit. They followed him throughout his training, like his metal name tags. Just as a soldier never forgot his Army number, so no soldier was ever separated from his mug, knife, fork, and spoon. Not if he wanted to eat, that is. You might change your battle-dress if it became ruined on exercise; you might receive another pair of boots when the first ones wore out; but you never changed your mug, knife, fork, and spoon. I shouldn't be surprised if, all over the country, there are, to this day, elderly National Servicemen who have, in some dusty drawer, or on a shelf in a shed, an Army spoon which they still use for measuring out weed-killer or getting cat-food out of the tin.

But we were new. We had only just arrived. We hadn't been issued with our mug, knife, fork, and spoon. No sympathy was available, much less help. Permanent Staff merely raised their eyes to Heaven as usual at improvident civilians cluttering up the counter. Catering corporals dug deep into their reserves of repartee to ask us what we thought this was – 'the bleed'n' Corner 'Ouse?' Without Eddie we should not have eaten at all. But it wasn't only the business of obtaining utensils.

It was Eddie who went first and showed us how to get served in military manner. Hold your plate too far from the vat of sausages and the soldier serving them stared at you until you shoved it up so that it was touching. Under no circumstances did he intend to extend his elbow more than forty-five degrees. The same with baked beans.

Potatoes and custard required a totally different technique. They were still prepared in the same sort of enormous aluminium saucepans, and they were still served with the same type of long metal spoons. But they were not hard like sausages, and they were not drippy like baked beans in tomato sauce. They were of a solid consistency approaching that of stale cream cheese, and just about as sticky. So, to get mashed potato and custard from the serving spoon on to the plate, it was necessary to hold the plate so that the rim was touching the side of the saucepan, but about three inches below the rim. The serving orderly then scooped up the regulation spoonful, poised his spoon like a Tower Green executioner's axe, and brought it down with a fearful crack on the rim of the saucepan, immediately above your plate. The resultant impact shot the contents off the spoon on to your plate at about three hundred miles an hour. If it hit the tomato sauce or the gravy or the fruit juice, you lost a good deal of your tomato sauce or your gravy or your fruit juice on to the hotplate, but the glare from the orderly halted any protest before it reached the larynx. The challenge in his eyes spoke more clearly than any words.

After lunch we sat around again, and welcomed more new arrivals. There was Albert Pegg, one of the Yorkshiremen I was talking about. Not quite one of your 'reet gradely lads', but definitely a Yorkshireman. A benign, cheerful fellow, in appearance and manner not unlike a sort of youthful Labour politician of the old school.

There was Irving Bryce, who actually looked as naïve and unworldly as we felt. Wore glasses. John Sly – another spectacle-wearer. (How did they all get into the Army? I had always thought that the medical standards were particularly stringent. But then, thinking back to my own medical. . . .)

Talking of health standards, there was another young man who stayed with us only a few days. He said he actually wanted to do National Service. It would be tempting to record that he was discharged on the spot on the grounds of insanity. But apparently he was destined for the priesthood, and had deliberately chosen to do his National Service (even though he might have been exempted, I believe) because he fancied that it would give him 'experience of Life' – which would, so he hoped, serve him well when he came to be let loose on the cure of souls, lost or otherwise.

No – the Army did not certify him. But they did discharge him. And on health grounds too. Flat feet? No. Curvature of the spine? No. Hay fever? Wrong again. You'll never guess, so I'd better tell. They discovered that he had an allergy. . . . You know that stuff, like green shoe polish, that the Army used to put on belts and other items of webbing equipment? Blanco. This keen-to-do-his-bit, seeker-after-experience, future saver of souls was *allergic to blanco*. Brought him out in rashes. Now, as we soon discovered, the average National Service recruit had more contact with blanco than with almost any other substance you care to think of – even water. Except possibly black shoe polish.

Well, anyway, the Army couldn't have one of their recruits coming out in constant rashes, and they certainly couldn't shield him from blanco (it would have been easier to cut him off from air), so they discharged him. Invalided him out. He was heartbroken. All that wonderful 'experience of Life' – the cup of wisdom, as you might say – dashed from his parched lips.

We were dumb with baffled envy. There were we, trying to think of ways to avoid the coming two years, and swapping anecdotes about legendary and successful conmen, and about how you could convince the medical teams that you were deaf or daft or whatever, and coming up with nothing. And there was Father Ignatius, who wanted – *wanted* – to do it, and they kicked him out. What a perfect escape. So simple – sheer genius. Not even Eddie the Gunge had thought of that one.

Finally, we met Mark Simpson. Well, not finally really, because there were over twenty of us all told, but you won't remember that number of names. I thought about six to ten was enough to be going on with.

Now, Mark Simpson. Solid, strong, heavy-limbed. Built on the lines of a Sherman tank. Yet another one with glasses. You began to wonder whether the Army had put all the goggle-eyed recruits in the same platoon for convenience. Yet another public schoolboy. Fraffly well spoken. Very serious. To be honest, not a greatly developed sense of humour. Keen. Quiet, but *very* determined.

He didn't say much, but, from his accent, his strength, his impassive face, his lowered brows, his earnest endeavour – his whole demeanour – you got the impression that he was going to try harder than any of us to overcome – and overcome well – anything that the Army chose to place in our path. It was not altogether too fanciful to build for him a distinguished country gentry family, whose male members had held commissions in every campaign since the Peninsular War, and whose female members had been memsahibs and consorts of consuls and company chairmen. The family honour was going to be preserved if it meant blood pounding through every vein – without of course showing any sign of it. That would have been bad form.

' 'Ey, Jack!'

Eddie, back again. Everybody was 'Jack' to begin with.

'What's up, Eddie?'

He sat down familiarly, with his feet astride a chair the wrong way round.

'Kit issue tomorrer mornin'.'

After only one day, we had learned not to be amazed at Eddie's sources of information, nor did we question them. In this case, though, the dumbest of us had worked out for himself that we should have to be given some military clothing pretty soon, so nobody collapsed with fear or shock. Eddie drew on a weedy Woodbine, inhaled, and looked round, as if timing his next remark.

'You're the P.L.'s, aintcher?'

'We're the what?'

'What I said. P.L.'s. Pertenshul Leaders. I thought you was a funny lot.'

'Thanks.'

Now what were we to make of that? Eddie wasn't finished with us yet.

'I've found out 'oo your platoon sergeant is.'

That did concentrate the attention rather more. We all thought we knew about sergeants. We had seen and heard enough about sergeants in films and songs and music hall jokes. William Hartnell had created the definitive hard-bitten sergeant in the film *The Way Ahead*. And we had come across countless stories about merciless martinets in anecdotes about wretched National Service recruits who had been reduced to weeping wrecks in two or three weeks.

Eddie flicked away some ash.

'Lugg,' he said.

'What?'

'Lugg,' he repeated. 'That's 'is name. Lugg,' he said again, savouring it.

He puffed, exhaled, and sniffed.

'Gungy bastard.'

5   First and last trump

THE AGONIES OF GETTING UP early in the morning have long been a cliché, so it will be no news to you to be told that we suffered in the same way the following day – our first military dawn. Strange place, strange bed, strange surroundings, ungodly hour – nothing much new about that either. And your average reader can work out for himself that most of us were thoroughly spoilt – either ex-schoolboys used to a tolerant parent calling up the stairs several times, or ex-undergraduates scarcely accustomed, some of them, to getting up at all. Even the tougher boarding-school survivors did not have to rise at six o'clock. And this was September – just after a very long summer holiday, when we had all, naturally, made the most of our remaining leisure and kept the most outrageous hours.

So the oaths, the groans, the hair on end, the groping for watches and the total incredulity when the hour was discerned through squinting Chinese eyes – these may be taken for granted.

But the Army did enhance the traditional, nay, hackneyed picture with two dimensions of its own with which the average reader may perhaps be unacquainted. Both were concerned with noise.

Now – I know bugles; so do you. I have heard them; so too, probably, have you. I have also heard them *en masse*, in a scout or cadet band. As close as the pavement when they march past with sock tabs fluttering and woggles at the slope. I must admit that I have never accorded bugles, either singly or in number, a great deal of my attention, or my consideration. Speaking personally, I have always been able to take bugles or leave them alone. This being a free country, I am generously prepared to believe that they do something for some people, so let them get on with it. For that reason I have for years put bugles alongside match-box collecting, morris dancing, train-spotting, and playing the ocarina. All right if you like that sort of thing, but it doesn't do anything for me.

Well, one particular bugle did something for me on that first morning in the Army, and nobody who has not been in the same position as I was can have the faintest idea of its cataclysmic impact. What I am about to offer is a feeble attempt, a pale reflection, a groping after imitative effect. It's like what they say about Dunkirk or Mafeking Night; if you weren't there, you can't possibly know.

For sheer volume I have never heard anything to beat it. If they had had the entire Royal Philharmonic Orchestra, with cannon effect, playing the '1812' Overture, they could hardly have exceeded its element of surprise, or its assurance of imminent Armageddon. And this was a single instrument. Maybe it was because it was being played between brick buildings and on an asphalt surface – you know, acoustics or whatever. Possibly there is something in the idea that the air is clearer at dawn and so the sound travels faster with fewer barriers. You get the full treatment, unalloyed by mere atmosphere. Perhaps Army bugles are some kind of super-bugle, hundreds of decibels away from the feeble braying achieved by the 4th/11th scout group on its asymmetric ramble down the High Street.

It makes you understand why the Light Brigade charged the Russian guns at Balaclava. Spurred by that awful sound, they would have galloped into the Valley of Death with a will.

I tell you something else too: if Joshua had had a dozen of these barrack-blasters at his disposal, it is small wonder that the walls of Jericho fell down. I should think the desperate inhabitants of Jericho would have been happy to pull their walls down with their own hands – anything to stop that noise. Come to think of it, perhaps that is what happened, and the scribes of Israel, ever eager to accord as much credit to Jehovah as they could, promptly labelled the incident as a miracle. After all, who would believe that city-dwellers would willingly pull down the walls of their own city? Whereas making walls fall down with a few brass arpeggios and harmonics was child's play for a god like Jehovah; compared with plagues of frogs and parting the waters of the Red Sea and pillars of fire by night, it was pretty low-key stuff – to coin a phrase.

We had no such choice. Coming as it did so suddenly, and so early, we had no means of knowing at first whether it was part of sleep or of consciousness. When something awful happens during sleep, it is some time before it forces itself upon you, and then you not only become aware of it, but you become aware that you have been becoming slowly aware of it for some time.

'Daah – dah-dah – dah – da-da-da da-da-da – daah – dah-dah – dah – da-da-da-daah!'

That made us restless. Something very unpleasant was happening, but we had no idea what it was.

The theme was repeated. (Never waste a good theme.) God Almighty! Some nightmare. But we had reached only the end of the first movement, as you might say. Then came the sort of scherzo in the middle.

'Dah da-da dah da-da, dah da-da da-dah; dah da-da dah da-da, dah da-da da-dah.'

Round about the end of the last 'da-dah', we began to realise that this was perhaps not a nightmare after all. The return to the main theme – *rinforzando* in the major key – swept away all doubts.

'Daah – dah-dah – dah – da-da-da da-da-da – daah – dah-dah – dah – da-da-da-daah!'

Then – just as suddenly – it stopped. The silence was so abrupt and so complete that for a minute, propped on our elbows, blinking and panting with shock, we wondered whether we really had had a nightmare. The silence continued. We eased ourselves off our stiff elbows, back on to our pillows. Must have been a mistake. God – that was a nasty moment. Ah, well. . . . blankets were pulled up again, and eyes were closed in relief.

Then it happened again.

'DAAH – DAH-DAH – DAH – DA-DA-DA DA-DA-DA – DAAH – DAH-DAH – DAH – DA-DA-DA-DAAH!'

We found out later that the first rendering of reveille was

perpetrated by the Depot Bugler just outside the guardroom. That was the one we concluded was a nightmare. After that he marched further into the Depot until he was standing between the two main barrack blocks, and right outside our windows. Then he let fly again.

That was the one that shot us out of sleep, heads splitting, eyes bulging, minds boggling. That was the Dunkirk element I was talking about; that was the Mafeking bit. If you weren't there, you can never know.

We lay there with our hands over our ears while the scherzo and the repeats of the main theme were hammered out.

'Jesus Christ!'

Was it going to be like this every morning for seven hundred and thirty days?

Incredibly, there were still a few unstirred bodies when it was all over. That was when the second of the two dimensions I mentioned took form.

The door of the barrack room burst open, and Corporal Bournville introduced himself to us. He didn't actually say, 'Oh, by the way, chaps, I'm Corporal Bournville, and I hope we're going to pull together and become one jolly happy team.' He went about it in a rather more informal way.

He stamped on the wooden floor – with hobnailed boots, remember. He slammed the door, re-opened it, and slammed it again – several times. He tore back bedclothes. He banged dementedly on steel lockers. He opened windows. He rattled buckets (no military interior accommodation, we were to learn, was allowed to be without buckets). He kicked the coal scuttle. He tipped up the ends of bedsteads and let them drop. He picked up a broom and banged with the handle of it on the side of the stove.

And he shouted.

His assertions cast aspersions on our sanity, manliness, military bearing, dignity, self-esteem, and of course parentage. His oaths, which we could see even in our extremity were carefully rehearsed and oft-repeated, combined the violent exaggeration of Long John

Silver with the prophetic vehemence of Jonah and Elijah.

So – by about eight and half minutes past six on our first morning in the Army, we had become acquainted with the military obsession with noise.

This deserves a small digression.

First of all – to be fair – I don't think Corporal Bournville's ranting was typical of this obsession. This was a non-commissioned officer of pretty lowly rank succumbing to the temptation to make life uncomfortable for a crowd of raw recruits at the moment when they were at their most vulnerable, and when they were totally unable to answer back, or even bridle with annoyance. Any overweening school prefect or playground bully, in similar circumstances, would have been tempted to do the same. The episode merely introduced us to the principle of noise, so that we were more prepared for its later, perhaps more genuine, manifestations.

If you stop to think about it, the Army can hardly avoid noise, because it exists to fight wars, and wars are somewhat tumultuous affairs. The most ill-disposed new soldier would, if he were honest, have to admit that. We knew too that much of our training would have to do with noisy things like guns and hand grenades and thunderflashes. If we were fair, we knew too that we would have to get used to drill commands bawled at us from the other side of the parade ground. The man had to make himself heard.

All that was noise from necessity. What we were not prepared for was the Army's assumption that noise for its own sake conduced to efficiency. Setting the foot on the ground was not smart, however quickly or firmly or elegantly the manoeuvre was performed; stamping was. Placing the hand against the weapon during a rifle drill movement was not soldierly; slapping it hard was. A sergeant-major did not march an offender to the colonel's office for trial with spoken commands; he roared them, even though the said offender was only three feet away and the long-suffering colonel about five.

This passion for raising the voice has provoked much bitter reminiscence from those who have recalled their recruit days during

National Service. Not only are we told, in books, articles, TV documentaries and interviews, that sergeants and sergeant-majors thrust their faces within inches of a recruit's nose in order to bellow what they thought of him; we are also assured, with much sense of injury, that the insulted recruit was required to bawl the abuse about himself back to the aforesaid sergeant or sergeant-major. This elevating interchange is enhanced by the sergeant (or sergeant-major) lacing his abuse with vulgarity, lurid innuendo about the recruit's private life, and outrageous exaggeration. Something like this:

'Private Lacey, your kit is in shit order. What is it?'

'IT IS IN SHIT ORDER, SERGEANT'!'

'It is the kit of a roaring queer. What is it?'

'IT IS THE KIT OF A ROARING QUEER, SERGEANT!'

'It is the worst kit I have seen in my whole life. What is it?'

'IT IS THE WORST KIT YOU HAVE SEEN IN YOUR WHOLE LIFE, SERGEANT!'

And so on.

A lot has been made of this technique by memorialists. They claim too that the abuse is much less printable and much more personal than I have indicated here. Sergeants' powers of invective have extended beyond the suffering recruit to embrace his whole family.

That may be so. I am not suggesting that these incidents have been totally fabricated. There is no smoke without fire. But you must speak as you find. All I can say is that I was an ordinary kind of soldier, and I had experience of three different types of training squads during my National Service, and no sergeant or sergeant-major ever did that to me. Nor did I see it done to any member of any training platoon I was in.

Of course I got shouted at. We were all shouted at. We were all chased. We all got sworn at from time to time. One of our sergeants repeatedly cast doubts on our heterosexuality. But it was done to all of us, from a distance. As often as not, it caused us to writhe – not with agony, but with suppressed mirth. No sergeant or sergeant-major pushed his stubbly jowl under my nose and demanded partnership in the vulgar operatic double act I have described above, nor did any of my fellow-recruits' noses ever quiver with a similar threat.

A few National Service lance-corporals tried hard to be unpleasant, but they had not the presence, the depth of nicotine stain, the richness of invention of their seniors. They were so obviously beardless little bullies trying to imitate their betters that nobody took them seriously.

I just thought I'd put the record straight.

Anyway, we were up. Now we had to get washed and dressed. Clearly, we couldn't all get washed at the same time, so by a combination of elementary common sense and Devil take the hindmost, some of us trudged off to the 'Ablutions' (a term I have found used nowhere but in the Army), while the rest made their beds (not so simple as one might think, especially for those spoilt young men who had hitherto had their mothers to do it for them; but as this was the Army, they felt they'd better show willing).

The washroom had once been decorated in green distemper, which was now flaking off at the slightest touch. The scars left by those who had tried, and failed, to fix mirrors to the walls with the aid of nails showed that the colour over the years had alternated between green and yellow no fewer than five times. Enamel on the sinks, like grass on an Australian test wicket, was a matter of form. And plugs were as rare as the dodo.

Here was another of Life's Great Puzzles, and I'm sure I'm not the first to speculate on it. Why do people steal plugs from sinks? Wherever you find sinks in public places – Army washrooms, public toilets, recreation grounds, cheap hotels, shower blocks in school playing fields – there the plugs are – gone. Yet they must have been there to begin with, as the pathetic amputated length of rusting chain testifies. I repeat – why?

They are not intrinsically valuable. They are not particularly useful for anything other than the purpose for which they are designed (unless by chance they are vital for the performance of some unspeakable sexual perversion which holds nearly the whole nation in thrall, knowledge of which I am precluded from having by virtue of my sheltered existence). They are not rare – easily obtained in any ironmonger's shop, or DIY emporium today. Possession of them has no special cachet.

Can you imagine a felon gloating over his latest coup – a twenty-seven carat, brass-centred, platinum-bound beauty from a millionaire's country house? Or one resourceful thief showing off to his rival in his garden shed – 'Look at that. Finest set of draughts you'll ever see. And you know what? Never cost a penny.' Or the compulsive collector who boasts to his fellow-enthusiast, 'Beat that – one from every hotel from Claridge's to the Dorchester. All I need is the Hilton and my set is complete.' Or the man who must keep ahead of the Joneses: 'Leicester Square? Leicester Square? Everyone's got Leicester Square. Now – if you had one from Holborn Viaduct Gents – like me. . . . '

However, tantalising as it may be to theorise about the possibility of a special sort of criminal mind – which may lead, from stealing plugs out of sinks, to depositing brass bedsteads beside stagnant ponds, heaving old fridges into ravines, and blacking out the teeth in smiling ladies' pictures on the Underground – I must return to the washroom and discuss water.

Luckily for us, it was still early autumn, so the temperature of the rusty fluid that sputtered from the asthmatic tap was quite tolerable. The horrors of late autumn and winter were in store for us. By that time we had learned that hot water issued from the taps only on the day of inspection by a visiting general.

Boilers existed, and, as with most other devices for providing for the common soldier's comfort and contentment, there was a laid-down means for putting them into operation. The trouble came when one tried to find out just where it was laid down. Depot Standing Orders were verbose in the extreme on the positioning and colouring and contents of buckets for the extinction of unlawful fires, but completely silent on arrangements for the starting and maintenance of lawful ones.

Responsibility for the boilers was largely a question of habit or rumour. One thesis held that it was one of the jobs implied by 'General Duties', thereby laying it squarely at the door of the Permanent Staff. Another theory suggested that it should come within the purview of the Sanitary Orderly – Craphouse Dan. A third school of thought maintained that it ought to be done by that lazy so-and-so of a civilian who supervised the delivery of coal to the Married Quarters. Now and then the Duty Corporal would remember to ask the night guard to 'have a look at the boilers' as they went round the barracks in the small hours; but if the guards happened to be Permanent Staff they would be too anxious to get back to their card game to be bothered, and if they were recruits they would not know where the boilers were anyway – and Duty Corporals were not always punctilious in informing them.

The Company Sergeant-Major was of the opinion that modern soldiers never showed enough initiative, and that they ought to get things like that done for themselves. But if any recruits managed to locate the boilers, they still had to find time in an overcrowded day to light them. If they found time, they had to procure wood and newspaper in an establishment where nobody issued anything for nothing and where untidy piles of scraps were not tolerated. If opportunity, wood and paper were to become available, the question of a coal supply presented itself; the ration was about two bucketsful per room per week. And finally, if by some providential miracle everything came to hand, the task of actually making the boilers work was one which demanded a combination of the patience of Robert the Bruce and the engineering skill of George Stephenson.

We all got washed after a fashion. We all got dressed – still in our civilian clothes. Can you imagine – collars and ties, and sports jackets! No wonder the Permanent Staff raised their eyes in disgusted disbelief when they saw us cluttering up the breakfast hotplate in the canteen. Even Hamilton managed to get there on time – thanks to some of us making his bed for him.

Corporal Bournville got hold of us immediately afterwards. Collected us back in the barrack room. He was tall, thin, and slightly emaciated, with a liberal collection of spots on a pale face. Man of few words – when he wasn't waking us up. But he turned out to be reasonably human when you got to know him.

We asked him once what it was that had induced him to join the Regular Army. Nothing short of an Act of Parliament had pulled us into National Service for two years, never mind the Regular Army for nine, so we were understandably curious.

'Box pleats,' he said at once.

'What?'

'Box pleats. I were on t'dole. An' this lad from our street coom 'ome from the Army on leave. In uniform. 'E were that streight. Streight oop, like a ramrod. An' smart. 'E were that smart. Loovly box pleats 'e 'ad, right across t'shoulders of 'is battledress. Ah said to meself, I want to be smart like that. I want to 'ave box pleats like that. So ah joined oop.'

And very smart box-pleats Corporal Bournville had, too. Knife edges. Sharpen a pencil on them. He was a good corporal too, as corporals go – and we were to become connoisseurs.

'Ey oop,' he said. ''Ere cooms yer sergeant – Sergeant Loog.'

It was useless for him to bring us to attention, because most of us hadn't the faintest idea of what that entailed. We stood up reasonably straight, because we felt that it showed willing. One or two of us tried addressing the sergeant as 'Sir', which occasioned much amusement, and the first of his heavy-handed jokes.

He looked ostentatiously all round the room.

'I can't see any officer. Can you see any officer, Corporal Bournville?'

'No, sergeant,' said the corporal, right on cue.

'I wonder where the officer can be hiding,' went on Sergeant

Lugg, squeezing the pips out of the joke, which wasn't much of a joke in the first place.

From this ponderous sarcasm, the sergeant conveyed to us that only commissioned officers were to be addressed as 'Sir', with the exception of the Sergeant-Major.

'Ya call me "Sergeant", ' he said.

'Yes, sergeant.'

Well, it seemed sense to get on the right side of him.

Sergeant Lugg fitted the Army, and the Army fitted him. To say that he had a coarse face was an understatement; he looked like one of those great Renaissance, not-quite statues that had been salvaged from marble quarry detritus at Carrara – you know, one of Michelangelo's false starts, abandoned on his way to roughing out Moses.

It may have been a face a mother could love, but I shouldn't think it had inspired much affection in schoolteachers, neighbours, shopkeepers, policemen, probation officers, or magistrates. Or employers, for that matter; I could not imagine him holding down a regular job for long.

But for all his lack of education and finesse, he was not without wit and resource. Not without guile and low cunning either. He had clearly entered the Army on the reasonable assumption that it could not possibly be worse than what he had had before. Now, after a decade or so, he was fed, clothed, and housed to a standard far beyond that of his civilian days, and he probably had more to spend on himself each week than most schoolteachers, neighbours, local shopkeepers, policemen, probation officers, and magistrates. His uniform, and more especially his rank, opened avenues of society to him that would otherwise have remained forever closed. This was particularly so in regard to younger members of the opposite sex, many of whom were prepared to grant the most intimate favours in return for the privilege of being seen out with someone who looked so dashing and smart. It was a common fashion to attend local social gatherings in Number One uniform – 'blues'. It was not too difficult in the late 1940's and 1950's to pick up a campaign medal or two – Palestine, Malaya, Korea, Kenya. Can't beat a tiny rampart of brightly-coloured medal ribbons to enhance a manly chest.

The Army appreciated him too. Characteristics which had been deplored by schoolteachers, neighbours, local shopkeepers, policemen, probation officers, and magistrates redounded to his credit once he had donned khaki. The furtive teenage hooligan who had been able to commit to memory the timings and distances of every policeman's beat from the Balham High Road to Vauxhall Bridge could, as an NCO, commit to memory the salient points of a military training pamphlet as easily as falling off a log.

The light-fingered thief who would take anything that wasn't nailed down would be appreciated by his platoon commander as a resourceful sergeant who could be relied upon to procure any desired item of equipment or furniture within days – so long as not too many questions were asked. Quick wits, a vocabulary honed by the whetstone of the gutter, a sound physique, and a raucous voice were the perfect qualifications for the successful drill instructor. Not strong on flexibility or imagination, perhaps, but you couldn't have everything, and no army could expect all its sergeants to be gifted Napoleonic heroes with field marshals' batons in their knapsacks.

6   What the well-dressed soldier wears

'FIRS' OF ALL, Y'ALL GOTTA 'ave Army 'aircuts. When y'get aht of 'ere, firs' lef', firs' righ', an' up the stairs. 'E's there from six till nine Mundis, Wednesdis, an' Fursdis.'

'What if we had a haircut just before we came in?' said Irving Bryce.

Sergeant Lugg brought the full range of his powers of wit and repartee to bear on this footling interruption.

'When ya comes inter the Army, you 'as an Army 'aircut. SEE!'

Irving jumped, swallowed, and nodded.

With one final glare of disapproval, Sergeant Lugg returned to the agenda.

He always enjoyed the first full day of the new intake's Army life. He could swagger and shout, and be respected almost to the point of reverence. He could unmask his admittedly limited battery of military wisecracks, and actually get a laugh with each one. And he could derive immense satisfaction from the number of jaws he could cause to drop by enunciating the standards of cleanliness, smartness, and efficiency he expected from one and all.

'Ya won't get no timetable till nex' week. You'll spend from nah tiwl Mundy cleanin' yer kit and getting' it stamped.' He paused, as if gathering himself for the forthcoming *ex cathedra* utterance. 'Ev'ry item of kit you possess mus' be clearly stamped wiv yer Army number. All woollen and other items of soft clothing wiwl bear a tape sewn on them, also clearly stamped wiv yer Army number.'

Before anyone could ask how we were to stamp numbers, or sew tapes, on to our Army kit, when most of us had little more than a fountain pen in our pockets, the sergeant took another deep breath and launched into another prerecorded message.

'The stampin' kit can be drawn from the Depot stores between the ahrs of nine-firty and ten-firty on all weekdays excep' Sattidis.'

The fact that it was now Friday, and already well past nine o'clock (and a full day in front of us), and we were expected, it seemed, to have all our kit stamped, sewn, numbered, and clearly identifiable by Monday morning, and the Depot stores were to be closed all day Saturday and Sunday, did not strike our sergeant as in any way anomalous.

But it was a crowded programme. The sergeant swept on to the next item.

'Reportin' sick.'

We forgot our kit-numbering and listened. What to do if we should become ill seemed far more important than a few crummy digits inside the waistband of a pair of pants.

Another deep breath. Another papal bull was about to be delivered.

'The Nigh' Orderly Cawprul wiwl come rahnd at six a.m. an' ask if anyone's sick. If y'wake up sick, y'tell 'im yer number, rank, and name. Then y'make y'bed up, dress fer y'firs' parade, put y'small kit in y'aversack – which shall consist of pyjamas, towel, cleanin' kit, shavin' kit, spare shirt, spare underclo's, P.T. shorts, P.T. vest, P.T. shoes, spare socks, mug, knife, fork, and spoon – an' be on parade ahtside the barrack block at seven-firty sharp, to be marched over to the M.O. Any questions?'

'Yes, Sergeant,' said John Sly, who had recovered first. 'What time do we have to be on parade if we're not sick?'

'Abaht eight-firty. Why?'

'Oh, nothing. I just wondered.'

After a glance of mild curiosity, the sergeant moved on to item three.

'Barrack Room Duties,' he intoned. 'Besides makin' y'bed boxes and cleanin' up y'bed spaces, each one of yer 'as a Barrack Room Duty.'

He waved a sheet of paper in the air, and pointed at it with the index finger of his free hand, the colour of which indicated a terminally carcinogenic consumption of cigarettes.

'I've written 'em awl dahn 'ere. I'll pin it up on the door arterwoods, and y'can each find aht wot y're doin'. I'll swop 'em rahnd ev'ry week, so's y'awl get a go at each one. My platoon,' he added meaningly, 'always 'as the cleanest barrack room in the 'ole Depot. Any questions?'

He glowered round like a cornered wolf.

'Yes, sir,' said Taffy Davies pleasantly. 'I mean, "Sergeant".' He corrected himself just in time, before Sergeant Lugg could go looking under beds for commissioned officers. 'What do you mean by bed boxes?'

'I'll show yer,' was the prompt reply. 'Where's y'bed?'

Taffy pointed it out.

'Get rahnd 'ere.'

We shuffled into an obedient circle like a cowed group of tourists.

Taffy had thrown up his bedclothes into a semblance of order before breakfast. I suppose we could consider ourselves lucky to have been supplied with blankets and sheets on our first day. They were there when we arrived. I was to hear stories of recruits in other depots having to lie for their first night on their bedsprings, or (probably preferably) on the floor.

Sergeant Lugg stripped Taffy's bed completely. He then proceeded to demonstrate one of the many ways devised by military morale-builders to fill each second of several unforgiving minutes of a soldier's morning. This consisted of arranging the sheets and blankets, by folds and packings of geometric precision, into a sort of bedding sandwich. You know – blanket-sheet-blanket-sheet. (Or was it sheet-blanket-sheet-blanket? I can't remember now. But there must have been a vital difference, and the Army would have stressed the importance of getting it right. Bound to have been in Depot Standing Orders.)

The sergeant took the last blanket – which had to be the green one (all the others were black or grey) – the 'bes' blankit'. He folded this into a longer strip so that it could be wound completely round the aforesaid sandwich, with the alternate folded layers of sheet and blanket (or blanket and sheet) still showing. Somehow or other the loose ends were tucked away. This unit now became a 'bed box'. The bed box was then placed at the head of the bed, and surmounted by the two pillows, the utmost care being taken that no such horrors as creases, dents, or rucks spoiled the visual, not to say, aesthetic harmony of *le tout ensemble*.

The sergeant spent some considerable time over this, continually stepping back to cock his head and admire the progress of his labour, and stepping forward again to make a minute adjustment here, or hide a stray thread of blanket there. The whole thing would have seemed ludicrous, but for the fact that the sergeant had an expression on his face of such rapt concentration as to preclude any question of open laughter. Or suppressed mirth, come to that. He had completely forgotten his audience, so absorbed did he become in the process of obtaining the absolute precision of folds, the exact width of sheet in proportion to blanket (or blanket to sheet). In that brief span of time, Sergeant Lugg's vocation in life was bed-box-building. To him, in that moment, the supreme question of existence, the ultimate pattern and purpose of the universe, was summed up in the achievement of the perfect bed box.

This quest for perfection became infectious, and, as so often happens when a person is watched while he is performing a task requiring patience and delicacy, the onlookers felt affected by his intense concentration, and were themselves consumed. When, therefore, the sergeant stepped back for the sixth time to view his masterpiece, and Jack Gatewood pointed out that one sheet was showing at least half an inch of width more than its adjacent blanket, the sergeant merely grunted in agreement, and pulled the whole thing to pieces, reassembling it with the same meticulous care.

At long last, he turned to his enraptured audience, who almost had to resist the urge to give him a round of applause.

'There y'are,' he said. 'That's wot y'do ev'ry mawnin'.'

It had taken him about twenty-five minutes.

The spell was broken.

'Christ Almighty!'

At that rate we'd have to get up at five o'clock, never mind six. And if we ever got it as perfect as that, we'd never have the heart to undo it again.

'I'd rather sleep on the floor,' muttered Albert Pegg.

Hamilton would never have time for breakfast. He'd be at it all day.

Sergeant Lugg stood up, placed his hands on his hips in an exaggerated attitude of alertness, and gazed round in satisfaction at our incredulous faces.

'Right! Any more questions?'

'Yes, Sergeant,' said John Sly, beaming through his glasses. 'When do we get leave?'

We sniggered. But the sergeant was ready for us. He stretched his neck forward and thrust his face in the direction of the speaker, in a gesture clearly intended to take him aback.

'When y'can wear yer uniform smart enough t'get pas' the Guardroom. An' that won't be fer some time. Which reminds me.'

He looked at his watch, and clapped his hands.

'All ahtside. Kit issue. Time for the RQMS.'

Even the sergeant, who, we were to observe, was to show total contempt for all forms of authority (behind their back) short of the Queen, was not willing to be late for an appointment with the Regimental Quartermaster-Sergeant.

The description I am about to give of Colour Sergeant Ernest Berryman is not an accurate picture of the man who actually gave us our kit on that first full day, for the simple reason that I can not remember him. But I met quite a few regimental quartermaster-sergeants in the course of my two years, and this portrait, though composite, gives off, I hope, the ring of truth. Ideally, in order to vindicate myself, I should like to receive dozens of letters from old National Servicemen, assuring me that my picture is absolutely spot-on.

Colour Sergeant Ernest Berryman was an old soldier. He had joined up in 1939, when the call came. He may have been a Territorial before the War, when the storm clouds were gathering in 1938. He may even have been a Regular before that – when soldiering really was soldiering. As a private, he had waited, and wondered, and cursed, and probably sweated, on the Dunkirk beaches. Rescued, re-trained, re-posted, and promoted lance-corporal, he had sworn, and sweated again (for different reasons), in the Libyan sands. As a full corporal, he had bounced and heaved (in both senses) in landing craft towards the beaches in Sicily and Salerno, and he had sloshed through the mud of the Gothic Line. As a sergeant, he had fought and fraternised his way – depending on whether he was dealing with German soldiers or French civilians (preferably female and young) – from Normandy to the River Rhine.

So he had probably earned most of the medals that spread across his ample chest – the 1939-45 star, the Defence medal, the Africa star, the Italy star, the Victory in Europe medal, and so on. When we joined the Army in the mid-1950's, there were still a lot of men there who had served right through the War, and who had decided, for a variety of reasons, that the military life they had been forced to learn up to 1945 offered better prospects in peacetime than the more pedestrian jobs from which they had escaped, or been drawn, in 1939. Ten years later, there they still were – often with little enhancement or rank, but with great enhancement of experience, a cosy little niche, and a very sharp eye to the main chance.

Sergeant Berryman found himself posted, in 1945, to assist at a demobilisation centre for those who wished to return to civilian life. Here he began to acquire some conception of the ramifications of the Army supply system. Here he learned the three cardinal rules of the quartermaster's profession:

The rigid understatement of one's resources and capabilities.

The blank refusal to issue items of kit one inch beyond basic requircments without the explicit instructions of at least a divisional commander.

The total embargo on any item of kit going past the store-room door that had not been individually and expressly signed for, and the unquestionable status of ownership – total and perpetual – that that signature implied for its author.

Ernest Berryman discovered, as so many men did in a variety of similar situations, that carrying a file and sitting at the back did the career a lot more good than carrying a rifle and marching at the front. So he sucked his pen and kept his ledgers up to date; he counted his stores at the scheduled times; he made lavish indents for equipment and sparing issues of it; he hid his reserves when the Ordnance inspection teams came round; and he kept his fire buckets clean and freshly red and filled with clear water (which always seemed to impress visiting generals).

He won one more promotion – to colour sergeant – and so became conscious that he now had a position to maintain. This feeling was enhanced by his belated venture into matrimony. Installed as Company Quartermaster-Sergeant at his Regimental Depot, he settled down for good and all into routine, and became to all intents and purposes a middle-aged suburban business man. He rented a modest house near the Depot. He bought a small motor car, which he solemnly drove five hundred yards every weekday to his office. He took out one or two endowment policies. He joined the local darts league. He developed a paunch. The only real difference between him and the assistant manager at a local agency was that instead of wearing a shiny blue suit, he ambled from his office to his store in an ill-fitting battledress, on which the insignia of his rank were conspicuous.

But whether you liked Colour Sergeant Berryman or not, you had to admit that he ran a good store. It was his private opinion that it was the best in the Brigade, and he could well have been right. It was certainly the tidiest. He knew from memory the exact shelf, locker, or drawer of every conceivable item from a Bags Kit to a Buttons Denim, and woe betide any of his storemen whom he caught negligently tossing a Gloves Hand Knitted in with the Gloves Wire Protecting.

Along with the ghostly absence of disarray went an adherence to routine as rigid as a regimental sergeant-major's pace stick. The Colour Sergeant laid down the hours during which the Depot stores were open for business, and outside those hours nothing short of a full admininstrative inspection by a lieutenant-general would induce him to pull back a single bolt. To give him his due, he swung back the doors for business at 8 a.m. sharp – set your watch by him – but any unfortunate who arrived so much as thirty seconds after the Depot clock had announced 10.30 a.m. would find those same doors closed with the implacability of the gates of Jerusalem against the infidel.

Routine, routine, routine. To Ernest Berryman the very worst sin that any human could commit was to break it. Sabotage the Depot transport; poison the canteen stew (an improvement, the wags would say); blow up the magazine; assassinate the Commanding Officer (another improvement) – all these were merely venial sins. The mortal sin of all mortal sins was to interrupt long-established routine.

And that was what we, the recruits, did, every five or six weeks. So he didn't like us much. When Sergeant Lugg assembled us outside his store that morning, dangerously close to his closing time, he met us with a baleful stare.

'Come in when I call your name.'

What happened next came under the heading of what the French would call *'mouvementé'*.

I hope I have been able to convey the impression that Colour Sergeant Berryman was a pretty efficient regimental quartermaster-sergeant. It barely needs pointing out that his storemen, after hundreds of issues of kit to newly-arrived National Service recruits, were also pretty slick. I can hardly resist summing up their skill by suggesting that they performed their duties just like well-drilled soldiers. Added to this was the Colour Sergeant's very natural eagerness to get his store closed as near as he could to the hour set in stone by hallowed custom. The result was that each recruit was shunted along the counter more quickly than a customer in a high-speed eatery whose staff were out to win the year's efficiency prize.

Certainly nobody was allowed to delay proceedings for an instant by asking questions, by seeking time to read the forms shoved in front of him for him to sign, by testing the fit of shirt collars, or by trying on battledress blouses.

Note – the forms came first. Before any recruit could receive so much as a Needles Darning, he had to sign for it. As soon as he had entered the Holy of Holies, he was propelled towards the end of the counter, where a storeman pushed several pieces of paper towards him. He got a blurred impression of a series of complicated grid layouts, and various disembodied words like 'Bags Kit' and 'Mugs China' swam before his eyes.

'Sign.'

A greasy biro materialised. Hesitation as to where to place one's signature was speedily resolved by a nicotine-drenched finger stabbing the paper.

As I write these lines, it occurs to me to wonder what would have happened if somebody had signed his name 'W.C. Fields' or 'O. Wilde' or 'A. Dumas'. I don't suppose any of those bored storemen actually read every signature – if indeed they read one. And I doubt too if those celebrity names would have meant much if they had. I remember a later colleague of mine telling me that, during his time in the RAF in the War, he was leaning out of his hut window, thinking of nothing in particular, when along came a harassed corporal, who had been saddled with the task of organising a camp concert. He was desperate to find talent, any talent. As he caught Denis' eye, he said anxiously, 'Do you know anyone who plays the piano?'

Denis promptly said, 'Yes – Moiseiwitsch.'

Relief blazed in the corporal's eyes.

'Which hut's he in?'

None of us was so inventive, or so seditious.

Once the signing was over, our heads span. We moved down the counter to the accompaniment of a sort of sartorial plainchant, led by the Colour Sergeant (with a master-form the size of an international treaty in his hand), while his storemen intoned the responses. As they did so, they awarded the recruit the article referred to, putting it in his kitbag (his first acquisition), or, as that became full, shoving it under his arms, throwing it over his shoulders, thrusting it into his belt, slinging it round his neck, pushing it into his pockets, and placing it on his head. Their infinite practice enabled them to achieve a machine-gun speed and precision.

'Shirts Angola three – '

'Shirts Angola three.'

'Vests Woollen two – '

'Vests Woollen two.'

'Drawers Woollen two – '

'Drawers Woollen two.'

'Vest P.T. red one – '

'Vest P.T. red one.'

The only breaks in the ceremony came when the recruit was asked what size he took in boots (well, we were the infantry, so they had to get our feet right), and when a storeman ran a canny eye over us before selecting a battledress blouse of approximately corresponding capacity. Thereafter the chant was resumed.

'Belts Waist one – '

'Belts Waist one.'

'Pouches Basic two – '

'Pouches Basic two.'

'Frogs Bayonet one – '

'Frogs Bayonet one.' (Yes, frog. I'll explain that later. Watch out for it in the chapter about rifle drill.)

The list seemed interminable. By the time the recruit had reached the end of the counter, he felt as if he had been over-endowed with equipment for a two-year trip to the moon. Two berets and a tin hat were perched on his head; his pockets were stuffed with buttons, button-rings, shoulder-flashes, cap-badges, and bootlaces; round his neck hung ties, socks, boots, and braces; his shoulders sagged beneath the welter of of flaps, straps, and packs that were reputed to be an inescapable part of the vital equipment of the well-trained soldier; one hand dragged an overfilled kitbag; every finger on the other grasped loops, holes, buttons, hooks, and straps on a shapeless mass of khaki clothing; and over everything was draped, in the manner of a bell tent, a colossal greatcoat.

'Ne'er cast a clout,' muttered someone as he staggered through the door.

When we had made it back to the barrack room, feeling rather like Scott's party arriving at the Pole, we strove to induce some kind of order into our mountainous baggage.

At least, some of us did. Martin Forrest and Albert Pegg each selected a Vest Woollen, a pair of Drawers Woollen, and a Belts Waist, put them on, and challenged each other to a prize fight. Bill Glover was on hand to record the event for posterity. I still have the picture.

Sergeant Lugg put an end to the jollity by informing us that we were all to get dressed properly – boots, gaiters, denims, and so on. That meant, first, getting the buttons into the holes on the denim jacket. The rings were small; the tension under which they had been constructed seemed to have been calculated to retain a horse trailer, never mind a button; the denim material of the jacket was thick, hard with newness, and totally unyielding. That cost us only our fingernails.

Then came the business of making the jacket and the trousers remain in a fair measure of proximity to the body; that cost us our dignity. Like so many items of Army equipment in those days (and, for all I know, now too), these denim overalls were manufac-tured with no variation in size. (Rather like the tin hats, which were clearly produced on a conveyor belt in the conviction that every recruit's head was uniformly spherical. They would have served well in Cromwell's New Model Army.) They were cut in the firm belief that every new recruit was about six feet five inches tall, with a forty-inch waist and a fifty-inch chest. Which said a lot about the treatment they were expected to get from Army laundries.

The Army braces kept the trousers at a height consonant with the standards of common decency, but they could not prevent them bagging out at the waist in the manner of a circus clown. So one of the mysterious webbing straps, the use of which we had no idea of as yet, was put into service, if only to stop the draughts.

Taffy stole the show at this point. He was, as I have said, rather short. He found that he could button the fly of the trousers right up to his chin, and he could put his arms through the pocket holes. He didn't need the jacket at all.

Then we put on the grey socks. They were rough, hard, and hairy, and would have driven the most ardent medieval hermit to give up his ascetic life in the wilds and go back to the fleshpots. Talk about mortification of the flesh. When we pulled on the boots, it pressed the socks even closer to our protesting skin. The boots were of course hard, and pimply, with about as much give as a pair of half-finished clogs. The leather laces were greasy and did not grip, and experiment soon proved that any tug exerted in sharp annoyance was too much for them. When we fastened the anklets, or Gaiters Webbing, that pressed the socks closer still against our martyred feet.

Standing was a feat (sorry about the pun). Walking at first appeared an impossibility. The thought of stamping the foot in a drill movement was beyond agony even in theory. Napoleon had once said that an army marched on its stomach. If it had boots and socks like these, I'm not surprised.

7   Smoke if you wish

'BLEED'N CHRIST – YOU LOOK like a twisted sick report.'

The epithet was not mine – I'm glad to say. It was the second of Sergeant Lugg's jokes. The first, if you recall, was his elaborate search round the barrack room the day before when someone ended a sentence with the word 'sir'; the ponderous pantomime was his way of informing us that one did not use the word when addressing non-commissioned officers. So we were treated to an exhibition of his histrionic skills.

Now, when we had at last dressed ourselves in Army clothing for the first time, and he surveyed one of our number from the front, we were regaled with his gift for repartee.

'You look like a twisted sick report.'

Well, OK, we showed willing; after all, it was the first time we had heard it. The Sergeant pretended not to have heard the polite laughter, like the comedian who rushes on to his next joke in order to show his audience what a clever throwaway humourist he is – and what a fertile one. Always plenty of jokes to come – can afford to cast them to left and right in abandoned prodigality.

He clapped his hands.

'On yer feet. Fall in ahtside. Time fer yer openin' address from the Commandin' Officer.'

Since we had not yet learnt any drill commands, and since, in our new Army boots, socks, and gaiters, even walking was a major achievement, I can hardly claim that we actually *marched* to the hut where we were to receive our speech of welcome. Sergeant Lugg bawled out 'Lef'! Righ'! Lef'! Righ'!' more to keep up appearances than anything else. We looked, and sounded, less like a body of able-bodied soldiers than a sort of composite human centipede with dyspraxia.

Anyway, we got there. The sergeant seated us inside and told us to wait. The silence gave way to mumbles of speculation. Then the sound of footsteps silenced them. It was only Corporal Bournville. He waited with Lugg just outside the door.

More footsteps sounded. A very large, fierce man appeared in the doorway. We leapt to our feet. It was only the Regimental Sergeant-Major. (Ha! Only!) We had never seen him before. He told us to sit down, while he joined Bournville and Lugg outside. We heard a match strike.

We waited. . . .

The Commanding Officer was a sort of lesser crested long-tailed osprey in human form. People got sightings of him. At least that was how it seemed to recruits. Those in authority over us laid claim to far greater acquaintance, and posed as experts on his moods and whims. They invoked him, in the way that harassed nannies used to call up the bogey man when every other ruse to quiet their charges had failed. The CO would do this; the CO wanted that; the CO would not tolerate something else. Corporals allowed a note of awe to creep into their flattened vowels when they spoke of him. Sergeants, even Lugg when it suited him, tried to use him to instil an extra sense of urgency into our drill – 'Nah, pull y'selves togevver. The CO said 'e migh' come pas' this mawnin'.' The Company Sergeant-Major would refer to him as a kind of divine being who could, if provoked, wreak terrible retribution on any trainee who fell short of the stratospherically high standards he was supposed to demand.

One and all they extolled his reputation, made admonitory remarks about his vigilance, drew fearsome pictures of his utter omnipotence within the confines of the barracks, and generally strove to inculcate a feeling of unthinking adulation of this distant deity.

This sense of mystic power was enhanced by his very seclusion. He was said to assume human form at about 11 a.m. on alternate mornings, in some temple of the Covenant, the approaches of which were guarded by the offices, and the persons, of the Chief Clerk, the Orderly Room Clerks, the Adjutant, the Second-in-Command, and the Regimental Sergeant-Major. A pretty impressive combination when you think about it – the remoteness of the Dalai Lama, the elusive ubiquity of the Scarlet Pimpernel, the omniscience of Hal the computer, and the capricious, awesome wrath of Baal and Kali.

As I said, people got sightings of him, and not always expected. There was the story of the soldier who nearly found himself on a charge for not saluting a tweedy civilian coming down the steps of the Officers' Mess one Saturday afternoon with golf clubs over his shoulder, his defence being that he had not the faintest idea who he was. The Sergeants' Mess once persuaded him to appear in uniform, to pose for a photograph in the centre of his senior NCO's on the occasion of their winning the inter-depot darts shield for that year.

In theory, there was a Commanding Officer's inspection of the barracks every Saturday morning, but somehow the task became deputed with mysterious frequency to some other Depot dignitary at the last minute. 'The Commanding Officer was busy', we were told (like nanny, who couldn't play today because she'd got a bone in her leg). Or he had been 'called away' (no doubt a crisis planning session to meet the latest Russian invasion threat up the Solent). Or – a favourite – 'attending a Brigade Conference'.

This remoteness, moreover, was not occasioned by his lofty rank; he was only a major. The Commanding Officer of the entire Regimental Depot was a major. But remote he was. The only soldiers who saw him with any regularity, apart from the senior captains – and there weren't many of those – and the senior NCO's, and of course his batman, were those few reprobates who made a habit of overstaying their leave, and were therefore accustomed every six months or so to spending two or three minutes in an attitude of rigid attention before his desk while he passed sentence on them.

The one occasion on which his physical presence could be predicted with accuracy was when the time came to make a few remarks of welcome and encouragement to the new intake of National Service recruits. As they had not yet been in the Army for more than a day – if that – no effort was to be spared in order to create an atmosphere of relaxation and informality.

The Commanding Officer's contribution to this effort was to wear his Number One uniform – blues. When his shape loomed in the distance, the NCO's furthered the effort by shouting at their charges till they were sitting in nice straight lines, and then by taking up alert stances in positions of vantage all round the Depot Sports Hut, from which they glared in exaggerated vigilance in all directions. Finally, when the CO was almost at the door, the Regimental Sergeant-Major, with a final scalding glance at the whole room to make sure that it was well and truly relaxed, bawled, 'Room! R-o-o-o-o-o-m – SHUN!'

The CO returned the RSM's rigid salute, proceeded to a makeshift desk, and removed his cap.

'Right, sit down, men,' he remarked genially. 'Smoke if you wish.'

Men!

Ever seen *Bambi*? Come now, you must have done. D'you know the bit where the rabbit, Thumper, is reproved by his mother for some verbal indiscretion, and is forced to recite his well-learned lesson: 'If you can't think of anythin' nice to say, don't say nuthin' at aawl.' By the same token, if you can't think of a suitable word, don't use any.

It would have been all right if he'd just said 'sit down'. The 'men' was so false, and so forced. For a start, we weren't. Men, I mean. We were school-leavers, or we were fresh from university lectures and playing fields. The most we had seen of the world was a few European country roads from the back of a lorry – the 'fifties saw the birth of the great hitch-hiking craze. (Students have always been poor, but the reader of the new millennium needs to be reminded that in the years following the War the allowance of foreign spending money allocated to tourists was laughably small by today's standards. And there were no 'Student' rates, no railcards, no

81

'Rover' tickets. If you wanted to see the 'world', you thumbed down a passing lorry.)

And in any case, commanders simply don't address their men as 'men'. I yield to none in my admiration of the film, *The Adventures of Robin Hood* – the definitive swashbuckler of all swashbucklers. But every time I hear Errol Flynn standing on that rock and beginning his tub-thumping address to the men of Sherwood – 'Listen, men' – I cringe.

Well, you may say, what else could the major have said? 'Lads'? No. Equally false, implying a sort of paternal relationship that takes a long time to build. 'Boys'? Ugh! Even worse. Reeking of instant familiarity. 'Chaps'? Again, no. Went out with Bulldog Drummond and Ronald Colman.

So you see? It's easy to sneer, but it's very difficult to think of something more apt. Which is why I suggest it would have been better if he'd just said 'sit down' and left it at that. It would have maintained his authority, without letting the cat out of the bag that he was trying, and failing, to establish an atmosphere of ease and informality.

The 'smoke if you wish' didn't get him much further forward either. Curious, this business of smoking as the talisman, the touch-stone, of relaxation. I am forced to guess that it was a by-product of the War.

We are now, in Britain, in a non-smoking society. One could almost say 'an anti-smoking society'. Fifty-odd years ago, when we joined the Army, this was not so. I'm sure that if we were to return to the 'fifties, we should find it intolerable, but, then, in the 'fifties, we accepted it. It would be silly to say that everybody smoked, but an awful lot of people did. Smoking was a simple fact of life, like radios blaring from open car windows and four-letter abuse and nudity on the telly today.

The health gurus would have had a fit to see what we, as kids, put up with during the War – railway carriages opaque with smoke, restaurants hazy with it. And cinemas – look up at the beam of light from the projector over your head, and you saw billows of the stuff like cumulus cloud on a summer's day. We did not even put up with it; we simply didn't take any notice of it. The majority of our parents, aunts, and uncles smoked too, all over the place. There remained one vestige of inhibition on all this permanent orgy of toxic exhalation: one often heard a 'gentleman' offer the opinion that he 'didn't like to see a woman smoking in the street'. I daresay such a nugget of reminiscence may well provoke a modern feminist to apoplectic fury, and I must admit that it would be difficult to know where to begin to criticise such a remark; you could come at it from so many different angles.

But I keep coming back to the War. This may be tiresome to younger readers – if indeed I have any – by this time – but the sheer fact of the War remains. There it is – the greatest single event of the entire century. It was our fate – luck if you like (good or bad) – to be part of it. It was enormous. It explains so many things.

Six years of menace, danger, separation, fear, bafflement, sacrifice, deprivation, loss, horror, trauma, and death – emotions and crises of a magnitude and depth unimaginable before. There were no counsellors, no social services to speak of, no escapist hallucinogenic drugs, no anti-depressants, no tranquillisers. If you got a headache, you took an aspirin; if you were constipated, you took a Beecham's pill. For everything else, you smoked. People smoked.

Hollywood put its weight behind the cigarette civilisation. Film stars smoked. In the films they worked in, cowboys, gangsters, tough guys, detectives, crooks, mystery men (and women), condemned criminals, heroes of the Resistance, soldiers on their death beds, the boys in the band, the firm, the organisation, the team, the back room – everyone smoked.

That was in the War. Now we were ten years away from the War. Most people still smoked. But it was now from habit, not from pressure. Gone were the days when the Commanding Officer gathered his troops around him to tell them what a devilish difficult job the General had given them to do, but he knew everyone would pull his weight and not let the team down, and he was sure everyone would put up a jolly good show and do their bit towards winning the War – and he always began proceedings by telling them to sit down and have a smoke.

Perhaps laughable now, but, in the middle of the War, not so funny. It really was bloody dangerous, and everyone was bloody scared.

It certainly was laughable to us, young knowalls ten years away from the real thing. We were sneering too at an officer who, ten years after the War, could not appreciate that things had changed. An officer, incidentally, who, for all we knew, had actually served in the War, and had been one of those frightened soldiers I mentioned just now.

'Smoke if you wish.'

Was it that the Commanding Officer was a stuffy old stick-in-the-mud who, ten years after being promoted acting major because four of his superiors had just been blown to bits, was still only a major (albeit substantive), and could think of nothing original? Or was it simply the whole Army? You know the old saying – Britain is always prepared – for the previous war.

We didn't think of all that at the time. I have only just thought of most of it as I write these lines. We just sat there and kept straight faces. More was to come.

'Well, now,' said the CO. 'I daresay you're all finding Army life pretty strange at the moment. But don't worry. You'll find you get used to things pretty quickly, if you knuckle down to it, work hard, and do as you're told.

'Take your uniforms, for instance. They probably don't fit very well, and you haven't got the hang of wearing them properly. I expect most of you look like a lot of pregnant ducks right now.'

There it was – the third Army joke. One – looking under the bed for a commissioned officer. Two – the twisted sick report. And now – the pregnant ducks. Unlike Sergeant Lugg, the CO waited for the polite laughter to die down before going on. Must have been a one-joke man.

'But you'll soon get the hang of things. Now – I daresay you all want to know what you'll be doing during the next ten weeks. Well, you'll receive training in drill and the handling of the basic infantry weapons, and of course physical training, in order to get you to the highest possible standard of fitness. You will be under first-class instructors who really know their jobs and who are genuinely concerned to turn you into efficient soldiers. And don't forget that all the Depot staff – officers and NCO's – are here to help you. Don't hesitate to go to them if you're in trouble of any kind.

'Remember you're in the Army for two years whether you like it or not, and it's up to each one of you to put his back into it and make the most of it. I wish you the very best of luck.'

Almost before the CO could reach for his cap, the RSM bawled 'Room! R-o-o-o-o-o-m – SHUN!' for the second time, and flung up another fearsome salute. Cigarettes were frantically stubbed out.

'Carry on, please.'

The speculations that assailed us during the gentle buzz that followed were pretty predictable:

Why was the CO wearing blues? We thought they only did that for things like Trooping the Colour and hunt balls.

What was the peak of physical fitness for someone like Martin Forrest, who got puffed running for the toilet when he was taken short?

How did we go about asking the kind gentlemen on the Permanent Staff for help when we got into 'trouble'?

How did you teach someone like Hamilton to take a Bren gun to pieces, much less put it together again, when he couldn't even make his bed?

It was difficult to argue with the last point the CO had made – that we were in for two years, whether we liked it or not. And we hadn't come across anybody who liked it, except our keen minister-to-be, who was going to be allergic to blanco.

We gazed about. What next?

Someone asked Corporal Bournville.

'Anoother talk,' he said. 'Trainin' Coomp'ny Commander. 'Ey oop – 'ere 'e cooms.'

'Room! R-o-o-o-o-o-m – SHUN!'

The RSM was right on cue.

The Training Company Commander, in businesslike battledress, walked to the desk and took off his cap.

'Sit down, chaps. Smoke if you wish.'

He had a row of medal ribbons too. Another wartime major who was still a major?

He put his thumbs under the flaps of his battledress blouse.

'Well, as it's your first full day in the Army, I feel it's as well that I, as your Training Company Commander, should say a few words to you, to welcome you here, and to give you some idea of what you'll be doing in the next ten weeks.

'I daresay you're finding things pretty strange to begin with. Don't worry; you'll get used to them. Take your uniforms, for instance. When you first put on your battledress, I can tell you now, you'll look like a lot of pregnant ducks – '

He paused for the flicker of polite laughter.

' – but a visit to the tailor and some hard work with the iron will soon put that right. In fact you'll find that hard work will be the key to most things. Knuckle down to it and do as you're told, and you'll find that the next ten weeks will go quite quickly.'

(Maybe. What about the next twenty-one months after that?)

'You'll go through a course of instruction in drill, physical training, and the handling of the basic infantry weapons. You will be under good instructors who know their stuff, and who are just as concerned as you are that you should master the various skills required of you. Don't forget they are there to help you – both officers and NCO's – and you should never hesitate to take any problem to them or me.

'You must face the fact that you're in the Army for two years whether you like it or not, and it's up to each one of you to put his back into it and make the most of it. I'm sure you won't regret it. I wish you the best of luck.'

'Room! R-o-o-o-o-o-m – SHUN!'

We went through the RSM salute-stubbing out-'Carry on please' routine.

The RSM turned his fearful glare on the gathering.

'Stand fast.'

He stalked out. We remained standing. Well, he had said 'stand fast'.

Lugg came to the front of the room.

'Sit dahn.'

Ah – so that's what it meant.

'What now, sergeant?' said Jack Gatewood.

Lugg lounged against the edge of the desk.

'Y're goin' t'get anuvver tawk – from yer Platoon Commander.'

A glare silenced any seditious comment before it could reach the tonsils.

A doctor's-waiting-room hush descended.

'Time to finish our smoke?' asked someone.

' 'F y'like.'

The smell of struck Swan Vestas had barely filled the air when the sergeant sprang to his feet.

'Room! R-o-o-o-o-o-m – SHUN!'

A pink-cheeked subaltern stepped nervously towards the desk. Even to our untrained eyes, it was clear that this second-lieutenant was only recently out of officer-cadet school. He returned Sergeant Lugg's salute much too correctly. The leather on his cane was very shiny. I was willing to bet that he was a National Serviceman too. I did not know many Sandhurst graduates – one, actually – but I felt sure they had a good deal more assurance and polish than this young man did.

He took off his cap – very carefully. He laid his cane on the desk, and prevented it rolling off the edge just in time.

He wrenched his eyes up high enough to look straight at us – though not for long.

'Right. OK. Um – sit, please. Smoke if you wish to.'

After the scrapings and the raspings, he licked his lips and cleared his throat.

'Well – er – as it's your first full day in the Army, I – um – thought it would be as well if I, as your Platoon Commander, said a few words to you. . . . '

* * * * * *

Sergeant Lugg had kept his promise. When we returned to the barrack room after our pep talks – refreshed and inspired, no doubt – eager to get stuck in – there was the list on the back of the door. The smudgy biro scrawl, and the title – 'Barack Room Dueties' – told us that the sergeant had given its preparation his personal attention.

Now, you may have heard stories about this. I certainly had. About whitewashing coal, and making adjacent floorboards gleam with polish of different colours. About the insertion of strips of cardboard inside the small and large packs, so that even when empty and out of use, they looked square and trim and generally absolutely beautiful.

I didn't see much of that. The jobs we were given were the sort you would expect to be given out by a sergeant whose boast – to us at any rate – was that his platoon had the cleanest barrack room 'in the 'ole Depot'. So I was sweeping the middle of the floor (each of us was expected to sweep in the immediate area of his own bed space), and Jack Gatewood had to dust window-ledges. Taffy got lamp-shades (which he couldn't reach), and Martin Forrest cleaned out the wash-basins. And so on and so on. Inevitably, some poor devil was put in possession of a bucket and brush and was told to get on with the lavatory pans. But the jobs were to be shared round each week, so. . . .

All very predictable. There were only two daft things. I expect every squad of trainees has its stories of stupid standards of cleanliness and order. Ours involved the coal scuttle and the brooms. The coal scuttle had to be sited in the middle of the floor not far from the central stove (logical, admittedly), but then all the brooms had to be leaned against it so that they constituted a sort of four-point compass, with the heads turned outwards. But before we did that came the prize idiocy; someone's 'Barack Room Duety' was to arm himself with a razor blade and scrape the day's accumulation of hand-dirt from the handles of the brooms.

'Any questions?' bawled Lugg.

No – there were no questions.

8   Who are we?

WE DIDN'T KNOW IT, BUT we were being watched. Studied. Assessed. All the time. While we demonstrated our soldierly qualities in vital tasks like polishing new boots, taming belt brasses, finding our way through the jungle of webbing straps, and stamping kit.

Because that was about all we did during the first few days, the days that followed our friendly, informal chats of welcome from those kind gentlemen who were so concerned to make our training fruitful and enjoyable. (So long as we put our backs into it, naturally.)

We certainly did very little of what we had expected soldiers to be doing – like manoeuvres, and shooting, and unarmed combat, and survival training, and so on. All those exciting things depicted, or at least hinted at, in the recruitment posters for the Regular Army. They usually showed a young, eager, jaw-set soldier in battledress and tin hat, set against a montage of tanks and skylines and hopeful dawns, with, underneath, in prominent print: 'You're Somebody Today in the Army'. Yes. Ironic, when you think about it, that it was not tanks and skylines that had got Corporal Bournville into khaki, but box pleats.

Be that as it may, there we were, for the whole of our first weekend and beyond, cleaning, polishing, sorting, and stamping. The bit that sticks in the mind from that time is the stamping. Not driving our feet into the parade ground, but stamping our Army number on our kit. And – when we were not stamping – engraving, stitching, sewing, writing, or any other technique you can think of for placing, permanently, an eight-digit number on an item of equipment.

Just think what we had to put it on – a greatcoat, two berets, two battledress blouses, two pairs of battledress trousers, two sets of denim tops and bottoms, two P.T. vests, two pairs of P.T. shorts, two woollen vests, two pairs of woollen pants, three pairs of cotton

pants ('Drawers Jungle'), three or four pairs of socks, the inseparable mug-knife-fork-and-spoon, two pairs of boots, a pair of
plimsoles, a 'housewife' (repair kit), two ties, and two towels.

So much for the clothing. Then there was the equipment – a
tin hat, a 'small pack', a 'large pack', two ammunition pouches, two
belts, miles of webbing straps.

I think the only thing they let us off was our darning needles.
And if they could have found a way of stamping them they would
have insisted on that too.

I forget now by what miracle we extracted the stamping kit
from the Stores, which, as you doubtless recall, was accessible for
issue 'between the ahrs of nine-firty and ten-firty on all weekdays
excep' Sattidis', but the box of individual dies for every digit and
every letter in the alphabet was open on a table in the middle of
the barrack room, with a hammer or two, and somehow or other
twenty-odd young men – all total strangers to each other – had to
find a way of sharing them without coming to blows in such a way
as to transfer eight-digit figures to all those bits of kit – and to do it
in about two days, in amongst all the bulling. It is small wonder that
nobody – nobody – ever forgets his Army number.

There was one item of kit with which the Army displayed an
inordinate obsession – identity discs. Or, in military vernacular,
'name tags'. These were the little aluminium plates that every soldier
was required to wear, on a length of cord, round his neck. Whatever
else you took off – and you took off most things, at one time or
another – many times – you never took off your Discs Identity.

It was not because you might have to show them to a suspicious sergeant of the guard at an unfamiliar depot; you had your
Army paybook for that, or your leave pass. It was not because a
drill corporal with incipient Alzheimer's needed a convenient means
of checking up on your name which had temporarily escaped him,
just in case you were bent on deceiving him with a pseudonym. It
was not because you might suddenly be called upon to prove your
identity to a physical training instructor in the showers.

Who are we?

No – it was, as the training staff informed us with lugubrious relish, in case we were blown to pieces in the front line, and the War Graves Commission needed to know whose name to put on the War Memorial in some corner of a foreign field that is forever England. Encouraging.

And the really comforting bit was that we were required to put on the disc, in addition to our Army number (and, presumably, our name, although I'm not sure about that), our religious affiliation. This was so that the Army chaplain, assuming he happened to be in the vicinity of your demise, could consign the few remaining shreds of your cadaver to the temporary shallow grave demanded by custom and front-line hygiene (before the War Graves Commission came along and dug you up again after the war) with the funeral rites appropriate to your individual view of the Almighty.

Very liberal-minded of the Army, you may think – until you discovered that your choice of engraving was a trifle limited. This was the 1950's, when most people thought of England as a Christian country. And, since the Army was about two generations behind mainstream opinion, the Army most certainly did. It took its cultural and religious tastes from mid-Victorian respectability. It had, to be sure, abandoned the rigid discipline of Mother Church, excommunication, and the Inquisition, but it still assumed that every soldier had only two choices when it came to attendance at church service. (Church Parade. It was still a 'parade'.) He either went and sat, stood, knelt, sang, and paid up according to ritual, or, if he had a tender conscience, he could jolly well stand to attention outside the church, whatever the weather, for the whole duration of the service. This was part of the Army's policy of religious toleration.

The other part was the broad-minded recognition of the fact that there had been a Reformation in the sixteenth century. This brings me back to the limited choice I was talking about. When it came to stamping your religion on your Discs Identity, you could put 'C. of E.' or 'R.C.'. Nothing else. As far as the military mind was concerned, Baptists, Methodists, Unitarians, and so on just did not exist.

John Sly caused a ripple or two when he decided to put 'A' (for 'atheist') on his tags. Somewhat to our surprise, he got away with it. So there were three classifications, apparently, not two. If John had ever got himself blown to bits and an Army chaplain had happened to be in the vicinity, no doubt the pieces of his unfortunate corpse would have been scooped up, shoved in the nearest shell-hole, and camouflaged with a few duck-boards, while the embarrassed chaplain muttered something to the effect that he hoped for the best.

Still, all that was a long time ago, and no doubt the Army is a lot more tolerant these days. I wonder what they permit in these multi-ethnic groupings. Can a man put 'H' for Hindu, or 'M' for Moslem, or 'B' for Buddhist? What do Sikhs do? Or Shintoists? Or Coptic Christians? And even if they are allowed to put these initials, does that improve the odds that a padre of their own particular method of approaching the Ultimate will be on hand when they are blown unrecognisably to smithereens? Or, alternatively, that an Anglican padre will be familiar with the Coptic funeral service or the Hindu regulations for death pyres?

And what if you're a Friend of the Earth, or a New Age Traveller? Yes, I know – you'd have more sense than to be in the bloody Army in the first place. But don't forget that, for us, in the 1950's, there was no choice. True, there were conscientious objectors, but it was very difficult to prove this to the satisfaction of the authorities. Most of us were swept up in the great military scoop – C. of E., R.C., A., and all.

And, when we'd finished stamping our religious affiliation on our Discs Identity, we could turn to our battledress, and our boots, and our belts, and our blanco, and our cap badges, and our brasses, and our bed boxes – just in case we should find time hanging heavily on our hands.

Bulling. That's what it was called. We 'bulled' everything – except our bed boxes, of course. We didn't have to put polish or 'Brasso' or blanco on them. And, curiously, the word didn't apply either to the stamping I have just described.

Who are we?

Have you noticed? It's the short, simple words that are often the most subtle or the most deceptive. For example, everyone knows what a fair is. But if you take the trouble to find out what a medieval fair was, you will discover some important differences. The word has not changed, but its meaning has, but we see the word as so simple that it doesn't cross the mind that it can trip us up.

All very interesting, you may say. But 'fair' is a proper word. 'Bull' is slang. Totally different. A touch, Watson – a definite touch.

But slang meanings change too. Or at least develop. Take this word 'bull'. Or rather 'bulling' – that's the word I first mentioned just now. A gerund, from the verb 'to bull', you would think. So, just out of curiosity, I looked up 'bull' in the dictionary. Lots of meanings for the *noun* 'bull', naturally. But few references to the *verb* 'bull', and none in the sense of cleaning Army kit.

I could use 'to bull' transitively in the sense of artificially raising prices on the stock market, or I could use it intransitively in the sense of a cow being on heat. Not quite what I wanted. There was one other; I could use it, if I were an American, in the sense of talking 'lightly or foolishly'. And I don't really want that either.

But going back to the column on the noun meanings, I came not surprisingly on the derivative 'bullshit', and was informed that 'bull' was short for it.

So over to the entry on 'bullshit', where I was told primly that it was not merely 'slang' but 'taboo slang'. But there, sure enough, was the explanation that it referred to '(in the British Army) exaggerated zeal, esp. for ceremonial drill, cleaning, polishing, etc.' This is still the *noun*. It referred only to the fact of exaggerated cleaning and polishing; it did not refer to the *action* of exaggerated cleaning and polishing. As we all know, if we know no other grammar, a verb is a 'doing' word, and if there was anything we were doing during those first days, more than anything else, it was most certainly cleaning and polishing.

So the dictionary is deficient. The verb 'to bull' ought to exist – taboo, slang, or otherwise. I ought to know; we did enough of it, and so has every soldier since – well, since the Crimean War, I should think.

And, while we're on it, I take issue with the dictionary definition of the noun 'bull'. We spent all those hours on cleaning and polishing, but it certainly wasn't from 'exaggerated zeal'; we did it because we had to.

I suppose we might have been a touch more 'zealous' if we had known the extent to which the Depot authorities were watching us. God knows what they expected to be able to deduce from the bent shoulders and spitting, smearing, rubbing, scraping, hammering, shaping, ironing, pressing, honing, and polishing that were going on in our barrack room.

The clue lay with the titbit of information that the encyclopaedic Eddie offered us.

Remember? 'You're the P.L.'s, aintcher?'

Potential Leaders. All of us. Wow!

So – we had to conclude – while we were wading through vats of blanco and shoe polish and 'Brasso' (all bought, incidentally, out of our week's wages of twenty-eight shillings a week – £1.40), and learning how to harness up our small packs and large packs, and tie bootlaces, and put on gaiters the right way up, and divine the difference between the positions of 'Attention' and 'At Ease', our 'potential' was being rigorously assessed.

The only discernible evidence of this uncomfortable fact was an interview we all had on about the Wednesday – that is, about five or six days after we arrived.

One at a time, of course. But all with the same man. We never found out his name. He was known as the PSO. We all fell in very readily with the Army's passion for initials. It was later discovered that it stood for 'Personnel Selection Officer'. At least I assume it was 'Personnel' and not 'Personal', because it turned out that he was a mite rude. Well, that was how it struck us.

He didn't query; he insinuated. Like the eagle-eyed lawyer after a quick conviction: 'I put it to you that. . . . ' 'Am I to understand

95

then? . . . .' His questions were not enquiries; they were challenges: 'What makes you think that you have the qualities that are required to be an officer?' With a stress on the second 'you'. Nasty.

Dammit – how were we to know? We hadn't been in the Army a week, and we had had no idea that we were 'Potential' anything; it was the first we'd heard of it.

It was easier when he asked us whether we'd been prefects at school, and whether we'd played for the first eleven, and whether we'd enjoyed 'positions of responsibility'. It was probably all down on his clipboard anyway, but there – we were happy enough to tell him that; it enabled us to draw just a fraction of confidence from remembered successes.

He didn't seem very impressed. Barely flickered a muscle. None of us could recall seeing him smile. When he listened to our feeble, concocted, cobbled-together reasons as to why we wanted to become officers, he seemed even less impressed. Doodled on our forms and tossed them into an 'Out' file.

'Send in the next one.'

From this searching analysis, the PSO decided that every single one of us was to be sent to another barracks for training in a Potential Leader platoon. Every one, that is, except Hamilton. The PSO did weed him out. We could have told him that by the end of the first day. Eddie could have told him after half an hour.

I don't know what happened to Hamilton. But I do know what often happened to young men *like* Hamilton. Due to disturbances, or civil unrest, or terrorism, or foreign infiltration, or outright war, the Army would decide suddenly that it needed experts in various languages for security purposes – monitoring, interrogation, counter-espionage, general intelligence work, and so on. A batch of Hamiltons scoured out of barrack rooms all over the country would be summoned to the War Office. After a short interview to ascertain whether their maternal grandmother had been born a British subject, they would be handed a clutch of newspapers in some outlandish foreign tongue. If they made a fair fist of reading them, they would be whisked off to some top-secret headquarters in the Home Counties, where they spent the rest of their time deciphering Iranian freedom fighters' coded messages or interrogating defectors from Azerbaijan or scanning the radical press in Cambodia.

They would be provided with an office, a telephone, quite possibly a secretary, and given access to all sorts of restricted information. Clearly such privileges could not be awarded to a humble private soldier, nor a corporal. Nor even, it seems, a lieutenant. No. These very special young men were given three pips to put on each shoulder.

So it was quite likely that the one reject from our 'Potential Leader' squad, who could barely make his own bed, was (while the rest of us went through months of rigorous training in spartan barracks to turn us into second-lieutenants) packed off to some comfortable office, where, without any further military training whatsoever, he was gazetted captain in the Intelligence Corps.

To be fair, I have no statistics for this, and it is equally likely that just as many Hamiltons were passed over, bullied, and humiliated, and spent miserable months in loneliness because they were not sufficiently worldly to defend themselves. They would be given unpleasant and servile jobs. Others again might have been canny enough to accept their lowly status, content to be left alone with their buckets and brooms, just so long as they could curl up with their latest scholarly magazine. I daresay that throughout the many years during which National Service persisted, the Army, did they but know it, possessed a vast reservoir of untapped talent in the shape of sanitary orderlies who could mop out lavatory pans and recite to themselves great chunks of Aeschylus or Tagore at one and the same time. After all, they didn't need *that* many captains in the Intelligence Corps.

Anyway, it was pretty clear why Hamilton had been turned down. It was not clear why the rest of us had been accepted – as 'Potential Leaders'. It was nice to know that we *were* 'Potential Leaders', and it is also true that many of us had harboured secret ambitions to become officers – at any rate to try. We all had friends and acquaintances who had done it, and when we looked at them, we thought, well, if he can do it, so can I.

All the same, we were curious to know what we had achieved, or what sterling qualities shone from our very demeanour, that made the military authorities classify us so promptly. So far as we could see, the only things we had done up to then were to clean kit and attempt some elementary parade-ground drill under Sergeant Lugg. And we were not very good at that either. Predictably, we all looked like 'pregnant ducks' or 'twisted sick reports' – or so we were repeatedly informed.

'It's to do with your "O" Levels,' said Irving Bryce. 'If you've got two or more, you're going to be a P.L. That's what I was told.'

Well, we certainly had those. There must have been at least a dozen university degrees among us. Bill Glover had three himself. But Martin Forrest took a more cynical view.

'It's not "O" Levels; it's Christian names. If you've got two or more, you're a P.L. If you haven't, you're not.'

'I've only got one,' said John Sly.

'Is it anything to do with the cadet force?' asked Mark Simpson, who had held high rank in his. I suspect he was more determined than any of us to gain a commission, and would have naïvely regarded his time in his school CCF as a worthwhile investment.

He was laughed down. Few of us had been near our school cadet hut.

'I suppose it was nothing to do with those tests we had, was it?' suggested Bill Glover. 'You know, a couple of days ago.'

For an hour or so we had been given relief from our stamping of kit and our tins of polish and blanco, marched to the Depot Sports Hut, and told to sit at the desks provided. We were given printed papers, filled with intelligence tests. All I remember is dots and squares. The answers, to some of them, seemed so simple that you hesitated to put them down, in case there was some dimension of fiendish cunning that had escaped you. We were prepared to credit the military authorities with absolutely anything in those early days.

But Bill Glover's argument was demolished by someone who remembered that Eddie had known about us almost from the start.

'You're the P.L.'s, aintcher?'

Which brought us full circle. We had no idea.

'I wouldn't mind betting that the Army hasn't either,' said Taffy Davies. 'They've forgotten why they did it.'

Well, forgetful or not, the Army had made up its mind what to do with us now. We were told that the next day we were being posted. To a whole company of P.L.'s, apparently. At Brigade Headquarters.

I should explain, for the benefit of the unmilitarised, that our squad, about twenty-odd, constituted a platoon in Army parlance. A company consisted of three platoons. Four companies made a battalion, and three battalions made a brigade. So 'Brigade Headquarters' sounded impressively strategic. Commanded, presumably, by a brigadier, who had no end of ironmongery on his shoulder flaps.

So, on the Friday, only eight days after we had joined up, we were bundled into our full battledress and kit – small pack, large pack, straps, kitbag and all – and given travel passes to the rural metropolis in the Home Counties where our new barracks lurked.

Nobody went with us to show us the way, or to ensure that we didn't desert. Perhaps, since we were now 'P.L.'s', and therefore some way towards becoming officers and gentlemen, we were trusted to behave ourselves and stay true to the colours. Perhaps it was some kind of initiative test to further their assessment of our officerly qualities. Who could tell? Looking back, we spent a large part of our thinking time wondering what motives lay behind the decisions of our superiors.

The great god Rumour never suffers from ill health. He is particularly vigorous in incestuous societies like the services, or boarding schools, or any similar closed institution. Not entirely spineless outside them, come to that. One instance lingered from my history studics: the Great Reform Bill, designed to modernise the English voting and representative system, was earnestly described by some, and believed by others, to be a plot to put the Duke of Wellington on the throne.

Anyway, we slurped British Railways tea on some mainline station or other, while we speculated on why we were being posted so soon, and why, if the Army had made up its mind so early, they hadn't posted us to the P.L. company in the first place and saved everybody a lot of trouble. We lugged our kitbags through the tube barriers. Some of us actually wore our greatcoats in the belief that it would make it easier to carry the rest. It was barely October; we must have boiled in the Underground.

Bill Glover went off to telephone his wife (he was the only one who was married), and found one of those narrow, old-fashioned booths with the folding doors. Folding inwards. He got in all right, and prudently dragged his kitbag in after him. His large pack was on his shoulders, and his kitbag was propped against his thighs.

When he had finished, he couldn't get out. Not for ages. We wondered if he'd deserted. He finally rejoined us, in a dreadful sweat, only seconds before we got on the train.

So – after eight of the most momentous and traumatic days of our lives, so far – we went to our Brigade Headquarters – to begin our ten weeks of basic training all over again.

9   Beginners' pains

WE LIVED IN A SPIDER.

There must be hundreds of thousands of ex-National Servicemen for whom that term not only needs no introduction, but for whom that term conjures whole volumes of reminiscence.

But, for the benefit of the uninitiated, it refers to domestic architecture. Our barrack block was more modern than the looming, mid-Victorian edifices we had just left. You got the flavour of those massive, workhouse blocks from the names of the various separate units – Alma, Inkerman, Khartoum. . . . you follow the general idea.

No – our new home was built in the sort of red brick they used to favour for 1930's primary schools. Low-slung like new primary schools too. For all I know, planned by the same architect. The sleeping accommodation was in units rather like the spokes of a wheel, which radiated from a central ablutions chamber. Hence, naturally, 'spider'. I think the overall picture was square rather than circular, but the metaphor is still valid. Anyway, square or circular, it was, to all of us, a spider.

Like pig-iron. Do you know why it's called pig-iron? Because when they tipped out the molten metal from the furnace, they used to pour it into sand moulds that had a long, fat central trough, with little side troughs at right angles throughout its length, and on both sides. Like a sow and its piglets. Yes. . . . Well, that's what it said in the books I read.

Now, the spider. A barrack block is a barrack block, and rows of iron beds are rows of iron beds. So we didn't feel any more cossetted. But it was, admittedly, cleaner and newer, and the distemper wasn't flaking off the walls. And we had no cause to fear the ghosts of Lord Cardigan or General Gordon.

There were several other training platoons there besides ours.

101

Some of them 'Potential Leader' platoons. The rest could be referred to, I suppose, as 'Potential Follower' platoons. I don't mean that patronisingly: we had had no idea we were regarded as being potential leaders; I don't suppose the inmates of the other platoons had had any idea that they were regarded as not.

With all those training platoons, it was a pretty big establishment. Brigade Depot, as I said. I never saw the Brigadier. Our Potential Leader platoons were lumped into the 'P.L. Company', which was presided over by a mere major.

Let us call him Major Ambrose. Another bemedalled war veteran. Still a major ten years afterwards. I suspect that, like other soldiers who had seen real service, he had little patience with or fondness for the formality and red tape of peacetime soldiering. Well, we were with him there. We had little fondness for any kind of soldiering at all.

Major Ambrose was rumoured to have very little time for office work – 'bumf', as it was universally known in the Services. The word was not so common in civilian circles then as it is now. Perhaps it was millions of National Servicemen who spread it. Just as they spread the word 'skive' right through the nation's life and language.

Just as they learnt to apply swearwords to a host of different situations – a skill garnered from the fertile imaginations and vocabularies of thousands of vociferous non-commissioned officers. Take the word 'bugger'. It was pretty strong stuff in the 'thirties and 'forties. I remember, as a small boy, being shocked to the core merely to overhear it being spoken in a bus queue. Its very existence was not referred to in polite circles. It became little more than punctuation in the Army, along with its four-letter corollaries. But the Army added a neat grammatical refinement.

By the time I had left university, I could take the word 'bugger' without flinching. But mostly as a noun. (There was a rare use of it as a verb, when the speaker colloquially invited the whole world to perform an unnatural act upon him: 'Bugger me.') It was the Army which made me familiar with the verb in a special context, and I do not refer to its anatomically correct usage. Anybody who has spent any time longer than a month in uniform knows what it is to be 'buggered about'. That was a unique Services process.

To go off at a further tangent (I haven't forgotten about Major Ambrose), the word 'bloody' has received similar extension. Coined originally as a corruption of 'God's Blood' or 'By Our Lady', it became a common enough adverbial expletive indicative of some extreme or other – 'bloody silly' or 'bloody stupid', for example. Then, at college, I came across it to mean the condition of not being up to scratch, often after an evening's drinking – 'I feel bloody'. An adjective, qualifying the pronoun 'I'.

Note – the 'bloody silly' usage is adverbial, not adjectival, qualifying the adjective 'silly'. To what extent is he silly? To the extent of being 'bloody silly'. So he is not slightly silly; he is very silly.

But see how the adverbial use of the word has been stretched in recent years. Nowadays the word 'bloody' doesn't qualify only an adjective; it can also appear as a sort of auxiliary to the verb. As in: 'Will you do so-and-so for me? I bloody won't!' Or: 'I went into his office and I bloody told him.' One can detect a similar adverbial use, and corruption, of the commonest four-letter expletive too.

Now – Major Ambrose. If he didn't spend much time in his office, what did he spend much time doing? Ah – a good question. We never saw a lot of him, that was sure. He gave the occasional lecture on military law, or officers' mess etiquette (which indicated a touching confidence in our ability to survive both officer selection and officer training), and that was about all really.

His lectures were hardly what you could call either technical or structured. (His penchant for informality again.) He sat down, never stood. He never wrote on a board, and I don't recall his ever bringing a prop or visual aid into the room. He leaned back on his chair, thrust his hands into his pockets, and launched forth into his lecture rather in the manner of Columbus setting out into the Atlantic – having little idea of where he was going, and therefore having little to prepare himself for what he might meet because he had no idea at all *of* what he might meet. He just hoped for some destination or other.

So, for example, if he were explaining to us the mechanics of section whatever-it-was of the Army Act concerned with insubordination, he would start, 'Now, suppose you come up to me one day, and say, "Major Ambrose, I think you're a bloody bastard" ' . . . . . That sort of thing.

He had a deep moustache. Not a thick one, or a wide one. A deep one. I think it must have got in the way of his diction, because he had a trick of eliminating whole syllables. So the word 'several' came out as 'sev', 'impossible' would appear as 'mposbl'. In print it looks like the slurring of a drunkard. This was not so. On the contrary he could be very vehement or emphatic. It was not that the syllables were slurred; they just weren't there. The Manual of Military Law would be disguised as 'Ma Mili Lawh', with great force on the 'Lawh'. He was fond of indicating the vital nature of anything by describing it as 'por' ('important').

Our day-to-day training was in the hands of one senior non-commissioned officer and a National Service corporal or two. Except for the specialist lessons like P.T. ('P.E.' now) and throwing hand grenades. More of that later.

For the first two or three weeks we were taught by a long, rangy company sergeant-major with a large Adam's apple called Jefferson. He was, not the apple. Prominent front teeth. Beaky nose. Very quietly-spoken man. Looked as if he could have been a reader. Light years away from Sergeant Lugg.

I never heard him swear, for a start. He certainly didn't thrust his face into yours and ask you personal questions about your family history. He was not sarcastic. He didn't hurry. Didn't need to. With those long legs he covered the ground just as effectively as normal people did in the rush hour. Like a sort of leisurely ostrich. Always impeccably dressed.

He was happy to socialise too. I have a permanent impression of him, in our barrack room of a late afternoon, leaning on the window sill, and answering our barrage of questions in his unhurried way. He would often gaze out of the window as he did so, as if seeking inspiration from the sight of another spider twenty or thirty yards away, and explain any problem as if the solution were the simplest thing in the world. 'All you have to do is . . . . '

When he had finished elucidating, he would turn inwards to us, pause, and say, 'And that.' Just as some of us cannot leave the house with a calm mind unless we have put our heads in the kitchen for the fifth time to see if the gas switches are turned off, so Company Sergeant-Major Jefferson found it impossible to end a sentence without adding 'and that'.

And there always had to be a pause. He could never stick it straight on like a brisk postage stamp. There had to be that hiatus. Either he took comfort from the empty moment as well as from the 'and that', or he would struggle every time to resist saying 'and that', and every time, in the end, he gave up the struggle. For his audience it was agony. It was like listening to the late King George, with his appalling stutter, trying to come out with the last word in a phrase during a broadcast. We would hang there, almost grimacing with anticipation. When at last it came – as it always did – 'and that' – we would all sigh, lean back, and relax. Until the next sentence.

Most of us have some speech tic or other – 'I mean', 'y'know', 'well, this is it', 'kind of ', 'like', or, just for a change, 'kindoflike'. But these are all to indicate hesitation or uncertainty or lack of fluency. Jefferson's 'and that' was not a preamble nor an interjection; it was a postscript. And it just had to come. You knew that any sentence he uttered would not be complete until it arrived. It was like the last gasp of an asthmatic engine that had just been switched off.

But when he wasn't stretching our nerves on the rack like this, Company Sergeant-Major Jefferson was fine. He was well-organised; he was clear in his instructions; he was fair. We worked for him with a will. Perhaps it was because we were so surprised to find any NCO in the Army who wasn't like the caricatures we had been fed on for so many years in stories, films, and music hall jokes. We actually liked him. As I said, he was light years away from Sergeant Lugg.

He took us through the early days of our foot drill. Well, to be strictly honest, not the very first days. Sergeant Lugg had done that, in between our marathon sessions of bulling, stamping, and sewing – with a bit of sag-muscle physical training shoved in here and there.

As the attentive reader with a good memory will have deduced, the sergeant had a prepared script for this too.

'Driwl,' he said, 'teaches yer self-controwl. It's the bes' way of getting' good discipline, and gettin' a sowjer to obey an order at once wivaht finkin'.'

Another deep breath.

'Neat turn-aht and good driwl give a sowjer self-respec', an' pride in the uniform 'e wears.'

Now, it may sound pompous and daft written down like this years later. It was not without its amusement quotient at the time. But my subsequent experience in the Army, and my later experience after that, taught me to accept that, pompous or not, there is a high degree of truth in it.

Put it this way. The Army has been doing it for a very long time, so one would be disposed to presume that it had been proved effective. Certain it is that the British fighting soldier, when I joined up, had a unique reputation in the world for professionalism, adaptability, and sheer usefulness. One could still argue that a system that has not been substantially changed for over a hundred and fifty years is a bit short on imagination and awareness. Further, if an outdated regime had produced such fine soldiers, what could have been produced by a modern one? You could say the same about the British Navy in the late eighteenth century, where the system was almost prehistoric (men were still being *paid* at the same rate as in the reign of Charles II, never mind being recruited, trained, and administered).

You could go further still, and cite the political system of the late eighteenth and early nineteenth century – a morass of cynicism, jobbery and corruption – which nevertheless produced men of the calibre of Pitt (both of them), Fox, Canning, Palmerston, and Peel. What geniuses could we not have thrown up with a clean system?

Well, maybe. But, in each case, that was the system we were stuck with. I suppose you could argue that any soldiers who could make such a system work would be bound to become the most adaptable in the world.

All I can say is that it certainly smartened up one squad of National Servicemen.

And, before we leave the scoffers to continue their scoffing, it is worth pointing out that foot drill may look mindless and pointless, but as a matter of sheer fact, it is not as easy as you might think. Not to begin with anyway. Take Sergeant Lugg's first lesson.

'Nah, the firs' fing y'gotta learn is t'get from the "at ease" position, where y'are nah, ta the position of "attention". It's a perfeckly nacheral position, wiv 'eels tagevver an' toes slightly apar', arms straigh', and 'ead up. When I give the word o' comman', y'come t'that position by pickin' up yer lef ' knee and drivin' yer lef ' foo' inta the grahnd beside yer righ'. OK. Let's try it.'

' 'Toon! Taaaaaooooowwn – SHUN!'

There was a noise like the staccato rattle of a machine-gun as each left foot in the platoon arrived beside its companion right foot at a different time. Some left feet had forgotten to raise themselves the required distance ('pick y'foot up nine inches an' drive it in twelve'), and so arrived before the others. Some did not travel far enough laterally, and so after landing were forced surreptitiously to shuffle the last inch. Others travelled too far; there were grunts of physical pain as steel tips of left heels crashed down on tender insides of right heels, and shudders of mental anguish with the realisation of how much painstakingly-applied polish must have been seared away.

It wasn't only feet either. It may come as a surprise to those who haven't done it that standing still and upright while lifting the left knee and driving the left foot into the ground can not easily be achieved. Not till you get used to it. There is a natural tendency to move the body as well. It is a case of isolating muscles. It's like trying to move the third finger of the hand without moving the second. It takes practice and confidence.

So a lot of us swayed this way and that. Arms flapped. Bodies bent at the waist. We looked down at our feet at the end to see the extent of the damage.

The sergeant's face was a picture of incredulity and agony.

'Hazhawere!'

The machine-gun stuttered again as left feet sought their original position.

Time for a taste of the sergeant's command of irony.

'In case y'don't know, y're supposed t'keep tagevver. An' when y'get ta the position of "Attention", y'supposed t'keep stiwl.'

Deep breath. Here it comes – another papal bull.

'The position of "Attention" is a perfeckly nacheral one – 'eadupchininchestoutarmssraigh'shouldersback'ands closedthumbsdowntheseamo'thetrousers. Any questions?'

John Sly put up his hand and grinned pleasantly.

'I'm sorry, sergeant. I didn't quite catch that last bit.'

'Ho, you didn't quate catch that last bit.'

The sergeant thrust forward his Neanderthal features.

'Well, catch this:

'EAD UP CHIN IN CHEST OUT ARMS STRAIGH' SHOULDERS BACK'ANDSCLOSEDTHUMBSDOWNTHESEAMO'THETROUSERS!'

John beamed through his glasses.

'Thank you, sergeant. That's much clearer now.'

Lugg shot him a glance of acute suspicion through half-closed eyes, but could think of nothing more to say. He resumed his original position.

' 'Toon! Taaaaaooooowwn – SHUN!'

We were at it for the entire lesson. One drill movement. But, as I have tried, perhaps a little ponderously, to stress, it was not as easy as it seems when you watch Trooping the Colour. Look at all the separate factors we had to bear in mind. Lugg was quite right;

we were not at the proper position of "Attention" until we were standing up straight, with our stomachs in and our chests out, and our arms straight at our sides. The hands had to be closed, with the thumbs straight and facing to the front. They had to follow the line of our trousers – thumbs down the seam, as the sergeant said. Oh – and the feet. Heels together, toes slightly apart. Slightly, remember – not splayed like some circus clown. Head up at all times, eyes gazing fixedly to the front, even when addressing the sergeant if he came up to interrogate us individually as to where we thought we were – 'Brighton bleed'n' sea front?'

The situation made great inroads into the sergeant's reserves of fresh simile and invective. We should snap to attention like – well, like 'a violin string goin' "twang!" ' . Alternatively, our leisure-liness of movement put him in mind of a wounded homosexual on vacation – 'like a bloody queer on 'olidy'. When, in our zeal to thrust out our chests, we succeeded only in making our new and ill-fitting battledresses look even more baggy, thereby giving the impression that half the front rank were in an advanced state of pregnancy, the sergeant seized the opportunity to tell us what he thought of our maternal contours, and speculated luridly as to how we had got ourselves into that condition.

Take playing a scale on the piano. No – hold on a minute; there is a connection. Bear with me. Eight notes, right? In the key of C, all white ones. Dead easy.

Not so. Not if you want to do it properly. Not if you want to please a qualified teacher. Just think of all the things you must remember if you want to get it right.

In no particular order – smooth playing; no stabbing of the keys. When you have struck the key, take your finger off it; don't leave it there for the sound to blur the sound of the next note. Sit up straight. Wrists poised above the level of the keyboard; no hanging them below, so that the fingers clamber up on to the keys like an exhausted mountaineer attaining a difficult summit. No waggling about – the old teachers used to put coins on the back of the hand to keep you steady. Going up the scale with the right hand, carry the thumb under the first and second fingers and strike F with it, and then continue up to C. Keep the elbows free from the sides. Play from the shoulder, not from the wrist or the elbow; certainly not from the hand. (Try that one.) If you play more than two octaves, move the body so that the hands and arms stay in roughly the same relation to the torso. When you turn round to come back down, stretch the elbow out, so that the arm stays at the same angle to the wrist. And so on and so on. The books say that there are up to fifty things a good piano teacher can look for when watching a pupil play a simple scale.

In the same way, there were very many things we had to bear in mind when we came from the position of 'At Ease' to the 'perfeckly nacheral' position of 'Attention'. And the position of 'Attention' was only the beginning. In the coming weeks we had to master the left turn, the right turn, the about turn, both when still and when on the march. We had to do close order drill, open order drill. We had to 'left form' and 'right form'. Even the simple 'halt' – coming to a stop in unison and in a 'soldierly manner' – was fraught with difficulty for some who were none too strong on co-ordination.

And all those commands assumed marching in quick time. There was a completely different set of rules for marching in slow time. And for changing from slow to quick and quick to slow. And so on. We had to learn them all.

Then there was the business of pauses. Just as important in drill as they are in music. Two types. First, the pause in the commands. There were always two commands for every movement. Well, three, if you count the explanation beforehand. Four, if you count the word of address. So it went like this: 'Platoon! Platoon will retire. Aybaaaaooooot – TURN!'

Why was the third part so drawn out? Because it was a warning of what was coming. What was called the 'cautionary' word of command. While the sergeant's voice lingered over this syllable, you were supposed to coil your body like some kind of spring (without moving it, of course – not yet), ready at the right instant, to let it flash into action in a crisp, soldierly (always 'soldierly') movement, in which part of your torso removed itself from where it had been resting and placed itself at great speed in another place, traversing the distance between in as straight a line as possible – or, in the case of feet, stamping into the asphalt of the parade ground as hard as possible. The sergeant's un-subtle admonitions about violin strings 'goin' twang' and 'pickin' y'foot up nine inches an' drivin' it in twelve' were not as inept as might appear at first.

Another reason for the long-drawn-out cautionary word of command was to enable the sergeant's voice to travel down a long line of soldiers on a big parade, and so prepare everybody, and get unity of movement. Well, that's what we were told. It makes a sort of logic. Certainly there was a certain suspense generated by that long wail, roar, or whatever sound it was that sergeants generated in the prolonged syllable.

So the executive word of command, when it came, really did act like a whiplash. We jumped.

The second kind of pause we had to learn was the interval between the two halves of many drill movements. Take the 'Left Turn'. We got: 'Platoon! Platoon will turn to the left in threes. Leeeeeeff – TURN!'

On the 'TURN!' we whipped our bodies round ninety degrees, but kept our feet in the same place, though of course swivelling them somewhat. So our left leg remained straight, and our right leg was slightly extended, with only the toe in contact with the ground. That, as you can understand, left our right leg stretched to form a sort of triangle with our left leg and the ground. We held it there, bracing our right toe, indeed our whole right leg. After an appropriate interval, we lifted our right leg so that our thigh was roughly parallel to the ground, and then we drove our right foot into the ground as hard as we could, in such a way that when the movement was complete we were again standing at the correct position of 'Attention', having turned through ninety degrees to the left.

The appropriate interval – that was the crunch. That was what we had to learn. How long to stay braced. There was only word of command to cover the whole movement. In the early days, we were encouraged to count. In the very early days, we were made to count out loud. 'ONE – twothree ONE!' It is difficult to convey the timing of this. The beats were not regular. You hung there for a sort of extra half-beat on the first 'ONE', paused very slightly, then counted 'two' and 'three' as a kind of composite beat, and finally belted out a staccato 'ONE' to complete it. 'ONE! – twothree ONE!' The Army didn't seem to appreciate that it was just as bloody difficult to learn this limping, syncopated counting formula as it was to learn the very timing it was designed to simplify. But, as with all the other things, we learned to do it in the end.

But next time you are tempted to scoff at square-bashing, remember what I have said. There is a lot more to it than meets the eye. And remember too that it wasn't just a matter of getting twenty-odd young men to perform all these movements correctly; we had to perform them in perfect unison. When twenty-odd right boots crashed into the asphalt, you were supposed to hear only one sound. If you still think it's a doddle, take twenty of your friends into a nearby car park and try it.

So – when we reached the Brigade Depot, Company Sergeant-Major Jefferson took us through these basic movements and drills, patiently explaining, repeating, and demonstrating. One thing you had to hand to these NCO's: their own personal drill, nineteen times out of twenty, was first class. They really could do it much better than you. And some of them were getting on for twice our age.

He was, as I have said, patient and fair, and we did our best. Or so we thought. We learned to turn right, turn left, turn about. We learned close order and open order. Quick time and slow time. We became able to put our thumbs down the seam of our trousers in our sleep. We marched miles on that square. We began to think we were getting rather good. We began to get rather pleased with ourselves.

On a crisp late October morning, it surprised us to discover that a good session of drill that went well – timing, smart movements, unison – could be something approaching exhilarating. I don't think we would readily have confessed this to anyone outside the Army, because it didn't do to say we liked anything about it. A bit like saying that you liked school dinners.

So three weeks or so of basic training went by, and the prospect of another six or seven didn't seem so awful. We'd got it pretty well worked out. CSM Jefferson didn't seem a bad chap. It was all getting rather cosy – and that.

We had not yet made the acquaintance of Sergeant Flynn.

10   Bull by the horns

IF 'DRIWL' WAS DESIGNED TO 'teach a sowjer self-respec' an' pride in the uniform 'e wears', so , I suppose, was bull. I hope I have been able to convey to the most cursory reader that they were both an integral part of a soldier's ten weeks' basic training.

This task has been made easier by the fact that drilling and bulling are the two legends about the Army that have passed into common knowledge. Everybody, from the oldest of old sweats to the most sheltered old maid, knows that the Army makes you do drill and makes you clean kit.

The legends have, of course, been stretched and inflated over the years, by cheap journalism, by lurid reminiscence on the part of veterans, and by innumerable second-rate books, plays, and films, the writers of which cannot drag their cliché-ridden imaginations beyond the obvious leaden jokes. Better writers too – the ones I mentioned in the first chapter – the literary ones, with joined-up writing, pungent metaphors, swearwords, blank verse, and plays with no nice characters – have added their weight to the scales, with their more pointed emphasis on 'mindless', endless, repetitive tasks which, if one is to believe them, practically filled the poor soldier's day. And we must take them seriously, because they were 'serious' writers – wrote stuff that people could rarely understand, got published in rarefied quarterlies, appeared on the Third Programme, marched in nuclear disarmament demonstrations, smoked and swore during interviews, got divorced, and won literary prizes for works that nobody had read except the sullen judges.

Naturally, then, when we arrived in khaki, we too were victims of these legends – particularly on bull. They made us prey to the rumour and anecdote that flew around every barrack room. So we were prepared to believe that in some depots they made you whitewash the coal; that in others they had two colours of floor polish, and hapless recruits had to bull one central floorboard in, say, red, and others in brown. In one regiment you had to buff up your darning needles; in another you had to make the hobnails shine on the underside of your boots. Beds that could not be slept in because the entire kit had to be laid out the evening before for a kit inspection in the morning, and there would be no time after reveille. Bicycle chains that knowing corporals wore inside their battledress trousers to make them hang evenly over the tops of their gaiters. Transparent nail varnish that smart-alec soldiers daubed over their toecaps to give them a permanent patent finish. (This had a cautionary rider to it: apparently, after several applications, the patina grew into a sort of crust that, in the end, suffered from a variant of adhesion fatigue. Some fine morning, when the wearer would come to a crashing 'Shun!', the crust would fly off complete, leaving the toecap defenceless, naked, and shrivelling, like a nymph surprised at an Arcadian spring.)

And so on and so on.

However, most legends have at their core a grain of truth. It would be ridiculous to deny that the Army made demands of cleanliness and smartness upon us that far exceeded anything we had known in civilian life. And it is also true that it did seem that the Army had gone out of its way to make the achievement of these demands wilfully more difficult than they need have been.

It was not enough that an item had to be clean. Belt brasses, for example, had to sparkle like the Crown jewels; toecaps, nail varnish or no nail varnish, would, if polished to the required standards of dazzle, make mirrors an irrelevance.

And to heighten the challenge, as I said, they did not issue you with kit that was just new, or even second-hand. Webbing would be oil-stained, and grubby from untold months in the stores (probably unused surplus from the campaign in the Western Desert). Brasses would be pocked and pitted like an elderly alcoholic's nose. The boots, in addition to being greasy and unyielding, were completely covered with minute pimples.

Here was the cause for another legend. Just think for a moment how many pairs of boots had to be made in Army boot factories. For during all those years of National Service, from the end of the War to the early sixties, millions of young men must have needed boots – two pairs each to begin with, and more when they wore out, as they did. To say nothing of the Regular Army – and Navy, and Air Force, and Marine Corps. How many millions of frustrated young men, bent over an obstinate boot that refused to surrender its pimples to the most frantic of rubbing, scraping, and polishing, must have wondered why they did it? Was it beyond the ingenuity of man – even of the managing director of a boot factory – to design boots without pimples? They clearly had no bearing on the efficiency of the boot itself – *qua* boot, as P.G. Wodehouse would have said – because the first thing the Army did was to tell us to remove them.

Had they really had the pimples put there simply in order to keep us busy during the first few weeks of our service? Surely it was far more difficult to devise a boot *with* pimples than one without. Was it, on the other hand, a subtle initiative test to which we were being subjected, just to see how we coped?

Silly speculations now, perhaps, and probably silly speculations before – if we had bothered to think about it at all – in the secluded comfort of our school cricket pavilions or our college libraries. But at the time. . . . I tell you that, after several long evenings bent over in poor light, with NAAFI Kiwi up to the elbow, and ahead of you many more long hours of attacking every obstinate pimple – one by one, it seemed – you were prepared to believe almost anything about the devious cunning of the Army authorities.

It helped if you did this bulling round the table that was usually set up in the middle of the barrack room. It was old, so it didn't matter how many stains you left on it. Uniquely, the Army didn't make us clean it every day, perhaps because we could fold it up each night and lean it against a wall out of sight behind a cupboard. When the evenings got colder with the onset of winter, it could be set up near the central stove, which was comforting (assuming it was alight, and one couldn't always guarantee that).

If you stayed in your own bedspace, it could be lonely; you were shut off from the next bedspace by your locker. And tackling the intractable problems of kit-cleaning on your own could be a frustrating, and therefore depressing, business. The pimples somehow became more permanent, as if they knew you were on your own and couldn't cope. Sneering at you. 'You'll never get rid of us. We're like the hydra-headed monster; smooth us out on this side of the heel, and there are seventeen thousand of us on the other side, waiting for you. And it's half-past nine already. And you've been at it for two and a half hours.' That sort of thing. There is no end to the tricks of the imagination when they go hand in hand with fatigue and depression.

So we gravitated to the central table, and pushed and pulled, and rubbed and scraped, and filed and honed, and thumped and slammed, and sweated and swore. We gossiped too, and told stories, and laughed. Quite a lot, actually.

We swapped stories about the best way to go about the business – things we'd overheard; things we'd been told by ex-service uncles and cousins; things we'd read in the paper; things we'd seen in other barrack rooms; things we thought we had deduced from bitter experience.

'Spit,' said John Sly. 'That's the answer. The chemicals in saliva. Over the course of time the pimples wear away. You know what they say – "spit and polish". It's right.'

'We're only in for two years,' said Albert Pegg. 'Not twenty.'

Irving Bryce blinked through his spectacles.

'I always understood the secret was to rub hard with something like the bone handle of a knife.'

'Where do we get those?'

Irving had no answer to that.

'It's spoons,' declared Taffy.

'What?'

'Spoons. Make the spoon hot and press it on the leather. Sort of melts the pimples.'

'Bit drastic,' observed Jack Gatewood. 'Suppose you damage the leather. How can we afford to pay for a new pair from our pay – twenty-eight bob a week?'

'Not if you're careful,' said Bill Glover. 'Look.'

He placed a large left boot in the centre of the table. We gazed as he revolved it. He pointed with the stem of his pipe.

'See?'

He had indeed made considerable inroads into the legions of stubborn pimples that arrayed themselves so disdainfully before our puny armoury of knowledge and technique. And they weren't just temporarily squashed down, inundated with a butterspread of polish, waiting to spring up again overnight. They were totally removed. No undulations or tidemarks to show where they once had been. Some feat – to coin a phrase.

'It's not so much the spoon as the heat,' said Bill.

We all stopped to listen. Bill had already made sufficient impression with his solid intellect and his imperturbability for us to consider most of his pronouncements worth listening to. He was no soldier, but he was a mighty thinker. All those degrees, you see. As with other problems, he had used his intelligence.

'As I understand it, the real problem is not the pimples but the oil. You will never get them to shine with that oily residue all over the place. Get rid of the oil, and the pimples will follow.'

'How?' said someone.

'Heat,' said Bill. 'Bring enough heat to bear, and the oil will dry up. Use something to get the heat into the leather, and you will eliminate the pimples. Get rid of the oil, as I said, and you will get rid of the pimples.'

'Show us.'

Bill did.

'You can apply the heat indirectly, by means of a heated object, like a spoon, straight on to the leather. Or – '

'Or?'

'Or you apply it directly.'

'How?'

'By applying a thick layer of polish, and setting light to the polish.'

'What!'

'You set light to the boot,' said Bill calmly.

'Christ Almighty!'

The risk!

Bill pointed with his pipe again.

'See for yourself.'

We gazed again.

'You set light to your boot?' breathed John Sly in awe.

'Yes. I'll set light to yours if you like.'

John snatched his boot away from the table as if Bill were an approaching dragon.

'No bloody fear.'

We continued for some minutes in deep thought, until someone slammed his cap badge down on the table, making tins of polish and blanco jump into the air, and detonating a barrage of protest like a colony of angry rooks.

'Oh, I'm sorry,' said Martin Forrest testily. 'But look at this badge. I've made no impression since the day it was issued.'

'Have you tried the cardboard?' said Irving.

'Cardboard? Cardboard? What cardboard?'

'Soak a piece of cardboard with "Bluebell", and run the badge up and down against it on the table. Takes a long time, and it's messy, but it works. And before that it helps if you put it in a tin with some "Brasso" or "Bluebell" and set light to it.'

'Set light to it!'

Martin threw up his hands.

'What is this place – a smithy? A foundry? Do we have to burn everything? You'll be telling me next that you have to hammer belt brasses into shape.'

'Well, it's a funny thing you should say that,' said Mark Simpson, 'because if you put them over the foot of the bed – you know, those iron feet the beds have – and tap them carefully with a hammer, it gets rid of the convex shape and – '

'Boys!'

Taffy's rich baritone cut into the conversation. He was stock still, his face alight with the sort of rapturous expression that had covered the features of Toad the minute after he had seen his first motor car. His left hand was swallowed almost to the elbow in a boot, his right enveloped in a once-yellow duster, through which his index finger was poking, black and shiny. The smudge of polish on the end of his nose, and his ecstatic, glowing-cheek demeanour, gave him an arresting pixie-like appearance.

'Specialisation,' intoned Taffy. 'Division of labour – the first principle of organised industry.'

'Who said that?'

'I did,' said Taffy, coming out of his trance. 'Don't you see? This is the way to beat this bulling. Each one of us must be good at one part of it or another. Look at Bill there.'

He pointed a shiny, admiring forefinger in Bill's direction.

'The touch of the professional – that's what he's got.'

And that was how it started. Well – make a few allowances for dramatic licence. It was hardly a Newtonian breakthrough. Bit obvious really, when you think about it afterwards. And it would be foolish to claim that we were the first platoon to tumble to it. Nor, having tumbled to it, did we extend the idea to cover the whole platoon; we didn't, overnight, have over twenty specialist craftsmen beavering away in their own workshops.

But it is fair to say that some of us did become adept at one particular process – hammering belt brasses, taming cap badges, boxing kit, pressing battledress blouses, and so on – and were frequently consulted by others more mystified. Not the blind leading the blind; rather the sharp-eyed leading the short-sighted.

120

And I do not exaggerate about Bill and the boots. He really did become an expert. He proved his point to us with the mirror shine of his own footwear, and with the speed with which he achieved this staggering standard. So, gradually, we came to trust him.

We started by coming to him for advice.

'That's a good toecap you've got there,' he would remark. 'There's still a bit of oil to come out around the sides and instep. But if you're going to burn it out, be careful. Put plenty of polish on, and make sure the flames don't damage the stitches round the sole. You have to watch it all the time, and turn the boot round constantly to get even coverage for the flames.'

Some of the more trusting souls actually gave their footwear into his care. They sat, transfixed with a mixture of envy, fascination, and mortal terror, on the edge of Bill's bedspace, watching as their precious left boot appeared to be going up like a guy on bonfire night. There were ghastly smells too. And sounds – the rasp of matches, the pop of ignition, the murmur of naked flame, the hiss of hot metal on leather. It was like Dante's Inferno.

Those of us who preferred to do it ourselves nevertheless hung on his advice.

'Don't overdo it with the toecap. You've made good start; be patient. Don't expect a glassy shine straight away. Just a little polish and water every evening for about a week. Rub it in gently and leave it overnight. Then a clean rag next day. If you get into trouble come and see me.'

'Thanks, Bill.'

The owner listened humbly, and carried away his boots like a mother with a newly-born baby leaving the post-natal clinic. Bill returned to his Devil's Kitchen, surrounded by boots in every stage of preparedness. As he held up another boot and watched the flames licking round, the light was reflected in his glasses. An expression of complete contentment settled on his face. He looked like Mephistopheles himself contemplating a cauldron of lost souls well stoked.

A final word about toecaps. Well, two actually.

First – you know how certain crimes can vary in dastardliness according to the society in which they are committed. I can't think of a very good example. . . . well, how's this? Let go of a rope in a tug-of-war at the village fete, and you only lose the silver cup; let go on a mountainside, and the rest of your team can die. That sort of thing. . . . No? Perhaps it'll be better if we forget the examples and just go to the real thing.

Toecaps, as I hope I have been able to convey, became of enormous importance to us. You could get away with slightly less than mirror shine on the instep and the sides and heels, but the toecap had to be perfect – absolutely perfect. More labour went into the few square inches of the toecap than into all the other surfaces of the boot put together. And we were all in this together, remember. So everyone knew how important a man's toecaps were to him.

So damage to someone's toecaps become the worst crime in the book. Pinch his cigarettes, screw up his bedding late at night while he's been out on guard, hide the firing pin of his rifle. Pooh! Mere venial sins, Father. Hit him, bully him, tell lies about him – well, yes, pretty serious. Insult his parents, malign his family, dishonour his sister – OK, OK, OK!

But to take a sharp metal object and scrape a line across his toecaps – that was the crime of crimes. That was the unspeakable, the inconceivable, the unimaginable.

And the last word? That lay with Bill. He became quite famous. Before very long, his reputation began to spread beyond the barrack room. Our P.L. Platoon may have hit no headlines with our drill, shooting, physical training, or pretty well anything else, but we were justly renowned for the high standard of our boots.

One evening, Bill was sent for.

'Why?' asked someone when he had gone.

'Jefferson wants him.'

'What for?'

'Search me.'

We continued bulling in silence for a while. Most of us had been on some kind of a charge for being idle, or having dirty kit, or whatever. Routine offences, which carried routine punishments. Part of the rich pageant of life, as they say.

But none of us had ever been sent for, without warning, late in the evening. Bill was such an inoffensive, convivial chap. Not the best of soldiers perhaps; he would have been the first to admit that he was no threat to the reputation of Hannibal or Marlborough. But he did his best. And his greater maturity enabled him to deal with the constant novelties, the regular inconveniences, the depressing problems that filled our days. And deal with them better than the rest of us.

After about ten minutes he came back, grinning all over his face, and holding something behind him.

'Well?' we all said.

Bill drew himself up to his full height.

'I have a special commission, from our Company Sergeant-Major – and that.'

He took his right hand from behind his back, and held up an enormous pair of new, oily, pimply boots.

11   Fit for purpose

THEY SAY THAT THE FIRST thing General Montgomery did when he took over the Eighth Army in the Western Desert in 1942 was to insist on everyone doing regular physical training. From privates right up to staff rank.

Well, maybe so. It makes a good story. And, as the comedian Dave Allen observed, the facts should never be allowed to get in the way of a good story.

What is odd is that the story should have been worth coining. You would have thought that any army would have insisted on regular physical training as a matter of course. Or is this assumption the result of the decade we now live in? A decade when everyone jogs, or 'works out', or 'does some circuits'. When we can buy little machines that monitor our blood pressure immediately after we have done our daily schedule (if you want one you can get it in those little freely-delivered catalogues that offer long-armed scissors to trim your toenails while you're standing up, or high-pitched whiners to frighten away all the savage dogs that infest the high street). When we can go into specialist shops and buy complete home gym kits that look like medieval torture chambers. When wealthy executives and celebrities have 'personal fitness advisers' (or, if you prefer, 'advisors'). When entire television channels are devoted to football, baseball, racing, and – for all I know – volleyball.

Odd again, when you think about it, that so much television is geared to transmitting sport, or at least to riveting people to their armchairs. You might conclude that the result of all this would be to make the population a vast mass of Coke-swigging, burger-wolfing, stomach-spilling sags, whose only exercise was throwing up their arms at missed goals, failed high jumps, or unfair marks for ice-dancing.

So what are we – a nation of brown-limbed, smiling, glowing, biceps-busters, or a great big squash of jeans-loafers, lolling back on our shoulders with the laces of our trainers undone? Or are we neither? And if we are neither, why have the fitness manufacturers and the television moguls and the Coke and burger advertisers spent so much money to get us to do things when we don't do them?

The point I am making in my usual digressive way is that we seem to be more fitness-conscious now than we used to be. So one must conclude – and I want you to follow me closely here – that we were less fitness-conscious in the 'forties and 'fifties. It called for comment then when even an organisation like the Army laid the emphasis it did on the need for physical efficiency. In our training anyway.

The way it reached us – this philosophy – was as follows. We were 'Potential Leaders'. We were going to supervise the training of men and lead them into battle. We had to be able to do all the things we were going to require from our men. And do them better. Fairness. Shining example. Can't argue with that, can you? If you did, it would be like saying you approve of sin.

So to the gym. Every day, practically. They hadn't issued us with Vests P.T. two and Shorts P.T. two for nothing. To say nothing of Plimsoles Brown – which, incidentally, had to be covered with *black* shoe polish. That's right. Black shoe polish. And made to shine. We were required to make our canvas brown plimsoles *shine* with black shoe polish.

Oh – and the other thing we often had to wear, when we did P.T. in the open air in cold weather, was our Army sweater. It didn't make you sweat; it made you cringe, in seven hundred and thirty-nine places at once. Why? Because it was about the hairiest garment you could possibly imagine in your wildest speculations on the martyr's mortification of the flesh. (The only garment I remember that was any worse was a khaki shirt I had to wear for the Scouts when I was twelve. It was one of the reasons why I left.) You had to wear these without the comfort of a shirt underneath. Apart from a skimpy vest with enormous arm-holes, it went straight against your skin. It would have been enough to give nightmares to a medieval hermit in Lent. Just as there must have been little men employed in boot factories to put the pimples on, so there must have been other little men in woollen mills whose job was to insert zillions of minute hairs on the insides of Army sweaters, hairs which had been chemically treated to cause the maximum possible level of itchiness.

So – once more – to the gym. Most mornings, we lined up outside our spider in the October mist or the November drizzle or the December frost, freezing in our shorts and squirming in our medieval hermit sweaters, our feet resplendent in our black-Kiwi-polished brown plimsoles, our toes wriggling in our prickly Army socks. One of our drill corporals marched us at the double to the gym and handed us over to the bear-like embrace of Staff Sergeant Barron.

Staff Sergeant Barron had long since lost the agility and lissomness of youth, but was still possessed of immense strength. And guile. He was typical of the senior non-commissioned officer who, as the years passed, made up for his declining physical powers by an ever-growing fund of knowledge, *savoir-faire*, quick wit, mendacity, and cunning so low as to be subterranean. Such men had been everywhere, seen everything, done everything, and escaped the consequences. Their resource was endless. It was easy to see why such repositories of experience, know-how, resilience, and capacity for survival became the backbone of an army. No officer with the smallest grain of sense neglected them.

Have you ever looked at a person in one set of circumstances and decided that you had a pretty good idea how they would behave in another set of circumstances? For example, have you ever looked at the office boor and decided you knew how he conducted himself with his wife and family? Well, I have no idea what Staff Sergeant Barron's private life was like, but it might give the flavour of the man if I say that you could make a fair guess how he would behave in a convivial gathering. He was the sort of partifier who would bore sullen subordinates and embarrassed superiors with hoary jokes of nauseating vulgarity. And whenever a piano was in evidence, he would insist on beating out nerve-jarring discords, because, as he would explain, he only played by ear. And you suspected that his capacity for beer would be measured in quarts rather than in pints.

But you had to hand it to Staff Sergeant Barron when it came to the old Army art of doing as little as possible, while at the same time drawing as little attention to yourself as possible. His capacity for evanescence was close to genius, and would have been the envy of the Scarlet Pimpernel. He had seen to it that most of the actual instruction was not done by himself; that had been shifted on to the capable shoulders of Corporal Duke. Some of the elementary training was left to a couple of P.T. trainee lance-corporals, whose progress Barron supervised in a remote sort of way from the tea-cups inside his gym office, which smelt of stale tobacco and perished rubber. These pale young men, Lance-Corporal Sykes and Lance-Corporal Tellman, were distinguished from the white-vested qualified instructors by long, rugger-type jerseys in red and black hoops that reached down to their buttocks. In style, rather like the jerseys that scout cubs wear. Barron would appear on important occasions, like the start of our fitness tests, or the end (if he had finished his tea). And that was about that. He was almost as elusive as the Commanding Officer in our Regimental Depot.

So most of the instruction was done by Corporal Duke. He was strong, fit, and unflappable, and his lessons went smoothly. So smoothly that I cannot recall a single individual incident in the gym. Which, I suppose, is a testimony to his efficiency. But there wasn't much light and shade. He didn't crack the usual NCO vulgar jokes. He didn't crack jokes at all. To be fair, he didn't lose his temper either, or pretend to. He had work to do, and did it very well. His job fitted him as tightly and as neatly as his spotless white singlet and plimsoles (no Kiwi polishing for him) and dark athletic trousers. We never saw him wearing anything else. If any of us had bumped into him, say, in the London Underground, we would have expected to see him bouncing out of the Stanmore train in white singlet and blue trousers.

One thing I do remember, though. He neither gave nor attracted much warmth, but he didn't miss much. And he had the knack of drawing the best out of people. Most of us made a greater effort if we thought he was watching us. We worked to earn his praise.

It was Corporal Duke's job to turn us – twenty-odd 'Potential Leaders' – into passable physical specimens within the space of ten weeks. Of course, like most healthy young men, we thought we already were passable physical specimens. Except perhaps Bill Glover, who had never made any pretensions to bodily prowess, and Martin Forrest, whose whole way of life was a challenge to the philosophy of *'mens sana in corpore sano'*.

Most of us played games of one kind or another, a few of us to a reasonably high standard. We had always had enough breath and strength to survive a weekly game of rugby or football or hockey. We conceded that we would have to learn new skills, but didn't foresee much trouble in meeting the other physical demands of Her Majesty's Armed Forces.

Our self-assurance received its first shock in the very first week at the Depot. Immediately after we had been selected by the sour PSO to be 'Potential Leaders', the Company Sergeant-Major took us in hand. I'm not sure why, because we had only about a couple of days left before posting to our next unit, and he must have known that.

He was an officious, smallish man with a toothbrush moustache. If it had been dark instead of fair, he would have passed in the evening shadows for Hitler. He was one of those senior personages that you find in any organisation who maintain that things are not what they used to be, and that it behoved the seniors to put the juniors in their place and make them appreciate. . . . well, just make them appreciate.

Understandably, one of our main preoccupations, from the moment we entered the Army, was the intensely important question – to us – of when we were going to get our first leave. Like a red rag to a bull to Company Sergeant-Major Fay. 'Leave,' he would say, like a priest intoning the catechism, 'is a privilege, not an entitlement.' We didn't care what they called it, so long as we got it, and as soon as possible, and as much as possible. What on earth did he expect our reaction to be? Were we suppposed to believe him? Did he honestly think we were going to wait around piously until the Army became so convinced of our virtue that they were going to grant us special privileges? Was his own sense of duty so blazingly pure that his last leave had been in 1937?

Perhaps our scepticism showed through our silence. Perhaps he was simply fed up, after only a few days, with the sheer cockiness of this bunch of ex-schoolboys and undergraduates who appeared to think that they knew it all. Perhaps it was the normal disdain that the professional Regular felt for the unwilling amateur National Serviceman.

Whatever it was, within hours of the announcement of our new classification – 'Potential Leaders' – he descended upon us. Because of our new distinction, he declared, we would now have to meet fresh standards of military efficiency. Moreover, he was now going to give his own personal attention to this matter. Or, as he put it, he intended to chase us 'from arsehole to breakfast time'.

We were to parade in full marching order – belt, pouches, pack, rifle, the lot. Boots and gaiters. Everything except greatcoats. We had been in the Army for little more than half a week. We had barely learned how to put the damned stuff on. Our boots were still stiff and unyielding.

And he took us for a six-mile march, which included a lot of double time, round the local park.

Now most of us could stand up to a six-mile ordinary journey on foot. But our feet were not ready for it in Army boots. Nor were our boots. We nearly all got blisters. And not just the little pimple that you get when you accidentally dab your hand on the iron. No, these were full dinner-plate jobs halfway across the ball of the foot, or right round the heel.

Fit for purpose

There was a great queue of us in the Medical Centre, where a stolid medical orderly inserted a long black needle in one side of the blister, out of the other, and then wiggled it about so that the juice came tumbling out. It was stomach-turning to see it done to somebody else; done to your own foot, it was – well, figure it out for yourself.

To give the Depot establishment its due, our Company Commander came in person to inspect our feet (we later discovered that it was a regular duty of company officers to inspect their men's feet). When he saw the devastated area that most of our soles and heels presented, he expressed his disapproval of the Company Sergeant-Major's misguided zeal. Which was some comfort, I suppose.

A small tailpiece to that. Two or three of us had to play a game of hockey in the afternoon. (The march had been in the morning.) I don't know how we got through it. Well, actually, we didn't. We collapsed with cramp halfway through the second half. The field looked like Wembley Stadium at the end of a World Cup match while they are waiting to set up extra time or the penalty shoot-out.

The second shock to our self-assurance came when Corporal Duke started to put us through the Army's more orthodox paces. Most of us soon discovered that we were lacking in agility, in self-confidence, in muscularity, in co-ordination, and in sheer puff. We got better, as you would expect, thanks to regular practice and Duke's patience and skill.

We passed the tests when they came. Things like forward rolls, long-jumping sixteen feet, climbing a rope. Incidentally, not quite as simple as it sounds, because you had to climb the rope twice – up, down, up, down – without touching the floor. It was the second 'up' that got you.

So far, so good.

Then came the stamina test – running a mile in six minutes. Pretty small beer these days, when they do the world record in well under four. But a reasonable test for non-athletes. Contemplating it now, after a gap of several decades, I am still pleased that I did it.

Staff Sergeant Barron honoured the occasion with his actual presence – in the flesh. We waited outside the gym, whipped by a November gale, shivering and twitching in our prickly sweaters and socks, till the door of his office opened, bringing a whiff of tobacco and electric fires into the winter air. He was muffled to the eyebrows in track suit and scarf.

'All right, listen to me. You'll do a measured mile starting from the park gates. Corporal Duke will go with you as far as the gates, and set the watch going. Then he'll bring it back to me at the door of the gym behind you. The measured mile ends here.'

I bet – right outside his office, with its electric fire and its teacups.

'Corporal Sykes and Corporal Tellman will act as markers.'

Those unfortunate young men had been sent off half an hour earlier to shiver and hover at vantage points in the park, like red and black wasps outside a pastrycook's window.

'You'll go to the left of Corporal Sykes and round Corporal Tellman. He'll have a list of your names, and he'll tick them off as you pass. So make sure you save enough breath to tell him who you are.'

See what I mean? Feeble jokes.

'Remember – the mile isn't finished till you pass me here.'

Outside the tobacco lounge.

Duke led us off at a brisk pace towards the park. Martin Forrest was puffed before we even got to the park gates.

'All right,' said Duke, when we got there. 'Pay attention.'

We did.

'See that small hill?' he said, pointing. 'Corporal Sykes is just over the other side. Then just round a clump of trees you'll see Corporal Tellman. Don't forget to give him your names, and make sure he ticks you off.'

He took out the stop-watch.

'Are you ready? Off you go – now!'

The willing sprint with which everyone started soon degenerated into something more processional. Except for the keen ones like Mark Simpson, who, naturally, wanted to be first in. The majority were chasing no medals, but their self-respect made them attempt a pace that bore a discernible resemblance to running. Bill Glover, characteristically, had done a sum on the back of an envelope, and had calculated that if he maintained a pace that was just within his scope, he would finish in five minutes, fifty-five seconds, and that was good enough for him. Those whose main activity at school or university had been moving from one chessboard to another stiffened their sinews, summoned up their goose pimples, and gave a moving demonstration of the eternal struggle between the spirit and the flesh. Martin Forrest, whose only unanswered question was exactly when he would be forced by an unwilling body to stop, prised himself away from the iron gates, and set his face to the mountain that Duke had referred to as a 'small hill'.

As our collection of military leader potential passed walkers in the park, it occurs to me now that it must have been something like this that had given rise to the old music-hall joke about the pensioner who saw something similar, turned to his veteran friend, and said, 'Thank Christ we've got the Navy!'

Well, we did it. Even Martin. But it was close. He was so short of breath at the halfway mark that he could not stammer out his name. He had got it into his head that if he broke his pace for any reason at all, he would not be able to start again. So he bounced and puffed in front of the gaping Tellman for several moments, struggling to get out the word 'Forrest'. In the end, after several unavailing attempts, he snatched the paper and pencil from the corporal's blue fingers. After a few seconds' focussing through a blur of sweat and jogging on the spot, he ticked his name, thrust the pencil and paper back, and began the toilsome half-mile return.

He came in last, of course, even behind Bill Glover. By good fortune, he had been passed on the return by the two lance-corporals, grateful to return to the warmth of the gym. One of them must have made a rude remark as they did so, because Martin did the last three hundred yards on sheer indignation. With purpling face and sagging knees, he arrived to a round of applause from the rest of us, and collapsed dramatically at Staff Sergeant Barron's feet.

Barron pocketed his stop-watch.

'Yes, not bad. Hundred per cent.' He nodded towards Martin's corpse. 'See to him.'

While Barron returned to his *Daily Express*, we half-carried Martin inside our spider and sat him down.

He blinked, coughed, and looked round blearily, oblivious of the congratulations.

'Anyone got a cigarette?'

* * * * * *

Ever done the fireman's lift?

The Army was very taken with it. Makes sense, I suppose. Rescuing wounded comrades on the field of battle, and all that. You can't always rely on having stretcher bearers in the offing, can you? As they do in the Hollywood films.

Have you noticed? Whatever the stage of the battle, wherever they are in the world, whatever the time of day or night, the hero, in acute distress at the plight of his comrade, gazes desperately about and bawls 'STRETCHER-BEAREEERRRR!' And sure enough, there are always a couple of them just off set, waiting for their cue. You can get stretcher-bearers on battlefields in Hollywood films almost as easily as you can get taxis in obscure London residential streets in English ones.

So it will come as no surprise for you to be told that we were taught how to do the fireman's lift. Nor will it surprise you to be told that it figured in our fitness tests.

'Pair yourself off with someone your own size,' said Barron.

God help Taffy Davies – the one who didn't need his new denim jacket, because he could button the fly of his denim trousers right up to his neck. And Heaven help the man who was left to carry some bastion of the rugger scrum like Mark Simpson.

Fit for purpose

The test was simple: you had to carry someone on your shoulder in the fireman's lift for a hundred yards in a minute. Simple, but far from easy.

You had to get him on to your shoulder first. That was included in the minute. Really this was the proper 'lift' part; the other was what you might call the 'fireman's carry'. Getting the body up there, that was the thing. Because it really was a body. Your partner – your 'liftee', as you might say – was under instructions to act relaxed, limp, unmuscled, dead. Liftees always thoroughly enjoyed themselves.

They gave you no help whatsoever. They let arms flop that you had just carefully balanced on your shoulder. They sagged in the middle. They slipped forwards, backwards, sideways. They slid off your shoulder just when you had got them in the right place. And, while you were puffing and sweating and beginning the process all over again, they lay there with a beatific smile plastered across their 'dead' faces.

There were ways of getting your own back. You could hoick them sharply into a sitting position. You could pretend to make a mistake and let them fall back. You could get them on to your shoulder, and then drop them. And above all, you could be careless about the exact position of their corpse in the completed lift, so that the point of your shoulder drove into their most sensitive parts. Their cries for mercy could be pitiable. You were too busy to listen, of course, because you were running to beat the minute deadline, and this involved much bumping and bouncing.

When, at the end, aggrieved liftees massaged the injured area, it gave Staff Sergeant Barron an opportunity to ventilate his flair for wit:

'Ha! Don't stroke 'em; count 'em.'

* * * * * *

That wasn't the end of it. There was one more physical fitness test – the ultimate, the *pièce de résistance*, the *ne plus ultra*, the one that sorted out the men from the boys.

Hardly surprisingly, therefore, it occupied a lot of our thinking and imagination in the days immediately before it took place. As with so many other tests to which we were subjected, we were not short of advice, comment, dire warnings, and nerve-jangling prophecies from every quarter. Most of it served only to excite our nerves rather than to settle them.

What was this fearsome obstacle? Running a mile in eight minutes. But if we had already done one in six, why the worry? Because we had to do this one in full Battle Order, that's why. It is time to explain an Army ritual that was as complicated as the investment of a medieval knight with the equipment of his trade.

Remember all those straps and pouches and packs I described? All that kit we were issued with by the RQMS? Incidentally, that shows you how quickly we slipped into Army jargon – the language of initials. If you are particularly quick on the uptake, or if you are extremely knowledgeable, you will have worked out that RQMS stands for 'Regimental Quartermaster-Sergeant', and you will have remembered that our Depot RQMS was Colour Sergeant Berryman. I suspect that the Army, like so many Government departments, loves initials for their own sake. We have already made the acquaintance of P.L.'s, the CSM, the RSM, the NCO's, the CO, and the ORQMS. There's a real mouthful for you – ORQMS. But the Army had a way of dealing with acronyms like that; they even shortened sets of initials. He was often referred to as the 'ORQ'. More simply still, he was known as the Chief Clerk, the Cerberus who sat on guard outside the CO's office. What does it stand for then? 'Orderly Room Quartermaster-Sergeant.'

Think yourself lucky you don't have to remember sets of initials like KOYLI (King's Own Yorkshire Light Infantry) or DAQMG (Deputy Something-or-Other Quartermaster-General).

Now, straps and pouches. All that gear that was deemed to be an indispensable part of the well-equipped soldier's kit.

The belt was the basic item. Everything else was built upon it. So it had to fit snugly. It would take drawings and diagrams to illustrate the means of adjusting the girth, but take it from me that you could make it any measurement you liked, from pencil slimness to gross obesity – from a drummer-boy's waist to a quartermaster's paunch.

Most of us, at eighteen or twenty-one, were pretty slender, but that did not prevent the military authorities from demanding extra standards of slimness that were a mile, or several inches, from civilian life. The belt had to be tight enough to prevent a suspicious sergeant from being able to insert his finger between belt and battledress blouse. There were few worse sins than a sagging belt – or, as the Army loved to maintain, an 'idle' belt – as if it were the belt's own fault. We were constantly amazed to discover how many inanimate objects could assume the very human characteristic of idleness.

But it was not enough simply to put the belt on, and wrench the two belt brasses together till they fitted. That left tell-tale folds and creases in the waistband of the battledress, and so created a battledress blouse that was also 'idle'. No. The answer was to get two people on the job. For the really important parades, we would work in twos. The one being dressed would put the belt round his waist and wait with the brasses poised to be fastened, one in each hand. The second, the dresser, would stand behind him, put his hands either side of the first one's waist, grasp the waistband of the battledress blouse, and pull towards the back. A knee against the lower spine also helped, or you would pull him over. The first, the dressee, would take a deep breath, hoist everything he could into his chest and away from his stomach, twist his neck to look down and so give himself half a dozen double chins, and press the belt brasses together till they clicked and locked the patient into the parade straightjacket. Then they turned about and did it the other way round.

On the back of the belt were two buckles. When we put on the other gear, the ends of two straps fastened to these buckles. The other ends were crossed and taken over opposite shoulders. These ends were then fastened to the tops of two ammunition pouches which had been previously fitted on to the front of the belt. So – we had a belt, two straps, and two ammunition pouches. This was known, by a charming archaism, as 'Musketry Order', and so had presumably been introduced by the Iron Duke in the Peninsular War.

So far, so good. They didn't mind quite so much about the belt being a bit floppy in Musketry Order, because you were usually wearing denim overalls, and it was accepted that denims were more informal than battledress. You were running about too, and you needed the extra space for sheer breathing. How reasonable of the Army.

Now came the pack on the shoulders. This had to contain 'small kit', by the way. Remember all the stuff you had to take when you reported sick? P.T. Vest, P.T. shorts, plimsoles, toilet gear, towel, spare underclothes, spare socks, mess tins, pyjamas, and the inseparable mug, knife, fork and spoon. (When the wretched invalid was swaying on his feet with dysentery, did they really count the socks in his 'small kit'?)

And you should see the size of the 'small pack'; they didn't call it the 'small pack' for nothing. Looking back, I am forced to doubt whether anybody actually succeeded in getting everything in. Getting even half of it in was enough to make the package somewhat dense. So the weight was inclined to drag it off the shoulders and down the back. If it slipped too far it began to bounce against the bayonet and the water bottle, which were by now fitted with webbing loops on to the belt.

But they'd thought of that. The ammunition pouches had been fitted not with one buckle, but with two. One took the shoulder strap I spoke about, and the other clipped on to another hasp on the small pack This would keep the pack high on the shoulders. It looked smart and effective at a stationary demonstration.

However, the minute you began running about, the greater weight of the small pack not only caused the pack to slip down the back, but also dragged the pouches, belt and all up the chest.

This could be counteracted, naturally, by tightening the belt even more than for a drill parade. So you were left with a choice: you either kept your pack and pouches in place by having the belt tighter than a dowager's corsets, or you paid for the privilege of breathing by having to tolerate a flopping pack at the back and a glorified webbing brassiere at the front. It was a bit like being asked by a torturer which leg you'd prefer to have broken.

Nor was the process yet complete. There was another webbing strap to go over a shoulder – the rifle sling, attached to nine and a half pounds of Lee Enfield rifle. Lee Enfields, I believe, came into use just before the Indian Mutiny. Indeed, it was the new cartridges, and the grease involved, which had helped to *cause* the Indian Mutiny.

So – Musketry Order from the Duke of Wellington, Lee Enfield rifles from the Indian Mutiny (modified no doubt since – at least, I should hope so).

Finally came the headgear – the famous tin hat. Looks fine in recruiting posters and war films. But you try to wear one, and keep it in place. The taut leather lining seemed to have been installed in the belief that every soldier's head was uniformly spherical. So one is forced into the speculation that this was a relic from the army of Oliver Cromwell.

The last relic from the past? Possibly not. I have to report that leather jerkins were often issued for wear on the rifle range, and they had a lineage going back to the Middle Ages. Archers wore them at the Battle of Agincourt.

And – Bob's your uncle – full Battle Order at last. We were ready for our mile run in eight minutes.

Staff Sergeant Barron started us off as before, and Corporal Duke saw us as far as the park gates, where he set the watch going. Sykes and Tellman had been sent off to their chilly signpost duty in the outback.

With the extra weight we were carrying, it was small wonder that before we had covered a quarter of the distance, many of us had degenerated into an undignified bag-flopping jog-trot. But, as Duke had pointed out, a steady trot was quite adequate; eight minutes at that speed, however uncomfortable we felt, was time enough, and more, to cover a mile.

However, it was not long before a gap opened between Martin Forrest and the rest, a gap which became progressively wider, and, for him, progressively depressing. He could manage nothing but a wild-eyed stare at the half-way mark, but Lance-Corporal Tellman remembered him from the previous run, ticked his name, and waved him on.

Everybody else drew further ahead than ever. Martin's rifle sling cut into his bony shoulder. His small pack flapped badly (he had opted for the 'loose-belt' technique). His ammunition pouches practically chucked him under the chin. His bayonet swung wildly, and his water bottle bounced like a Ancient Greek sprinter's genitals. The weapon on his shoulder felt more like an anti-aircraft gun than a rifle. He sweated heavily beneath the leather lining of his tin hat. He now realised how foolish he had been to wear his hairy sweater underneath his denim jacket, but he had known they would have to wait some time outside Barron's office, and it was a cold morning, and Martin was a great one for his creature comforts. He was now paying for it.

He felt a blister coming on his left heel. He was still sore from someone else's attempts at the fireman's lift on him (we had had to do both tests the same morning). Not even the ribald comments of the two lance-corporals as they overtook him on their return run could conjure any more effort out of him.

Indeed, they had scarcely passed him when they were brought up short by a wheezing gasp and muffled thump behind. They had to go back and unravel the pitiable pile of webbing, sweat, and misery that was all that was left of Private Martin Forrest.

But the Army was not finished with Private Martin Forrest. Nor were we. Not yet.

If you had told any of us a few weeks before that we would consider a set of Army physical training tests important, we would have laughed or snorted in scorn. But I am here now to tell you that we thought it was a pity that we had broken our hundred per cent record. Not that Martin had, please note; that *we* had. I don't know quite what that shows you, but it shows you.

Not only that. We cast about for a way to *restore* our hundred per cent record. When I say 'we', I rather fancy that Martin himself may not have been as eager as the rest of us. After all, he was the one who was going to run the risk of collapse again. Still, we worked on him, and he came round.

A few days later, a small squad of us paraded outside Barron's gym. Martin was in full battle order again. The rest of us were in P.T. kit. It says something for Barron that he was willing to bend the rules of his training programme just for this. Maybe he was impressed that a platoon of his actually wanted to do it.

Anyway, whatever the reason, he had posted the hapless Sykes and Tellman to the park again – and it was further into winter for them. Poor devils. Just for one more man. He might even have left his electric fire to come with us himself to the park gates to start us off.

We had reasoned that Martin would run better if he had somebody with him. He had freely admitted that it was a tremendous blow to the spirits to see the whole platoon vanish over the skyline and leave him with nothing but a pair of bursting lungs for company.

As soon as Barron was out of sight, we sent Mark Simpson on ahead. He was the fittest. It was his job to look out for stray lance-corporals, and report back. John Sly divested Martin of his rifle. Taffy removed his tin hat and carried it. Albert Pegg ran immediately behind him, and took the weight of his small pack. Jack Gatewood grasped one of Martin's elbows, and someone else took the other. All Martin had to do was stay upright.

We made good time. The only bad moments were, predictably, when we came across Sykes and Tellman at their lonely outposts. Mark gave us good warning, and when Private Forrest ran past them, he was wearing full Battle Order, and the rest of us were running beside him, though at a virtuous distance – just giving him moral support, as you might say. True, his rifle sling sagged over his right forearm like a stripper's shoulder strap. And he was complaining mysteriously of a headache.

But Sykes and Tellman wanted to get back into the warm, and asked no questions. Barron was secretly tickled that we should want to go to such trouble to maintain our unblemished pedigree, and he too made no comment on Martin's strange silence when we at last arrived back at the gym, well within the eight minutes.

The Army, whether we liked it or not, was making a platoon out of us.

And no doubt a cigarette soon put Martin on the road to recovery.

12 A soldier's best friends

THE MORE ATTENTIVE READER WILL have noticed by now that, though I dropped a hint about somebody called Sergeant Flynn at the end of Chapter Nine, so far he has not yet made an appearance in this record of our basic training. The more cynical reader might begin to suspect that the dropping of Flynn's name was simply for effect, rather in the way evocative names were quoted in the past – Captain Swing, Captain Moonlight, the Scarlet Pimpernel, Ned Ludd, Macavity. The result was usually to create an aura of mystery, menace, and ubiquity, while hiding the truth that such personalities did not in fact exist.

Not so in the case of Sergeant Flynn; he existed all right. And the effect he had on us and on our lives for seven weeks or so was huge and dramatic. But any writer will tell you that a vital feature of creating drama is timing. You don't toss one of your best characters on to the page as soon as you think of him; you wait for the right moment.

Drop a hint or two by way of building up a little suspense, by all means, as I am doing now. But get the actual arrival dead right.

Chapter Nine, if you recall, was about arriving at our new barracks and making the acquaintance of our new training staff. Sergeant Flynn was not there at that time, so it would have confused things to have introduced him then.

The next chapter was about bulling, and the worst of that happened during our first two or three weeks, for most of which time our chief training NCO was Company Sergeant-Major Jefferson. So to have started talking about Sergeant Flynn would not have done justice to him, or to Jefferson.

Chapter Eleven, as you have just read, was about P.T., and Flynn was not a Physical Training Instructor. He was as skilful at getting a burst of effort out of us as Corporal Duke was, but he never, so far as I can remember, put in an appearance in the gym, or in the park. So he didn't belong in Chapter Eleven.

This chapter is going to be all about weapon training, and Flynn didn't do any of that either. One can begin to hear scepticism raising its head: if this mysterious man wasn't connected with our arrival, our kit-maintenance, our physical training, and our developing skills in the handling of weapons, what on earth did he do? What scope did he have to exert the influence on us that my hints have suggested? Not kit-maintenance, not physical fitness, not skill with weapons. A soldier had to be smart and well turned out; he had to be fit; he had to be able to fire his guns accurately. What else was there of importance?

Quite a lot actually. And we were working at it long before Sergeant Flynn arrived. I don't wish to leave the impression that we spent our first three weeks bulling kit and cleaning lavatories, jumping over gym horses and climbing ropes, and taking Bren guns to pieces – and nothing else. But, in a chronicle like this, you have to organise. A week-by-week, or, worse, a day-by-day account of what we did would prove almost as mind-numbing, as tiring, as boring, as wearying, as we often found the real thing to be. You have to break it up a bit.

There is another dimension to this matter too. It takes no great intelligence to work out that there is a military activity conspicuously absent from my account so far, an activity that everyone knows about the Army, or thinks he knows about. I refer of course to square-bashing, military drill, marching about the parade-ground in complicated rhythms and patterns. For once the clichés are right. We did do an awful lot of square-bashing, and we were doing it regularly in between the bulling and the rope-climbing and the rifle-cleaning.

It will also take little intelligence again to deduce that Sergeant Flynn might well have had something to do with this square-bashing. So why the mystery? No mystery really. I am only trying to create a little atmosphere. I want you to keep in mind that for the first three weeks or so of our training, we had never seen or heard of Sergeant Flynn. By keeping him back till the next chapter, I want to try and create for the reader something of the shock he himself created when he did finally arrive.

So – let me now turn to the subject of the chapter – weapon-training. Let us start with the rifle. After all, we were the infantry, and the rifle was known as the infantryman's 'best friend'. (Only three men in a platoon got to fire the Bren gun regularly. Sten guns were not normal issue, and only officers carried pistols.) However, any idea we may have had that it was our best friend, or any kind of friend, had long since been dispelled by our constant cleaning and oiling of it, and by our continual practice with it during rifle drill (of which more later). Over nine pounds of iron and steel, bristling with knobs and rivets and a variety of other projections – designed originally for the British Army of the 1850's. I presume there had been modifications since, but it was still known by its original name, which was scarcely reassuring. (And, when the time came to issue us with live ammunition, we noticed that the date stamped on the cartridges was 1943 or 1944 – over ten years before we joined the Army.)

However, after we had spent three weeks learning how to clean it, hold it, port it, slope it, present it, take it to bits, pull it through (clean the inside of the barrel), and put it together again, it was considered to be about time that we were permitted to fire it. This first attempt would take place, we were told, on the miniature range. Twenty-five yards. Did this mean that they didn't trust us yet to hit anything further away than the length of a cricket pitch? Coincidentally, we were to be dressed in 'Musketry Order' – which reminded us of the armies of the eighteenth century, whose weapons could barely be relied on, at that distance, to hit a barn door. Again, not conducive to confidence.

What little we had left was eaten away in the days running up to our first outing into ballistics. Every large Army establishment has a group of people who are further into their course of instruction than you are. In National Service, every sizeable depot had several squads of recruits at varying stages of their basic training – in some cases only a fortnight apart. It is amazing what status of seniority and omniscience was provided by only fourteen days' advantage that one training squad had over another. One of the delights of such a senior squad was to descend upon the 'younger' group shortly before a worrying test, and to augment their worries by describing in minute and horrifying detail the risks that would be strewn before them like dragon's teeth in front of Jason and his Argonauts.

The first dragon's tooth was the rifle butt. It was apparently alive, and bent on mischief.

'The recoil, you see. Especially when you're not ready for it. Well, you can't be – not the first time – can you?'

As Eddie would have put it, rather more colourfully, 'Y'get a bash in the chops ev'ry time y'pull the bleed'n' trigger.'

Well, we were ready for that one. Had not our Sergeant-Major Jefferson told us repeatedly that 'you don't pull the trigger; you squeeze it – and that'. If only Eddie had had the benefit of the sergeant-major's training, perhaps he wouldn't have got all that bashing in the bleeding chops – and that.

But the prophets of doom were just getting warmed up.

'It's not only the recoil; it's the noise. Again, you see, you're not ready for it. And they never tell you beforehand. Some blokes have been invalided out – shattered eardrums. Very painful, I believe.'

'It's not just your cheeks that cop it. Don't forget that it doesn't only jump up; it jumps back. Straight on to your collar bone. There's usually one that gets it. Broken. Just like a stick. Puts him back three weeks in his training. Got to do it all over again.'

Then there's the helpful one.

'What you need to do is get hold of some of that foam rubber they have to line the tops of ammunition boxes.'

Now how on earth were we all to do that? When they didn't

open the box until five minutes before we fired, when there was only one strip per box, and when there were over twenty of us for it to go round?

So there we were – worried to death, told of the existence of a remedy, and then made aware that the chances of obtaining it were practically nil.

We didn't have a very good night.

Things didn't seem much better when we stood on the grass bank next morning and gazed down the range. The target cards looked damned small, for all that they were only twenty-five yards away. We were told that, in order to get ourselves into the 'First Class' category, we had to place all our five shots into a circle with a diameter of one inch. One inch! Not even Wild Bill Hickok was expected to do that.

Bill Glover adjusted his spectacles.

'I'll be quite happy if they all go into the target.'

'Yours? Or somebody else's?' asked John Sly, adjusting his.

'Details of four!' bawled the Firing Point Sergeant. 'Sort yourselves out into details of four. First detail get your ammunition from Corporal Johnson. Then go to the firing point. ALWAYS KEEP YOUR RIFLES POINTING DOWN THE RANGE.'

We milled about.

'Other details keep well away from the firing point. First detail – stand fast. Don't lie down or stand up till you're told.'

Those of us in the later details watched, genuinely interested. What sort of marksmanship was going to be displayed? Was there anything we could learn from their mistakes? Were we about to witness four crushed cheekbones, a couple of broken clavicles, and two bodies writhing in the agony of fractured eardrums?

'Load!'

We watched the first detail fumbling and fiddling. We had all practised many times with the drill rounds, and it really was quite easy. Curiously, live rounds, exactly the same in every feature save the obvious, presented much greater problems. It was some time before all four lay, legs splayed according to the drill pamphlet, hands on the rifle, waiting.

'Two rounds into the bank – and five rounds at your target in front – in your own time – carry on.'

More fumbling and fiddling. Rear sights flipped up. Rifle butts shoved into the crook of the shoulder, taken out, and re-adjusted. Several times. Fingers flexed and tightened on stocks.

When the first shot was actually fired, we all jumped. Christ Almighty! If that was what it sounded like when you were standing fifteen yards away, what was it going to be like when the thing was right against your ear?

Two sighting rounds into the sandbank. That shouldn't be too difficult. We reckoned we could all hit a sandbank. Five into that tiny little piece of paper – that was going to be interesting.

The rifle fire hardly crackled along the thin red line (Musketry Order or no Musketry Order), but somehow everybody discharged his 'five rounds'. Whether they all went into the 'target in front' was another matter; they seemed to be kicking up sand over an extraordinarily wide area.

'Clear your weapons.'

This meant working the bolt and trigger several times to make sure that there were no more rounds 'up the spout'.

'On your feet. For inspection, port arms.'

The first four had to stand with the bolt of their rifle drawn back to show an empty breech – while at the same time remembering to KEEP THE RIFLE POINTING DOWN THE RANGE.

Corporal Johnson inspected them.

'Ease springs.' (Close the breech.) 'All right – second detail.'

That was me.

I did as I was told mechanically. My head was buzzing – with the awful noise I had just heard, and with the lugubrious prophecies about bruised jaws and broken collar-bones. I looked at the foreign object lying in my hands. From the deep past sprang, unbidden, incongruous memories about marksmen in boys' adventure stories who got the thing to 'nestle gently' into their shoulders, while their fingers 'curled lovingly' round the trigger.

'Load.'

I'll say this for the Army. I did as I was told. All those worries, all those nerves, all that – let's be honest about it – fear. And I was still carrying out my orders.

I adjusted the back-sight and flipped it into position. I brought the rifle into my shoulder, which at that particular moment felt harder and bonier than it had ever done before. I should add that it was my left shoulder. I am left-handed. The bolt on the Lee Enfield rifle is on the right – understandably. I don't suppose left-handedness was officially recognised in the middle of the nineteenth century, when this weapon was invented. But with unexpected liberality of mind, the modern Army – well, the Army of the 1950's – did not mind their infantrymen being left-handed. So long as they found their own way of working the bolt. This necessitated taking the left hand right over the breech, grabbing the end of the bolt with the edge of the palm and the little finger, and operating it that way. Next time you hold a Lee Enfield rifle in your hands, try it. Not easy.

I gripped the stock with my right hand, which felt clammier than at any previous moment of my life. So much for a 'firm grip'.

I peered through the hole of the back sight, brought the target into view, and waved the muzzle about until the top of the foresight seemed to be round about in the middle of the hole.

Then, just in time, I remembered that the first two rounds had to go into the bank. So I had to repeat the whole business of sighting. Once again, I'll say this for the Army; I was so busy concentrating on all the things I was supposed to be doing that I have no recollection of anybody else discharging his weapon. They could have laid down an artillery barrage beside me, and I would not have noticed.

At last, having pointed the thing to my satisfaction, I harnessed my entire physical and mental resources to preventing it from leaping from my hands, shattering my jaw, or fracturing my collar-bone, or any ghastly combination of the three. So much so that, when I finally squeezed the trigger (not 'pulled' – 'squeezed'), I could not honestly have sworn that I was looking through the sights.

I felt my head ringing as if someone had crashed a couple of dustbin lids over my ears. The remaining shots went off almost without me. I was conscious of little else. In fact, it was not until I returned to the barrack room that I realised that the forecast of swollen cheeks had proved both prophetic and accurate.

'On your feet – clear your weapons – port arms – ease springs. Go and get your targets.'

Corporal Johnson put the measuring ring on my target. To my amazement I had a two-inch ring. Mind you, I had no proof that they were all my shots. Someone else arrived back with six shots in his target.

Probably Bill Glover's doing. He never made any bones about his poor eyesight. When we went to the full-sized range and fired from two hundred yards, he was lucky to get more than two or three on the target – anywhere on the target. When we moved back to three hundred yards, he solemnly swore that he could not see the target at all. And there he was – in a rifle platoon of the infantry.

Actually, a day on the range was quite enjoyable. It meant a day away from the Depot. A day away from the gym and the square. A day away from Staff Sergeant Barron and Corporal Duke. And from Sergeant Flynn. There was an hour's ride each way in a three-ton truck (not exactly Rolls Bentley comfort, but it was an outing, and a chance to gossip and moan – as if we didn't do enough of that during the long evenings bulling). We were sometimes issued with those medieval leather jerkins I spoke about – again, not designer clothing in themselves, but they were thick, heavy, and above all broad; they made you look extremely tough. And we got a better than usual hot meal when we came back.

The Army spared no effort to lay on extra attractions. Paving stones of sandwiches for lunch. Miles of shingle that doubled the fatigue of walking. A November wind specially imported from Siberia.

But for all that, it was a good day out. I have no bad memories of it.

I don't think any of us showed deadly talent for marksmanship. Several of the platoon wore glasses. Bill Glover, as I said, couldn't even see the target at three hundred yards.

But they let us loose with the Bren gun as well as with the rifle. And not only single rounds – bursts too. Just like the Marines in all those Hollywood films. No palm trees for Jap soldiers to fall out of, but a great satisfaction to have this instrument in your hands – similar to the ones that had been held by John Wayne and Randolph Scott and Robert Taylor – that was *capable* of making Jap soldiers fall out of palm trees. Power!

Don't misunderstand. I do not mean that the Army was turning us into mindless killer zombies. Such an idea would have been ludicrous. We were just young men – very young men – playing at being film heroes. If a Japanese soldier really had leapt up out of the shingle and waved a machete at us, we would probably have dropped our guns and fled.

We also did variants of rifle firing – variants of single-shot sniping, that is. There was 'Snap Shooting', where the man in the target butts held up a largish yellow disc for just a few seconds, which was all you had to see, sight, and fire. The men in the butts had a lazy time while this was going on – very few holes to paste over.

Then there was 'Rapid Fire'. That was much more like it. They kept the target up for about thirty seconds, and in that time you had to get off ten rounds. It was in this exercise that I once achieved my greatest military feat. I was credited with twenty-nine points out of a possible thirty. It was like the batsman given out out 'lbw'; no matter what he thinks about blind umpires, that's what the scorebook says – 'Out'. I cannot remember coming near that standard ever again, but there it is in the record – well, in the record of my memory. It must be true; it is so outrageous that I would never have dared to make it up. And that feat, may I remind you, was by a left-hander, who had to do the contortion with the bolt every time. My moment of military glory.

The only other achievement of mine which came close was when I was about ten. I had spent a year or two, at opportune moments in my school holidays and weekends, watching proceedings in a men's snooker club near my home. Inevitably, I was able to seize chances to push a cue myself, and I soon became fascinated by the symphony of colours that the snooker table presented, its subtlety, its serenity.

One evening, I was helping to empty the pockets and set the balls up for the next frame. It so happened that the cue ball lay right up at the top of the table, close to the top-left pocket. The black was near the green spot – miles away. On impulse, a man shoved a cue into my hand and said, 'Go on son, pot that black.' To his amazement, and mine, I did. I have never done a shot like it since. You treasure those moments.

I repeat – we usually had a good day on the range. Satisfying.

That did not mean that we didn't have more laughs back at the Depot, with some of the other weapons. This was largely because much of the instruction was carried out by lance-corporals. And National Service lance-corporals at that. They had been in the Army barely four or five months longer than we had. One of them was younger than most of us graduates. They knew little beyond the bare bones of the training pamphlet. They carried hardly any clout, and were, alas for them, fair game.

One of them – Lance-Corporal Johnson – you have already met on the range. He was saved by his sense of humour. After we had had our laugh, he was always able to pull the lesson together again. Lance-Corporal Victor was another matter. No sense of humour at all. Fresh-faced lad. Keen to impress both us and his superiors. And he tried. He really did. Incidentally, both corporals and lance-corporals were formally addressed, and referred to, as 'Corporal'.

Poor Victor did not have much imagination either. There was a section in the training pamphlet which allocates a whole lesson to making recruits bend and straighten their index fingers, as a means of conveying the exact pressure required on the trigger. (Remember, YOU DON'T PULL THE TRIGGER;YOU SQUEEZE IT.) Half an hour flexing and straightening one finger. Corporal Victor was baffled to see the extent of the laughter, and took it as a personal affront to himself.

He didn't have much better luck when we moved away from the rifle. One of the basic infantry weapons was the two-inch mortar. It was little more than a tube, a base plate, a firing pin, and a lanyard. And a mortar bomb, of course. Still, we had to learn how to take it to pieces and re-assemble it, and naturally many of us made a botch of it at first.

'You idiot, Davies,' Victor would say, trying to sound like a tough sergeant. 'Clockwise.'

Taffy would pause, stand up, and shake his head in contrition.

'I'm sorry, corporal. You were quite right. I was completely in error there.'

We all turned away, while Victor glared in mystification.

Then again, there was the time when he pounced on Martin Forrest at the beginning of a revision lesson on the mortar, and demanded, 'What is the first thing a member of a mortar team ought to know?'

Martin shrugged.

'The subscription?' he suggested.

We had no time to turn away. The lesson dissolved.

It wasn't much better with the hand grenade. When we were first shown hand grenades, naturally they were only the drill variety. But, as usual, we had to learn how to take them to bits. Without going into too much detail, there was a retaining bar, which was in turn held in place by the pin – the famous pin, which John Wayne was always pulling out with his teeth. Take out the pin, relax your grip on the bar (which you did when you released it to throw), the bar would fly off, and a spring was released which drove a rod against the fuse and detonator. This was in live grenades. In drill grenades there was no fuse or detonator, of course. Just a space at the end of the grenade. So the detonating rods, if and when released, could fly out, very fast.

You could stop this happening by holding the bar in place *after* you had taken out the pin. In fact you could replace the pin, if you were careful, and the whole thing could be put back in the box. Naturally, we were allowed to throw it only when we were outdoors. Indoors, we were restricted to taking it to pieces and putting it together.

But we were warned, sternly, about these wayward detonator rods. By an odd conceidence, it was always in Victor's lessons that careless fingers forgot to hold the bar in place, and no end of detonator rods flew about the room. Quite dangerous actually, but worth the danger to see the look on Victor's face.

Any large organisation, however well-arranged and however well-intentioned, is capable of inflicting endless pinpricks of annoyance on its large body of subordinates. Because of negligence, lack of communication, sheer numbers, pressure of work, forgivable human error, whatever. If to this mixture you were to add the fussiness of unimaginative junior officials, the pompousness of office staff, and the sheer ill-will and bad temper of a minority of others, you will be in a position to appreciate the extent and range of pinpricks to which a platoon of National Servicemen could be subjected.

We probably didn't suffer more than any other group. And as for training staff, taking the situation all round, I think we were quite lucky in the men allocated to us during our ten or eleven weeks. But that didn't mean that we didn't have plenty to moan about – both imagined and real. And don't forget that none of us wanted to be in the bloody Army in the first place. Dramatic remedies like assault, mutiny, and desertion were obviously out of the question. Dammit, it wasn't the *Bounty* or Devil's Island. So we got back at the Army any way we could. And the stolid Corporal Victor was unlucky enough to be on the receiving end of some of this rebellion.

When we threw live hand grenades – real ones – it was a different story. We had gritty sergeants at our shoulders. We were taken out into the throwing bays one by one, so we had no audience to play up to; we had no numbers to fall back on. And – now, what was it? – there was one other point. . . . Oh, yes. We were scared stiff.

We looked at the greasy pineapple in our sweating palm. With its safety pin secure, its ring flopped over and relaxed, like the still discs of a sleeping rattlesnake. Supposing you dropped it. *After* you had taken out the pin! All that grease round it – only too easy. This thing could kill you – KILL YOU. And anybody else in a range of several yards. Within the narrow brick walls of the throwing bay, the blast would be unimaginable. From what we had been told, all they would need to clean up the mess would be a few teaspoons.

John Wayne and his gritted teeth were suddenly a long way away. When you stop to think about it, it is hardly surprising. I mean it is hardly surprising that John Wayne, and all those real soldiers in real battles, were not nervous like us. They had far too much going on around them. Far greater dangers. If they didn't chuck that grenade, and quickly, a far worse fate was awaiting them. If you are being chased by an irate bull, you climb the tree; you don't worry about falling off the branches; you're far more frightened of the bull.

Well, we recruits had no war going on around us – thank God – to distract our attention. All we had to think about was the inanimate killer in our hand. Waiting to be detonated.

Luckily, we had one companion. A sergeant went with each of us into the throwing bay when our turn came. And these sergeants don't get themselves into the funny books and the corny films and the music hall sketches. And they don't get mentioned in those bitter memoirs from the tender plants who had their artistic lives blighted by the military machine. They were too good. No strutting, no bellowing, no sarcasm, no abuse. Just seasoned professionalism, stillness, quiet reminders, and vast resources of calm and confidence.

'All right, son, now remember what you've been told. Stand up straight. Put it in your throwing hand. Check it. That's right. Now take out the pin. Hold it firm. Take your arm back. Check again. Right. You're doing fine. Extend the aiming arm. Aim. Lean back. And. . . . throw. That's good.'

We were so relieved to be shot of the damned thing that we forgot the last part of our training. This – believe it or not – was to watch its flight. Until it landed. Until it landed!

But if we had forgotten, our sergeant had not.

'Stay up. Watch it.'

Those who had vanished into a prenatal position at the foot of the inside wall with their hands over their ears were dragged up by the scruff of the neck so that they could look out over.

'It's a seven-second fuse, remember? Now follow it, and count – three, four, five. . . . . . .'

Those three seconds were interminable. It seemed half an hour before the sergeant, in his fireside-chat voice, said, 'Right, down we go.'

And even then it was another second or two before it went off.

Nerves of steel, those men.

I repeat – I don't know for the how-many-th time – there were occasions when you just had to hand it to the Army.

Curiously, the weapon which gave us the most trouble was the one that seemed the simplest, the pistol. Probably because we knew it best. Or thought we did. It was in fact a revolver – the one with the drum of chambers that went round as you fired – but it was always referred to in the Army as a pistol. We had seen thousands of revolvers in countless westerns, and we had been raised on stories in wartime comics about intrepid officers (from all three arms of the Services) who, when they were not stealing the secret weapon plans or dealing swift upper cuts to the greasy chins of foreign agents, were saving the situation by some pretty deft handling of a thirty-something-calibre revolver that they had just come across in an office drawer. Pausing only to weigh it thoughtfully in their hand, and to observe that it was 'quite a few years' since they had 'used one of these things', they then embarked on some fancy shooting which would have drawn gasps of admiration from Wyatt Earp.

In the Army, it was an 'officer's weapon', of course. Regulation issue. As we were 'Potential Leaders', it was considered fitting that we should be given some training in the handling of it. We got one lesson, I believe. Well, two. One to show it to us, and to pass on obvious details about loading and range and calibre and so on. Nothing came to pieces. And the other actually to fire it.

We couldn't wait.

'You'll be lucky if you hit a barn door.'

That was the considered opinion of the veterans who were two weeks ahead of us and who had just done it. Almost certainly the opinion of our sergeants. The masks of expressionlessness that our marksmanship produced on their faces told it all.

The world was right. We were awful. The gun jumped all over the place. These were the days when we were still allowed to fire it with only one hand. Look at any self-respecting police TV series nowadays, in Britain or the USA, and the agent or copper or the undercover man or the female minder, at the first sign of hostility or escape on the part of the villain, goes at once into a game of statues. Body hunched, head buried in the shoulders, brow lowered, arms extended, both hands locked round the butt of their Biretta or Kalashnikov or Armstrong-Siddeley or whatever it is, they scream 'Freeze!', almost as if they are annoyed that they are playing statues but the dirty rotter at the other end isn't.

We weren't much better with the Sten gun, in the one lesson we had with that.

We fired the Bren more often, because, as I explained earlier, it was, along with the rifle, standard issue for the infantry section. There was only one Bren per section, but we had training in it. And quite thorough training too. We became almost as familiar with the Bren as we did with the rifle.

The Army must have been pretty familiar with it too; it had been standard issue since before the War. A fitting companion for the Lee Enfield rifle and Musketry Order and the Agincourt jerkins.

When they found something that they thought was good, the Army hung on to it with touching loyalty. I believe the Browning revolvers I was talking about just now went back to the First World War. It would be interesting to find out how far back belt brasses went, or mess tins, or webbing, or greatcoats. Or Drawers Woollen – there's a saga in itself, I should think.

Anyway, the Bren was reckoned to be a good weapon. Or so our elders and betters informed us. It was called the Bren because of a merging of resources and effort between two armament factories – at Enfield (where they also made the Lee Enfield rifle) and the one at Skoda, near the Czech town of Brno. Take the first two letters of each – 'Br' and 'En' – and you have 'Bren'. Well, that's what they told us.

It wasn't difficult to learn how to handle it. It was versatile; it could fire bursts or single shots. It you held it properly, it stayed steady under firing conditions. And it seemed pretty accurate. We were pleased with our results; whether the Commandos or the Foreign Legion or the Waffen SS would have been equally pleased we were never to know.

But it had its shortcomings too. The magazine was clumsy and heavy, and had to be loaded by hand. And left-handers like me found it awkward, because the sights were so placed that there was only one way you could fire it – right-handed. It weighed a ton – twenty-eight pounds, to be precise. But, if you were the unlucky wretch who happened to be the head of the Bren detail when your platoon or section was engaged in a rapid withdrawal, and you had to lug the thing over rough ground at the double for half a mile, it certainly weighed a ton by the time you arrived back at base. There should have been some kind of mathematical formula which measured the increase – say, if w = weight, and d = distance, and c = the coefficient of increased mass, and ma = the rate of muscular atrophy, you arrived at an expression something like this:

$$\frac{28w \times d \times 880c \times ma}{\text{local temperature x the square root of sweat loss}} = 2240$$

The other annoying thing about the Bren gun was that it stopped a lot. Gave up. Conked out. Just as a car stops when it runs out of petrol, so the Bren stopped when it ran out of bullets. Pretty basic stuff, I know (I do hope I'm carrying you with me on this technical detail), but it is not always easy to estimate how many shots you've fired when the thing is in 'machine-gun' mode. I must point out that the official nomenclature for this weapon was 'LMG' – Light Machine Gun. (Not – for once – 'Guns Machine Light', which must have been a major breakthrough.) There was also in existence a Medium Machine Gun – the MMG. A fearsome weapon – another relic from the First World War. Awesomely consistent. This was the instrument of slaughter that accounted for most of those countless thousands of unnecessary deaths in No Man's Land in Flanders. I tell you, when the Army found something good, they stuck to it. Interestingly, I never found out what a HMG was, a Heavy Machine Gun. It must indeed have been a slavering agent of Armageddon.

The point I nearly got to in the last paragraph was that an inexperienced recruit could easily get caught unawares by the sudden stoppage of the Bren for the simple reason that the magazine was exhausted – or, less frequently, blocked. There was of course a drill for dealing with this emergency. These emergencies were labelled 'IA's' by the Army – Immediate Aids. Now that the second of those words has recently acquired a much more emotive meaning, one wonders whether the Army has continued with this old phraseology, at the obvious risk of ribald misinterpretation by barrack room wags. (Actually, it may have been 'Immediate Action' – long time ago now.)

The Immediate Aid (or Action) for this situation I have described was not to have a squint at the magazine to see what was wrong; it was to wrench off the offending adjunct, to bellow 'MAGAZINE!' (just in case your partner in the Bren section, two feet away, had not noticed), to snatch a new one from his startled hand, and to ram it home on top of the barrel. Speed was of the essence. Naturally. It didn't make much sense if you were peering into the half-empty magazine, locating the two badly-loaded rounds that were causing the blockage, and shouting 'Eureka!', and a couple of the enemy had arrived at the top of your trench in their bayonet charge and were preparing to deliver the *coup de grâce*.

Speed. Speed. Learn to do it fast. In difficult conditions. With your eyes shut. In the fog. In the cold. In the dark. Yes, yes, yes, we could see the value of that.

That was the first IA. Changing the magazine. (We liked the shouting bit. 'MAGAZINE!' Jolly tough. Always hard to keep a straight face.)

It was even harder to keep one with the second IA.

Bullets spin very fast as they are being discharged. They make the inside of the barrel very hot. This heat spreads rapidly and causes problems all over the gun, the chief of which is that of making the gun stop firing – again. The Bren detail then springs into action. Well, more action. Having ascertained, by the process of the first IA, that the trouble does not stem from the blocked or empty magazine (and having glanced over the top of the parapet to make sure that the enemy is not about to transfix them with its bayonets), the well-trained Bren team goes into the procedure for the second IA – changing the barrel.

For most people the idea of changing a barrel on a gun in the middle of a trench halfway through a battle may sound ludicrous, as ludicrous as changing the chassis of a car on the hard shoulder of the motorway. But believe me, the Bren was so constructed that the barrel could be detached and a new one fitted (it was carried as standard kit by the second man on the detail, along with all those new magazines) – in seconds. If the men were properly trained, that is.

We were shown a training film in which the Bren detail was *not* properly trained. With the aid of some skilful editing, involving shots of bloodthirsty charging enemy, sweating Bren gunners, gleaming bayonets, frantic fumbling with new barrels, and grisly deaths, the Army made its ponderous point.

So, under the sharp, if slightly worried, eyes of Corporal Johnson and Corporal Victor, we went through the drill of barrel-changing again and again. There was more shouting involved – naturally. I forget now whether it was 'CHANGE!' or 'BARREL!' or 'CHANGE BARREL!'. But we bellowed with a will, and fumbled with as few thumbs as possible.

In an effort to relieve the tedium, and to inject a spot of fun into the proceedings, we would be divided into four or five teams. Each team was given a Bren gun. (I should point out, by the way, that other parts of the gun came off besides the barrel and the magazine.) At the word 'Go!' the first member of the team ran out and took off the first part, laying it on the grass several yards ahead. He ran back, and the second man ran out to the Bren, took off another part, and laid it on the grass several yards ahead of the first part, and so on. This went on until the entire weapon had been dismantled as far as it would go, and pieces of Bren were strewn over a park-like area. In theory, in straight lines, out in front of the stripped Bren corpse. In theory.

That was the halfway mark.

At another 'Go!' the process began again, though naturally in reverse. We had entered into the spirit of the thing, and all of us wanted to be in the winning team. That meant speed. It also meant a lack of attention to detail, and a certain amount of lack of scruple. The hectoring of the two corporals, the ribald comments of rival team members, the haste and the sweat all produced a vortex of fumbling, dropping, disputes over ownership, stumbling, and general disintegration that would have been the despair of Sergeant-Major Jefferson had he witnessed it. Sergeant Flynn would simply have gone up in smoke.

The confusion and total lack of military aptitude were so absolute that most of us ended up crying with laughter. An imperishable memory is of Martin Forrest writhing on the ground, clutching a Bren barrel to his bosom, quite helpless, his jaw rigid in a rictus of hysterics.

I don't think there was a third IA on the Bren. Probably just as well. Some of us would have had a seizure. No wonder one of the oldest jokes in the Army concerned the distraught weapon-training instructor who wearily told his fumbling recruits that their best course of action was to fix bayonets and charge. . . .

13   A touch of the Irish

IT USED TO BE A cliché that everyone could tell you where they were at the very moment that they heard of Kennedy's assassination. It was the same with the outbreak of the War. I have no doubt that, now, thousands can do it for the news of the death of Diana, Princess of Wales.

I cannot do that for the arrival of Sergeant Flynn. It is an irony that I can recall many details of my basic training, as this book testifies, almost as if they had happened yesterday, yet I cannot call up any incident of the day that Sergeant Flynn entered our lives – and, looking back, he proved to be the biggest single influence on our lives in the whole ten or eleven weeks.

I have no recollection of our first meeting with him, our first drill lesson with him, indeed our first anything with him. All I can do is to record the fact that he made an impact of seismic proportions. It was as if God had suddenly said, 'Let there be Flynn.'

And there he was, without warning, in our midst.

It might be tempting to say that, like so many sergeants right through the Army, he was a double-barrelled, triple-starred, gold-plated, First Division, Premier Cru, copper-bottomed bastard, and leave it at that. But Paddy Flynn was more than that. He deserves more comment than that.

I suppose we felt strongly about him right from the word go, because he suffered from comparison with Sergeant-Major Jefferson – and that. We liked Jefferson. We respected Jefferson. We worked for Jefferson. Dammit, we almost thought he was nice! We were to throw a lot of adjectives in Flynn's direction in the coming weeks, but 'nice' was never one of them.

Jefferson did not hector. He was sparing with words – and that. He was given neither to invective nor to vulgarity. Paddy Flynn had a command of colourful epithet which would have been the envy of a soapbox politician or a Welsh preacher.

Jefferson handed out praise if he thought we had done well. He could laugh at a joke. Flynn hoarded praise like Silas Marner with his money. His leathery features rarely showed much animation. Like Jeeves, a miniscule ripple at the corner of the mouth was about as near as he got to smiling.

What we did not realise at the time, and what Paddy clearly did, was that our relationship with Jefferson had gone cosy. We were bowling along very nicely, thank you very much. If this was all there was to basic training, then we had come close to getting it all sewn up. I think Paddy reckoned we were capable of better things.

When Jefferson was posted to another unit, Paddy did what all good NCO's do as soon as possible; he 'got a grip'. He gave an altogether different interpretation to the word 'drill'. That was what he took us for most of the time. He was officially our Platoon Sergeant, and there was, officially, a subaltern in overall command. But this young man was only a National Serviceman himself. Paddy had been in the Army almost as long as he had been alive. There was little interference from that quarter.

Other specialist NCO's supervised our physical training, and there were those tough sergeants in the mortar bays and on the firing range. Corporal Victor and Corporal Johnson helped out with the weapon training, but it was Sergeant Flynn who was in charge – at least as far as we were concerned. It was he who carried out all the drill instruction, and God knows we had enough of that. Then there were the various lectures, interviews, marches, parades, and the hundred and one things that helped to fill a tired recruit's day, most of which Flynn either planned, organised, supervised, or criticised.

So in terms of sheer man hours, I guess we saw more of him than we did of anyone else. But he would have made an impact if he had had us for half the time. Why? Because he made himself memorable, that's why.

He was not especially impressive to look at. Later on in what I laughingly call my 'military career' I was to meet much bigger, and, frankly, much more frightening men. Paddy was of average height. He did not have a particularly athletic figure. I should guess he was in his late thirties – early forties at most. Probably been a sergeant for quite a long time. But that was common in those days. Many a soldier, at the end of the War, decided that soldiering was the only trade he knew, or the only trade he fancied (peacetime did not hold many attractions for a lot of men after six years of action). They stayed on. Hundreds and thousands of them. So promotion was difficult. I came across many officers who had been captains and majors at the end of the War, and there they were, in the mid-1950's, still captains and majors. I should guess the same thing happened to sergeants and warrant officers.

So Sergeant Flynn turned his long experience to good use, training National Servicemen. I don't suppose he was particularly enamoured of the job. Maybe he hankered after a more active posting. (There were certainly plenty around – non-stop NATO exercises in Germany, chasing the Mau Mau in Kenya, tracking terrorists in Cyprus, cleaning up after Communists in Malaya, and so on). But to his credit, whatever he thought of his duties, or of National Servicemen, he did not let it colour his outward attitude.

You could guess very little from his flat, leathery face. It had that slightly yellowish, permanent tan that one associates with a long spell in the tropics. Two baleful eyes looked out over a child-ishly small nose. The slight pursing of the lips that was almost a permanent part of his face indicated that whatever it was his eyes fell on – our appearance, our kit, our drill, our barrack room, our skill with the rifle – he disapproved of it.

He was not a quick mover. For a man who got our squad to move faster than any of its twenty-odd members had done in their whole previous lives, he was annoyingly deliberate. He didn't march; he didn't walk; he processed. He didn't look at things; he surveyed them.

164

He didn't shout much – except for drill commands, of course. He had an Irish accent all his own. Certainly, I had never heard one like it. He could tip more weight of significance on to one syllable than anyone I had met before.

For example, he showed his professionalism by learning our names very quickly. One morning, while we were stiff at the 'Shun', he walked through our three ranks, stopping behind each of us, pausing, and reciting our surname. Got them all right too.

But it was what he did with those surnames that made the impact. By meticulous pronunciation of every consonant of, say, 'Gatewood' or 'Forrest', he was able to imply that the owners of those names were prime examples of inferior life forms. With single syllables, he was even more devastating. When he got to 'Sly' or 'Coates', he contrived to load the names with so much disapproval and suspicion that one almost looked around for plainclothes members of the CID. Ever seen *Mutiny on the 'Bounty'*? When Charles Laughton says 'Mr. Christian'? It was a bit like that.

Now let me correct a possible misunderstanding. I can hear some of those tender plants who had their lives blighted by the Army – remember? – the ones who wrote all those long-haired books and realistic plays – I can hear them saying, 'There you are. What did I tell you? He's got to admit it in the end. His sergeant was just as sarcastic a sadist as all the others.'

Not so. I have left to the end the final, and most important ingredient of Paddy's alchemy. Humour. Paddy would have been a credit to the acting profession. I don't know how he did it, but he was able to say those names in such a way that, while it *sounded* as if he were being sarcastic, the effect was completely the opposite. We stood there, naturally. We stood there, very quiet and very still. But I guarantee every one of us had a smile on his face. Paddy was funny. And clearly intended to be. The quintessential flatface humourist. He had got the mixture dead right. He had us totally obedient (and very wary of him), and he had us laughing, if only inwardly, at the same time.

165

That does not mean that we liked him. As I said, we would never have thought of applying the epithet 'nice' to him. We applied plenty of others in the coming six weeks or so, I can tell you.

We had good reason. He revolutionised our drill.

All those left turns and right turns and about turns. We thought we had done quite a lot, till we met Paddy. It was a wonder there weren't holes all over the square, the number of times we drove our feet into it. We did all the turns, both at the halt and on the march. We learned close order and open order. We 'advanced', we 'retired', we turned about. We did everything in quick time. Then we learned everything all over again in slow time. We learned to switch from quick time to slow time, and back again – on the march. We saluted; we did 'right form'; we did 'dressing' from the right. We set off 'by the right', 'by the left', or 'by the centre'. I think we even did the posh Guards manoeuvre – 'advance in review order'.

If we were too slow for Paddy's liking, he would suddenly march us round the square at a furious pace – a hundred and eighty to the minute. (Normal heavy infantry pace was about a hundred and twenty.) Only for a short while, but it was enough to make his point. I'm told that horses cannot sustain a full gallop for very long, despite what the cowboy films tell us. Well, no squad could keep up a hundred and eighty to the minute for very long either. But, for those twenty or thirty seconds, it had the desired effect of shaking us up. If our turn-out was not up to scratch, round we went. If our first movements were, in his opinion, too sloppy, round we went. If we showed signs of weakening half way through a drill lesson, round we went. (It was at such times that the epithets flew around under the breath – what breath we had left. Paddy lost more parents during those frantic hundred-and-eighty chases than a whole orphanage of Barnardo's children.)

He would bring us to a puffing halt, and stride up close to us. A gaze of deepening disgust would settle on his leathery face as he ran his eyes down the length of the front rank.

'Well, dhat's a bit betterr. . . . But only a bit. . . . Like of load of

166

tarts this morning. . . . Do you hearr? . . . . A load of tarhts!'

His pauses could be just as devastating as his curses. By the time he had finished we were already grinning through our sweat.

Then there was the business of the right marker. Every squad had to have a right marker. He was the right-hand man on the front rank. In formal parades, he was the one who had to march out alone to the required spot on the square, and the rest had to fall in accordingly. I don't mean we ambled gently out towards him, passed the time of day, and discussed the weather while we sorted ourselves into some semblance of three straight lines. It all had to be done to time, to commands, with much slapping of rifles and much stamping. But for the first minute or so, the right marker was out in front, on his own. The eyes of the whole platoon, and, more to the point, of its sergeant, were upon him.

So his drill had to be pretty damned good. If platoon sergeants were in a bad mood, the life expectancy of right markers could be about as short as that of subalterns on the Western Front. It gave sergeants a regular alternative to marching their squads round at the double as a means of 'getting a grip' on a cold morning. To make everyone jump, you sacked the right marker. Heaven help the poor devil who had to take his place. I don't know how many right markers Paddy dismissed during our six or seven weeks with him. If he'd had us for six months, we would easily have been going round again. However, I believe the record for short service was held by a hapless wretch in another platoon. He lasted for precisely one 'Shun!'.

Drill was hammered into us practically every day. Time and again, we were told by pompous officers and warrant officers that if we expected to become officers ourselves, we should make it our business to see that our own personal drill was better than that of our men. Higher standards than normal were expected of us. It wasn't Paddy who doled out this moralising; it was his job to make us do the drill.

Another little device for developing our 'potential leadership' was to make us each take turns to be 'Squad Leader' for a few days. It was the responsibility of the Squad Leader to see that everyone turned out of the barrack room on time in the morning. He had to get us from the end of each lesson to the beginning of the next. If this involved movement out of doors, we had of course to do the moving in military fashion – as a proper drilled squad, in column of threes, at the march, in time, with the Squad Leader calling the beat. For this purpose, he was empowered to issue the required drill commands.

The perils of this practice were numerous and obvious. We did not have the necessary experience, and our words of command lacked Paddy's sharpness and timing, to say nothing of his accuracy. It was common for a nervous Squad Leader to throw the platoon into amused confusion by giving the executive word of command on the wrong foot. No matter how keen a Squad Leader was, or how hard he tried, he was never able to inculcate the same sense of urgency into his charges as the sergeant did. Not only that; he would have to put up with a good deal of rear-rank banter.

Occasionally, by the law of averages, we would get a movement dead right. If we were able now and again actually to bring our feet down in unison on a turn or a halt, there were murmurs of surprise and mutual congratulation all round.

The 'orderly movement' that was officially required of us usually degenerated into a conducted stroll. We did have the decency to maintain three columns, but that was about all. Feet were barely in time; arms were not swung with the orthodox straightness; heads would be turned for the odd comment. One Squad Leader after another found from nerve-wracking experience that the most successful means of achieving anything remotely resembling smartness of movement was by appeals to the better nature of those who had already done their turn, and by threats of dire retribution to the others who had their turn to come.

We got too careless. It took one unfortunate episode for us to become more vigilant.

One day, under Martin Forrest's offhand leadership, we were 'marching' chattily back to the barrack room at the end of the morning's training, when a voice hit us with an almost physical blow.

'SQUAD HALT!'

No mistaking Paddy Flynn's voice. He was not normally a bawler, but he could shout with the best of them when it was necessary. Now – he had clearly decided – it was necessary.

'Christ!' muttered Martin. 'Now what have we done?'

We waited, rigid and perplexed, while Paddy proceeded in his leisurely, stiff-armed way towards us. He had a trick of slightly splaying his wrists so that his hands stuck out like small fins. It gave him a disturbingly predatory air, like a shark descending noiselessly and mercilessly upon its prey. It could afford to be leisurely, because it was utterly confident that the prey could not escape.

He came to a halt in front of us. The usual long, raking glance of inexpressible disgust. The usual long pause. At last:

'Ya call dhat marrching?'

Martin, true to the colours, decided that, as Squad Leader, it was up to him to cobble together a flimsy rampart of explanation. Very noble of him. Deserved a medal.

'We've just finished the morning's training, Sergeant, and we were on our way to lunch.'

He winced even as he said it, agonisingly aware of the gaping inadequacy and total irrelevance of the answer.

'Mincing!'

Paddy's verdict was crushing.

'Mincing along therre – just like a bunch of quearhs!'

It finished us.

I suppose I ought to explain to a reading audience of the twenty-first century that the simile about homosexuals was common usage among NCO's in the nineteen-fifties. I don't know whether in these days of gay rights a sergeant would be allowed to get away with it now. I mention this in order to answer any possible criticism about incorrectness. There was none, either in the event or in the narration of it. Paddy didn't use the epithet because he had it in for homosexuals, and we didn't nearly burst with the effort to prevent ourselves laughing because we were a gaggle of homophobes.

We laughed because Paddy was funny. It you weren't there, you can't possibly know. You will just have to take my word for it that it was, as Paddy said it, very funny.

It wasn't funny a moment later, because it will take little imagination on the part of the attentive reader to work out what we spent the next forty or fifty seconds doing. . . . That's right; round we went again, at a hundred and eighty. At least it gave us a better appetite for lunch.

I hope I have succeeded in getting it across to the same attentive reader that Sergeant Paddy Flynn made a huge impression upon us. He made us work harder than we had ever done before. He made us jump. He made us wary of him. All the time we were laughing at his jokes he maintained that last ditch of inscrutability between us and him that is one of the hallmarks of the good teacher. There was never any danger of anything going cosy with him.

It would be false to say that we liked him. Liking did not come into it. We moaned about him; we frequently consigned his eternal soul to perdition; we questioned his parentage.

To that extent, yes, he was a typical, music-hall, traditional, *Oh-What-A-Lovely-War* sergeant. But he was more. Much more. The fact that I can fill a whole chapter with reminiscences and musings about him must indicate that.

Perhaps a useful way to explain this is to say what he was not. He was not a bully. He was not loud, he did not pick on people, and he did not engage in the sort of personal invective that, it is often alleged, characterised the language of most drill instructors. No jowl-thrusting for him. I can not recall his moving any part of himself from the rigid perpendicular that he maintained every day on the square. As I said, even when he was walking, he stayed upright; no inclining of the body in anything as undignified as haste.

He swore at us; of course he did. That was the point – 'us'. As a group, we could take anything that a dozen Paddy Flynn's could dish out. And he knew this. He wanted us as a good squad, not as a rag-tag of cowed recruits, or as a tangle of Pavlov-conditioned zombies.

I think this enlightened attitude went back to his wartime experiences. I have no proof for what I am about to say, but it makes sense to me.

Paddy, we were told, had spent three years as a prisoner of the Japanese. That probably explained the slightly yellowish, parchment texture of his face. It might also have explained his unwillingness to evince much emotion. I have read books about prison-camp life in Burma or Malaya or wherever. I know about the beatings, and the malnutrition, and the forced labour, and the contempt of the Geneva Convention.

But I got a much clearer picture from the reminiscences of another survivor whom I knew as a friend, many years later. Ted knew me for a long time before he opened up. Then, without warning, as we were sitting in the garden in the afternoon sun, he began talking.

One tale that impressed me was about his razor blade. Apparently every soldier was expected to be clean-shaven, every day. If he wasn't, he was beaten. But if he was found with a knife, or indeed anything sharp and therefore potentially threatening, on his person, he was beaten again. Ted had a razor blade – no razor. Every day, he sharpened this blade on a stone, shaved, then hid it under a rock. He was never caught. He did this, with the same blade, for three years.

Yes, I may be a sucker for a tall story. Can razor blades last that long? I have no idea. But it is my experience that people who have been through a harrowing time (and the most hardened sceptic would admit that three years in a Japanese prison camp is a harrowing time) are usually reluctant to talk about it. And when they do, the tendency is to understate, not overstate. Ted had known me for several years before he told me this. The fact that he told me anything at all I took to be a great compliment.

But understatement or overstatement, even whether it is true or not according to the strictest laws of evidence, I think the story is a clear illustration. It was that sort of resilience, that sort of resource, that was required for survival. Ted was not a big man – far from it. He was not an officer. He had no lofty education. He had no connections, no clubs, no old school tie, no social clout of any kind. And by the end of the War, his weight had gone down to six stone. But he survived. And he survived when many men of his acquaintance – dignified, scholarly advocates of the Geneva Convention, well-covered officers bursting with the King's commission and the Manual of Military Law, tough commandos full of chin and challenge – lasted barely a few weeks.

He kept his sense of perspective. He maintained his overall strategic objective. No considerations of defiance, dignity, rank, playing the game, or anything else got in his way.

I suspect that Sergeant Flynn had a very similar experience, and I suspect that he reacted in a very similar way. Like Ted, Paddy was not a big man. He was not an officer. He had access to no privileges of birth, wealth, upbringing, or education. But, also like Ted, he had a sort of hot line to the centre of the earth, which gave him the wherewithal to get through. If life became a matter of surviving for the next week, or the next day, or the next hour, so be it. The trick was not to be shaken by the latest horror, the latest crisis, the latest surprise. Everything was to be taken in the stride. There was no room for rage, for exasperation, for a sense of injustice, or for self-pity.

When it was all over, Paddy was armed against life. Whatever else it was to throw at him, he was prepared. Nothing in the future could ever be as bad. He had proved himself in the worst possible of tempering fires. His shoulders had taken so many beatings that there was no room for any chips. He had no need for ego-bolstering. Any ego that had survived intact after three years with the Japanese was in no need of bolstering. He did not need to make any gestures; he did not need to take it out on anybody.

Which explains, I think, why he did not bully us. He did not need to; he had seen the very best, or the worst, bullies in the world. It enabled him to see his fellow-men much more clearly. He saw us at once for what we were – a bunch of bumptious, but likely lads who'd had it a bit soft (and in his opinion nearly everybody had had it a bit soft), and who needed a spot of licking into shape.

He did it by a combination of hard work, sheer force of personality, inscrutability, and humour. It united us. First, it united us in self-pity. We had never come across anyone so apparently hard as he was. He had no capacity for sympathy, no human feelings whatever. No concern for our welfare. We spent the first fortnight massaging our injured sensitivities.

'But sergeant, how can we clean our rifles again and get them over to the armoury for inspection right now? We'll be late for lunch.'

A baleful stare.

'Wel, dhat's jost too fockin' baad.'

The sod! The unspeakable bugger! He doesn't give a damn.

He united us too in hatred.

Perhaps the hardest part of foot drill is slow time. It looks impressive when the Guards do it in Trooping the Colour, but it is a pig to get it right. As with so many things that look easy, it is very difficult to do it well. And Paddy was never content until we had done it well. It involves a lot of stiff limbs, and a lot of staying poised in mid-air. It needs to be demonstrated really; it's hard to give the full flavour of it in cold print. Just take it from me that it was wearing, it was tiring, and Paddy made us do a lot of it.

The worst part was the marking time. Standing on the spot, and raising and lowering the legs alternately. Raising them until each thigh was parallel to the ground, before crashing the foot into the ground in normal seismic fashion. All the time remaining totally upright, with head still and arms straight. Bad enough in quick time; in slow time it was spirit-crushing. As we became tired, we got sloppy. Legs would not be raised high enough, arms would flap about, heads would oscillate. Asking for trouble. There were times when we felt that if our eyelashes moved, he would not be satisfied.

Paddy's cure for such forms of gross idleness was to bring us to the 'Shun'. He would then gaze in disdain down the whole length of the front rank, purse his lips, and deliver his verdict on our general level of performance. It went without saying that comparisons were made with loads of 'tarhts' and bunches of 'quearhs', in each case to our detriment.

Then he would make us raise one leg, as if we were going to do some more marking time in slow time, and leave us there. In that position. Still. With this leg raised, the thigh parallel to the ground. Straight up, chin in, chest out, arms straight, thumbs down the seam of the trousers. As the seconds ticked away, our disbelief at this novel form of refined cruelty fought a battle with the growing pain of fatigue in our unaccustomed muscles.

As a further refinement, Paddy would go into the same posture himself. Still, leg raised, thigh parallel to the ground, arms straight, and so on. He would turn his head to left and right, taking in the whole front rank with his challenging glance.

'I can do it; you can do it.'

The bastard!

I don't know how long he kept us there. It doesn't matter. What does matter is that, in spite of the pain, and the sense of disbelief, and the red faces, and the spluttering of effort, there was also a vein of comedy. We knew that Paddy, besides being a bastard, and besides toughening us up, was also playing a joke on us. And he knew we knew. As you are no doubt well aware, you can't chase anyone who won't run. The fact that we were prepared to run, and the extent to which we were prepared to run, are in themselves an indication of the respect we came to have for him.

There were times when the humour broke through completely, and destroyed us.

When it was considered that we had gained some control over the basics of foot drill, we were introduced to the subtleties of

Rifle Drill. As I am in the process of tailoring an anecdote, I must pass quickly over the ramifications of 'Order Arms', 'Slope Arms', 'Present Arms', 'Port Arms', sentry drill, and so forth, and come to the refinements of Bayonet Drill.

For weeks now, our bayonets had been bouncing ineffectually on our left hips as we flogged round the square at a hundred and twenty, -thirty, -forty, or any rate up to a hundred and eighty according to Paddy's mood. They were retained in a loose sort of webbing strap hung by a loop from our belts. For some reason that I have never been able to fathom, it was called a frog (the dictionary says it may be of eighteenth-century origin – which takes us back to Musketry Order again).

Since we possessed bayonets, and since we were the infantry, it followed that the Army envisaged circumstances when we might have to fix bayonets and charge (for example, if you recall, when our Shooting Instructors gave up on our marksmanship). Naturally, it followed too that there would have been evolved various drills for fixing bayonets on to the muzzles of rifles.

The experts at the War Office had, with commendable passion for simplicity, reduced the number of movements to three. On the first command – 'Platoon will fix bayonets. . . . Fix!' – we had to push out our right hands – the ones holding the muzzles of our rifles – as far as they would go. Simultaneously, our left hands were to flash to the top of the frogs on our left hips. Once there, they were to seize the handle of the bayonets, invert the whole bayonet (the frog was very pliable), and push down hard. This would have the effect of pushing the bayonet out of its scabbard, which would still be retained by the frog.

All right so far? On the first command – 'Platoon will fix bayonets . . . . Fix!' – right arm out, left hand to left hip, grab bayonet handle. You should note that although the command was 'Fix!', it did not mean that we were to fix bayonets, only that we were to grab hold of them.

The second command was, quite simply, 'Bayonets!' At that

word, we were to bring our left hands round to the front (holding, it was hoped, the bayonets), make contact with the muzzle of the rifles that the extended right hands were holding, and actually fix the weapon. Note once again, that the actual fixing of the bayonets was enjoined by the word 'Bayonets!'

The third command was a simple 'Attention!' We brought our right hand back to our sides, now holding the rifle freshly armed with the correctly-fixed bayonet. Our left hand returned to our left side, hoping against hope that in our desperate struggle to free the bayonet from its frog and scabbard we had not wrenched the scabbard out of its frog and let it fall with an unconcealable clatter on the parade ground.

All pretty complicated to the beginner. Paddy had his own version, which he used to make sense of it to the clumsy recruit.

First, the pause. Second, the raking glance along the front rank. Third, the pursing of the lips.

'For the firrst movement of the "Fix Bayonets", you put yurr left haand on yurr left hip – like a quearh.'

Another, longer, pause. Another glance of inexpressible disgust. 'It should come easy to most of you.'

It was as much as we could do to hang on to our rifles, never mind grab our bayonets.

Yet, even while we were falling about with laughter, there was never any temptation to take advantage. We could never be sure about him – not totally sure. There was a lot about Sergeant Flynn that we didn't know, and were never likely to. We didn't even know, for instance, whether he was married or not. Come to think of it, I cannot recall how we found out about his wartime prison camp experience.

Ours was a purely working relationship, and none the worse for that. We came to realise that Paddy was turning us into a reasonably efficient platoon, and, National Servicemen or no National Servicemen, we became grateful for it. In spite of ourselves, we came to take some kind of pride in what we were doing. That is firm testimony to Paddy's professionalism, and I feel sure he would have been content with that.

As the years have gone by, I have often thought of him, and I have often told these stories about him. Whenever I think of him, a smile comes to the lips. And that dismissive comment of his, that comment that we thought so shockingly cruel, has come to assume the proportions almost of a philosophy of life.

'Wel, dhat's jost too fockin' baad.'

I have not come across any other snappy sentence that encapsulates so neatly the fact that we must take in our stride what life throws at us, that nothing is as good or as bad as it seems at the time, that there is usually something, however small, that we can do about it. Whatever we do, we don't feel sorry for ourselves.

And, note, its impact has nothing to do with its vulgarity. I think this came about partly because Paddy's Irish accent (which I have tried to render, however inadequately) somehow ironed out the obscenity of it. No. Its force came from the deep philosophical truth hidden in it, the vast worldly wisdom, quarried in pain from the very worst of adversity. Paddy turned it from a coarse oath into a life-enhancing proverb. And of course he delivered it with such superb *panache*.

'But Sergeant, we've got a kit inspection tomorrow.'

'Wel, dhat's jost too fockin' baad.'

'But Sergeant, we had our BCG injections yesterday. We can't possibly lift rifles.'

'Wel, dhat's jost . . . .'

'But Sergeant, it's pouring with rain out there.'

'Wel, ...'

And he was right; it was never the end of the world. It never is.

14   Down the NAAFI

WE LIKED FRIDAYS. WELL, FRIDAY evenings, to be precise. It meant that we were going on leave the next day. The famous weekend pass. If all went well, we would be free from midday Saturday till dawn on Monday morning – in practice, Sunday evening. Thirty-six hours. Not much, is it? But you have to live in a spider day in, day out, in constant and intimate contact with twenty-odd other young men, being chased by hectoring non-commissioned officers, to appreciate fully the urgency of our desire to get away for whatever period of time was remotely practicable.

Our barracks was in the Home Counties, and most of us lived in the Home Counties. In the balmy days before Dr. Beeching had wielded his famous railway axe, we could all get a train to pretty well anywhere. The connections may have been a mite tortuous, but there were trains. None of us owned a motor car. If we had, I don't suppose there would have been any space allocated for us to park it. So, the minute we had been issued with our thirty-six-hour leave passes, signed by Second-Lieutenant Sanders, our platoon commander, we shot off to the railway station.

Not everyone, though. There were a few unfortunates, who, thanks to the whims of the agencies responsible for posting recruits, lived much too far away for a thirty-six-hour pass to be practicable. I have never been able to fathom the logic by which a chap like Dai Davies, our barrack-room Welshman, was posted over two hundred miles to our depot – when there must have been a dozen regimental depots within half a day's ride from his home. Why make Albert Pegg, a Yorkshireman, travel the same distance? Didn't they have depots in the West Riding? Gordon Dewar and Martin Forrest had to come from Scotland. So they never got home for a weekend pass.

I did. But my journey took me four hours, and it couldn't have been much more than forty or fifty miles. I had to change trains three times. Each one was a cross-country crawler. Perhaps the toughest test was to resist the temptation to spend what was left of my week's pay of twenty-eight shillings (£1.40) on cups of tea in station buffets while I was waiting for connections. My mother, bless her, always paid for my fare; otherwise I couldn't have done it.

My first trip home caused an unlikely problem. It so happened that my mother had moved house only days after I went into the Army. I don't think I have mentioned that the Army doesn't let you out of the barracks for at least three or four weeks after you arrive. The idea is that, during your basic training, you must wear Army uniform at all times. So far, so good. But I have most certainly mentioned that wearing unfamiliar items of Army clothing presents difficulties to the most resilient of recruits. Remember those clumsy jokes about all of us looking like 'pregnant ducks'?

They weren't far wrong, actually. Army battledress straight off the Quartermaster's shelves doesn't do much for the image. So after a week or two they marched us all off to the Depot tailor, who drew mysterious lines across our stomachs and the smalls of our backs with a sliver of tailor's chalk. When we got the battledress blouses back, we had to admit that, well – yes, they were a slightly better fit.

It also took us some time to get used to Army berets. New, they were huge and unyielding. They stuck up from the tops of our heads like great big black mushrooms. On our early drill parades, we looked like a gathering of Basque pensioners. In time we got used to them, and learned to pull one side down over one ear in required fashion. But no two recruits pulled them down in the same way. You wouldn't think, would you, that a humble beret could lend itself to so many different styles and shapes of wearing. True, though. By the end of our ten weeks, not only did every member of the platoon wear his beret in a distinctive way; but I could also have told you who the wearer was simply from his silhouette.

But back to the point. It was one thing to have a uniform that roughly fitted; it was quite another to get it up to the standard of smartness required by regimental *amour-propre*. To say nothing of our personal drill. Put more bluntly, we were not to be allowed past the Depot guardroom, and out into the big wide world we had so harshly been required to forsake, until our standards of dress, saluting, and general smartness were deemed to reflect credit on the cap badge we wore.

Of course, we managed it in the end, but it meant that, although my mother had been resident in her new house for three or four weeks, I had never seen it. So I found myself in the odd situation wherein I had to ask directions to my own home.

Still, uniform or no uniform, saluting drill or no saluting drill, long journey or no long journey, unknown domicile or no unknown domicile, we treasured those thirty-six hours each weekend, and were prepared to perform prodigies of bulling each Friday evening to ensure that we got out at the end of Saturday morning in time to catch the first available train. We had to make everything – everything – perfect.

For there was the hurdle of the Saturday morning inspection to be surmounted before those envied pieces of paper called 'leave passes' came into our possession.

First of all the room was to be inspected. Fixtures and fittings. So barrack room duties had to be attended to with especial diligence. Not much agony there, unless a bad-tempered subaltern was actively looking for trouble.

Then came our kit and our beds. Everything that could be extracted from our lockers and laid out on our beds was indeed extracted and laid out. And not only laid out neatly, but laid out in line. And not only laid out in line within the space of the area of the visible blanket on top of the bed, but laid out in line *between* the beds. That is to say, if you were to kneel down by the top bed and squint down the whole line of beds, you would see every spare pair of boots lined up with every other spare pair of boots, all the way down. Not only boots, but plimsoles, P.T. kit, and, inevitably, mug, knife, fork and spoon. Oh – and the spare boots had to be laid on their side, so that the newly-polished insteps could be easily examined. There were stories of some regimental depots where they insisted on the hobnails being polished to shine as well. We were at least spared that ignominy.

So – lines, lines, lines. Then there were the lockers. There was no chance that a harassed recruit could arrange what was necessary on his bed, and then save time by hurling any unwanted item of kit into a locker and locking it. Lockers had to be laid open. Inside, everything that could be piled, folded, displayed, stacked, and generally arranged in a pretty pattern, was indeed piled, folded, displayed, stacked, and generally arranged in a pretty pattern.

The recruit had to stand to attention at the foot of his bed, while the inspecting officer, behind him, sniffed at the kit laid out so painstakingly on it and peered into his locker, and he could only guess at what was going on.

To be fair, they didn't always insist on our lockers being open, but they did insist on top kit being on show.

Top kit.

To ask any survivor of National Service (in the Army, at any rate) about having his top kit inspected is like asking a garrulous old lady about her operations. Both are engraved in the memory. Put two garrulous old ladies together and they can keep going on horror stories about stitches and relapses for hours; put two NS veterans together, and they can bore the rest of the company under the table with tales of marathon bulling sessions, show parades, kit inspections when you slept on the floor the night before, hours cut off weekend passes, and eagle-eyed sergeant-majors with standards of cleanliness that would have made Florence Nightingale look like a slut.

The pettifogging ramifications of this have been discussed, perhaps at inordinate extent, in Chapter Ten. However, I'm afraid you have not heard the last of it.

Chapter Ten was concerned only with our clothing, our uniform. In order to pass the Saturday morning inspection, we had to clean everything else. I have already mentioned barrack room duties – the window-sills, the lampshades, the floors, the buckets and brooms, the wash-basins, the toilets, and so on. Then there were the rifles – the outside bits, the sling, the moving parts, the barrel.

Oh – and one piece of uniform that was rarely worn, but which had to be spotless and creaseless – the greatcoat.

And finally – the top kit. This was short for all our webbing equipment – the small pack, the large pack, the ammunition pouches, and the various straps which were designed to hold them in some proximity to the body.

Webbing. That meant that every square inch of the stuff had to be blancoed. Think of the trouble we had with our belts. Well, there were acres more of it on the surfaces of our top kit. That was not the end. How did a soldier stop the ends of his straps from fraying? Because the nice Army had provided him with brass clips on the ends. How did a soldier keep his packs securely closed? Because the nice Army had provided him with buckles, also of brass. How did a soldier fix the straps to the back of his belt? Because the nice Army provided him with more brass buckles. I never counted the brass buckles and brass clips on straps and belts and packs, but it must have exceeded a couple of dozen. Brass.

I expect you are ahead of me. Yes, they *all* had to be polished. Back and front. Bad enough to be put on show parade for a dirty brass, but if it was for the front of a dirty brass, well, you had it coming. But when they pulled the brasses down, straining them against the webbing loop that held them, in order to detect the smallest vestiges of dried 'Brasso' *on the back*, then we felt we had the right to call ourselves hard done by.

Show parade, by the way, was what it suggests. The offending recruit had to present himself at some much later, and very unsocial, hour, carrying the offending piece of clothing or equipment, which he then had to display under the suspicious eye of an Orderly Sergeant (the Duty Sergeant for the day). Show parade at half-past five on a Saturday afternoon, was, for obvious reasons, particularly inconvenient – as it was expressly designed to be.

So, Friday evenings, we were busy. This may seem inconsistent at first glance with my first sentence in this chapter. Until you recall what focussed our hopes for the weekend. If getting home meant several hours of bulling, so be it. It was a price worth paying.

Incidentally, cleaning and polishing and blancoing the top kit was not the end of it. Every item of it had then to be arranged on top of the locker. Arranged tidily, of course. So that it looked smart, and soldierly. Here is where the cardboard came in. I should have made some reference before now to cardboard padding. Perhaps you may have been intrigued to know what I meant by it. I meant exactly what I said. If you were a keen recruit (or one who wished to avoid show parade), you procured pieces of cardboard, and cut them so that they fitted exactly down the inside sides of the packs and pouches. If you did the job properly, it made the small pack, the large pack, and the ammunition pouches look rigidly rectangular. It was known, appropriately, as 'boxing kit'.

It was still not the end. The entire top kit had to be displayed, on top of the locker, in such a way that every buckle and brass that could possibly be made visible was indeed made visible. And, just to finish it off, the tin hat was placed above, like the fairy on the Christmas tree. It was a mercy they didn't make us polish that too.

So an inspecting subaltern had a pretty fair amount to inspect at half-past ten on a Saturday morning.

We were lucky in that our Platoon Commander, Second-Lieutenant Timothy Sanders, was also a National Serviceman, and he too looked forward to his thirty-six-hour leave of a weekend. Unfortunately, not every weekend. He was a rugby player, and was called upon now and then to turn out for the Battalion or the Depot or the Brigade on a Saturday afternoon. Our Commanding Officer, Major Ambrose, was indecently keen on games, and on members of his command playing representative sport.

Alternatively, it might be his turn to be Orderly Officer for the weekend. So he could not go anywhere.

Either way, he did not care about getting away promptly at midday. Naturally, he was feeling sorry for himself. Naturally, too, he found he had plenty more time to devote to the inspection of his platoon. And if he had to stay at the barracks for the whole of Saturday and Sunday, human nature dictated that he saw to it that everyone's kit was up to miraculous standards before he would be satisfied, before he would agree to march to the Orderly Room and sign the leave passes.

He was moreover anxious to make an impression on his men. He had watched superior officers, and he had watched senior warrant officers. One of their favourite ways of indicating disapproval of standards – apart from the obvious and hackneyed 'Never seen anything like it in all me life' – which was vulgar and not befitting the Queen's Commission – was to tackle a man's top kit.

The time-honoured way was to use the officer's baton or the sergeant-major's pace-stick to sweep the entire top kit from the top of the locker on to the floor. All the poor owner of this top kit was aware of was the sound, because it happened behind him. But it was unmistakable. It was one of the unforgettable sounds of a recruit's life – top kit being swept off a locker and on to the floor.

Second-Lieutenant Sanders decided that this was the way for him.

The trouble was that we did not know which weekends he expected to get away, and which weekends he didn't. So we couldn't gauge the extent of our bulling accordingly. It was chancy. Particularly chancy for people like John Sly, who made it a point of principle never to spend more than two hours bulling on any one evening – inspection or no inspection. More chancy still for Martin Forrest, who, having once cleaned all his top kit to what he considered to be a serviceable standard, arranged it in the prescribed pattern and left it there. On subsequent Friday evenings, his bulling of his top kit consisted of climbing on a chair, blowing off the dust that had accumulated from a week's cleaning of the barrack room, curling up in bed with a cigarette and an unexpurgated novel, and hoping for the best. He was also not above using his ammunition pouches as ash-trays, during breaks in indoor weapon-training periods. (I refer to the favourite Army technique for male bonding – 'Smoke if you wish to.') And if we received mail half-way through the morning, or during a NAAFI break, an ammunition pouch was the natural place to stow fond postcards from southern universities which were signed 'Francesca'. (The postcards were, not the universities.)

Martin wasn't being insubordinate; he genuinely forgot. But it didn't make a very good impression when our Platoon Commander, having already been shocked by coming across what looked suspiciously like verdigris on the back of a buckle, upended a pouch and watched the Players butts and the pictures of Pisa and Siena tumbling out.

So – yes – out would come Mr. Sanders' baton, down would come the top kit, the whole platoon would have to parade again, and we would miss our lunch-time trains.

I once nearly missed it because of a hockey match. I was quite keen on hockey, as it happened. I had heard that the barracks had a pretty mean hockey team, and I harboured ambitions of being selected for it. I religiously lugged my hockey kit to and fro between home and the spider for a few weeks – just in case.

I was not selected. So after a while, I thought – well, never mind what I thought. My hockey kit stayed at home. And then, life being what it is, I was informed one Friday afternoon that the Depot team was a man short, and would I play.

It is a measure of what the Army can do to a man. A year before, or four years before, if I had been told, after weeks of hoping, that I had been selected for the jolly old college or the jolly old school, I would have yelped with delight and said 'yes please'. Now, I thought, 'Sod 'em. I want my thirty-six hour pass.'

So I said – well, I didn't say 'sod 'em', but I did say no.

Within hours I was summoned to the office of the Company Commander, Major Ambrose. He was, incidentally, besides being crackers about sport in general, a keen hockey player, and the captain (inevitably) of the Depot team.

'Ah, Coates,' he said, snorting into his moustache, and glancing down at the paper in front of him to make sure he had got the right name.

'Yes, sir?' I said innocently. He was going to have to make all the running.

''s about this hock' ma', on Sat'y aft'oo'.'

'Yes, sir?'

'We wa' 'ou t'play.'

'But I have a weekend pass, sir.'

Which he knew perfectly well. I wasn't going through all that guff about not having my kit. He would say nonsense, we can easily get some kit for you – which would put me back at square one. So I was going to meet him head-on. I didn't want to play in his bloody hockey team.

'I would rather have my pass, sir, if you don't mind.'

Well, of course he minded. I knew that, and he knew I knew. He screwed up his nose and breathed down through his rampart of a moustache.

'It's a spesh' league match.'

'Yes, sir, I know.'

'It's ver' 'por'.'

I stood to attention like Horatius on the bridge. Silent but firm. He tried the appeal to the better nature.

' 'Course, y'know , can't *force* you. 'Has t'be y'r own 'cision.'

A long silence, while Horatius sweated at attention and the Major bristled his moustache and waited for better nature and natural British sportsmanship to take over.

Well, I thought, if I really did have a choice – I'd come this far. If he'd asked me three weeks before, I'd have jumped at the chance. Now, as far as I was concerned, the hockey team and the league and all could go to the Devil. I was only a substitute; they wouldn't want me next week.

'As I said, 's ver' 'por'.'

Deep breath.

How to let him have it diplomatically?

The silence must have gone on longer than I realised, because at last he gave a wave of his hand. He could see that better nature and natural British sportsmanship were not going to take over, and that one of his Potential Leaders had not displayed the sense of adventure and willingness to rise to challenges that he expected.

I don't think the episode did me much good, not in Major Ambrose's eyes anyway. I have no recollection of his ever addressing another single remark to me during the rest of my basic training. I had clearly let him down badly, to say nothing of letting down the side, the Depot, the league, the Brigade, the Army, the Queen, and the entire British Empire.

What did we do the rest of the time? During our hours off, that is. As the ten weeks progressed, we managed to screw more and more minutes out of our relentless bulling schedules. Take the mornings.

In the first fortnight or so, it was, as the Army designed it to be, a rush. An undignified one too. Getting up at ungodly hours; fighting to secure a place at the wash-basins; dressing; making sure we had the right kit – P.T., denims, musketry order, or full drill order; having breakfast; completing our barrack room duty; and any other special chore that happened to have been laid down in our training programme for that week.

By the seventh or eighth week, we had become so adept that, instead of rushing breathlessly out of the spider at twenty-nine and a half minutes past eight, with straps still flapping and gaiters awry, we were able by eight o'clock to enjoy a post-breakfast cigarette and read the morning paper.

The same principle applied to the evenings. As the condition of our kit improved, and we became more used to the standards required, we found we had the odd hour to spare more often. So what did we do?

We went to the NAAFI for a start.

NAAFI?

I don't know the extent to which this acronym is still common knowledge. For those not privy to the secret, it stands for 'Navy, Army and Air Force Institutes'. It's an organisation, as Collins' Dictionary says, for 'providing canteens, shops, etc., for British military personnel at home or overseas'. The acronym was used also to refer to the actual shops and canteens. So one of the commonest phrases you would hear in any British barrack room – in my time anyway – would be 'let's go down the NAAFI'. (It was pronounced 'naffy' by the way – not 'narfy'.)

Curiously, the acronym does not appear in the latest edition of the *The New Shorter Oxford English Dictionary*, which I have recently purchased. At least, I thought it didn't. I looked at the two columns of abbreviations immediately under the letter 'N'. It wasn't there. It should have been just between NAACP – the 'National Association for the Advancement of Coloured People' – and NACODS – 'National Association of Colliery Overmen, Deputies, and Shotfirers'. (Shotfirers!) I was just about to close the book when I glanced at the third column, and there it was – NAAFI – under the 'word' section. So there's fame for you – the acronym has become so old and so commonly used that it has been dignified by the OED with the status of 'proper word', and it has been entered in the appropriate place, between 'na' ('enclitic form of NO') and 'naam' ('the action of taking another's goods by distraint' – and I bet you didn't know that!).

Now the fact that the OED recognises it as a word does not mean that it is still common knowledge. After all, the OED mentions 'ossature', 'molebut', and 'ugsome'.

It is also quite possible – I have done no research on this – that the Armed Forces have been so truncated in recent years that the NAAFI has become unable to justify its existence. It may be that Services welfare has improved so much that 'British military personnel at home or overseas' have no need for canteens and shops; that they are so well paid and cossetted that they can buy, and afford, everything they want in local civilian establishments wherever they are posted, or through the Internet.

It may be.

Certainly I have no idea of the extent to which the NAAFI is still part of the nation's general knowledge – nay, folklore. But it certainly used to be – in the way that AIDS or LGBT are now.

It was the same with NAAFI. I would give you even money that seven or eight soldiers out of ten couldn't have told you what NAAFI stood for. The NAAFI just was. It was simply 'there', like regimental sergeant-majors or Everest. Like primary school playground games and rituals. Nobody took the trouble to explain to you what they were, or how they had been derived. Probably nobody knew. You simply tried to repeat what you heard (nobody wrote them down to ensure an authorised version), or tried to copy what you saw. You accepted.

So we had no idea who ran the NAAFI. Was it military? Could you be a Lieutenant-Colonel in the NAAFI as you could be in the Hussars? Or was it civilian? Was it sponsored and run by an organisation of do-gooders – mature ladies with double-barrelled names and a social conscience (and husbands with fat bank balances)? What was the chief executive of the NAAFI called? Major-General? Commissar? Top Lady Bountiful? Were the NAAFI represented at the British Legion Festival of Remembrance? Did an ample dowager sporting a huge sash (what were the NAAFI regimental colours?) march down the steps of the Albert Hall carrying a miniature silver urn while the massed bands played *I Like a Nice Cup of Tea in the Morning*?

It is, and was, easy to make fun of the NAAFI. The canteens were unromantic, unfussy, strictly functional. The staff were not noted for their conviviality. NAAFI accommodation was at the whim of the Depot authorities; that is to say, it was housed wherever the CO (more likely, the Adjutant or the RSM) thought suitable. So it could be anything from a barn-like room in a disused building that had been put up to house veterans from the Crimean War to a pensionable Nissen hut. Recreational facilities could be, and often were, dog-eared and out of date. An ill-disposed chronicler, keen to satirise the institution, would refer to six-week-old copies of *Titbits* as the only journalism on offer. Tables with four legs of equal length would be rare. Wall decorations might be limited to faded sepia photographs of Queen Alexandra or Lord Kitchener. If there was a piano, the box in the piano stool would offer sheet music of a tantalising variety, ranging from *The Sheik of Araby* to *Goodbye Dolly Gray*.

Those are exaggerations, but, like many distortions, they outline the shape of the truth. In the memory, the NAAFI was a place of chairs scraping, slatted shutters coming down right on time, bare light bulbs dangling like corpses on a gibbet, khaki bodies hunched over cups, berets stuffed under epaulettes, and cigarette ends flattened on stone floors.

A lot of the merchandise they sold was unromantic too. Dusters, boot polish, blanco – stuff like that. Made a big hole in our puny pay packets of £1.40 a week. And there was no choice; we had to buy it.

But they did sell food too. And tea of course. And they were cheap. Above all, they were there. As I said, like Everest.

And there was nowhere else. Not on the Depot premises anyway. It was no more comfortable than the barrack room – probably less if we had got the stove going. But it was different. It was simply *somewhere else* to gossip and moan and speculate.

What else did we do?

We went to the cinema. Or the 'pictures', as it was universally called then. People who were rich, or arty, or fraffly well brought up, called it the 'cinema'; everyone else called it the 'pictures'. This was the 1950's. Half a dozen giant Hollywood studios were still churning out scores of new features every week. Cinema chains up and down the country were still doing pretty good business. Television was only just beginning to make its impact. There was only one channel until 1953 or 1954. Every town had its cinema; many had two or three. (The university city where I studied had fourteen.)

So we would think nothing of walking a mile or more to the local *Odeon* or *Embassy* or *Roxy* or whatever it was to savour the talents of the current hearth-throbs and sex-bombs. Nobody took any notice of a dozen or so noisy young soldiers. Every young man over the age of eighteen had to do National Service. There were millions of us. Nobody took any notice of uniforms either. This was only ten years after the War. We had won it; we were not under threat from terrorist assassins who would home in on khaki or Air Force or Navy blue.

More differences – two films in one evening; a trailer or two; a newsreel; perhaps a cartoon; and, if you were lucky, a theatre organ too. All for your eight or ten pence of today's money. (We still had enough left for the next duster or tin of blanco.) Nor did anybody take any notice of the billows of cigarette smoke that swirled around in the beam of the projector's light.

On one celebrated occasion, we visited the local picture house the evening after we had had our jabs.

Jabs – there's another evocative subject.

Everyone knows the clichés – the faceless white orderlies, the tight-lipped doctor, the enormous syringe, the fainting recruit. One or two us may have passed out, but nobody bothered much. If the doctor was anything like the other doctors I had come across in connection with the Army, he was too bored to be tight-lipped or loose-lipped or anything else – just anxious to get through the upper arms of the fifty or so recruits lined up before him, and with as little incident as possible.

The Army had co-operated with this worthy, and very human, desire by combining two or three injections into one. The process was known to one and all as 'TABS'. I think it was yet another kind of acronym, but what fell diseases it gave us protection from has now long faded from the memory.

What remains is the pain. Not, curiously, the pain of the actual injection. It hurt, of course. But we could cope with that. We had all been to the dentist; we had all been vaccinated. So we made hackneyed jokes about huge needles, and about passing out, and about limbs swelling to grotesque proportions. Ha! Ha! All very droll.

We got dressed. We returned to 'duties'. Slight discomfort, but that was to be expected. Nothing much. Probably go off by the morning. It got worse. Tea was an uncomfortable meal.

Bulling that evening was painful. If we migrated to the NAAFI, even lifting a cup of tea to the lips was fraught. Undressing to go to bed was more painful still. Wherever you put your arm made no difference. It was like toothache; whatever you did brought no relief.

We eased ourselves gingerly down between the sheets. A good night's sleep – that was what would do the trick. Be as right as ninepence in the morning. I don't know if there is a collective noun for nightmares, but whatever it is, we had it. Pain, delirium, horrors, more pain, running, chasing, more pain, an incomprehensible agony the provenance of which was totally mysterious, and totally inescapable.

All the morning brought was greater awareness of the pain and where it was coming from. I think we felt more sorry for ourselves that morning than we did in the whole of the remaining weeks of training. You can imagine Paddy Flynn's comment when we complained.

Then we discovered that was only the first! There was to be a second TAB a few weeks later.

We were ready for it next time. Teeth were more gritted. No more flopping about watching the pain get worse. Meet it head on. Do something.

So the evening after the second TAB we all went to the pictures. Take our minds off it. Now I should explain that one of the symptoms of the TABS was to make the upper arm unbelievably sensitive. If you merely tapped someone's arm lightly to attract his attention, he would howl with anguish and nearly leap into the air.

Imagine therefore a row of about a dozen of us in the stalls, watching stolidly and hoping to have our minds distracted. One of our number would lean sideways to take a handkerchief or a packet of cigarettes from his trousers pocket. At once the person next to him would lean away in fright lest his tender arm be even touched. The next in turn would do the same. The patrons (customers in cinemas were always plummily referred to as 'patrons') in the row behind would be treated to the mystifying manoeuvre of a dozen young men leaning to the left or to the right in perfect unison, and then leaning back again. And doing the same again several minutes later when someone else of our number decided he needed to blow his nose.

We didn't go to pubs much – couldn't afford it.

But there was one other activity many of us became taken up with, which may come as a surprise.

We sang.

Yes. Sang.

Not because we were especially happy – God knows! Nor because we were especially talented. God knows again!

No – it was because we had a Welshman in our midst. Dai Davies. That little Welshman I spoke about. I told you we really did have one. Just as we had a Yorkshireman and a Scot. Well, this is the proof of the truth of what I have said. Taffy taught us to sing – in harmony! (I am afraid I cannot prove the existence of our Scot by our new-found skill in caber-tossing, or that of our Yorkshireman by our new-found passion for Yorkshire pudding and mushy peas.)

But we sang all right. Taffy taught us to do separate parts. He would sit up in his bed and conduct us while we sat round him like acolytes. We sounded pretty awful. But I tell you this – the minute Taffy joined in we sounded good. He had a wonderful baritone voice – and he was such a tiny chap.

I don't claim that everyone in the barrack room joined in this impromptu choral histrionics, and, looking back, I don't suppose everyone there enjoyed it. Perhaps we were a bit of a pain to some.

(If there was anyone there who felt put out by our efforts and who is reading these lines, may I at last take the opportunity to apologise.) But those of us who were part of it enjoyed it enormously. It was a great lift to the spirits.

I can still see Taffy, on the rare occasions when we all not only came in on cue, but stayed in time, and in harmony, right to the end of a phrase. When we had finished, he would drop his arms, shut his eyes, take a deep breath, sigh blissfully, and say, 'Ah, boys, that was rich – rich.'

15   The show goes on

I THINK THAT, LIKE TOPSY, it 'just growed'. No bright spark brought up the subject as a good idea. None of us sat in the NAAFI or round somebody's bed and discussed the pro's and con's of it. It was a bit like Paddy Flynn's arrival. In neither case do I recall the manner of it. In both, we were presented with a *fait accompli*. In Paddy's case, as I have described, one day he wasn't there, and the next day he was, as if he had been there all the time. Just the same now: one day, nothing could have been further from our minds; the next, it was as if the project had been in existence all the time.

I am pretty sure it was largely Martin Forrest's doing. Abetted by Jack Gatewood. If we wanted to join in, fine. If we didn't, well, it was going ahead anyway. Before we could turn round, it had an unstoppable momentum. The show would go on.

That is not a metaphor, by the way. I mean 'show' – literally. Martin and Jack had decided that we would mark the end of our basic training with a show, a happening, an extravaganza, a performance of some kind. Certainly most of us felt that the end of such a traumatic ten weeks as we were nearly completing deserved to be marked by something dramatic. The situation, we felt, would not be adequately commemorated by a squad of Potential Leaders reeling across the parade ground in the small hours in a state of advanced intoxication. Nor would the needs of the occasion be met by the hanging of some common toilet receptacle from the roof above the Regimental Sergeant-Major's office. We thought we could do better than that.

Our final week would come to an end in the middle of December, so the proximity to Christmas was a further incentive to devise something festive, with, ideally, some ingredient that would provide a modicum of entertainment to others besides ourselves.

Martin's show fitted the bill exactly. I suppose that was why we accepted it. Certainly it was not because many of us were frustrated thespians. Martin had some dramatic experience; and he certainly had the drive. He would have produced plays on a desert island. (He later went on to be a professional.) Jack Gatewood played the guitar a bit, and had written some scripts for college revues. Some of us had no doubt carried a spear or two in stilted school renderings, or rather rendings, of Shakespeare. But that really was about that. Oh – Taffy and his singing of course.

It says a lot for Martin's confidence, not to say his cheek, that he expected to drum up a tame audience for a performance by such unpromising material. But he had learned one useful thing during his eight weeks or so in the Army – namely, that is to say, *i.e.,* and *viz.* – military personnel will come to see almost anything, and they will laugh at almost anything. Well, consider the alternatives open to them.

It says a lot for his cheek too, and for Jack Gatewood's breezy charm, that before long most of the Depot's dignitaries had been persuaded that the presentation of such an event would be a good thing. Paddy Flynn pursed his lips (well, he would, wouldn't he?) but went along with it. I think he was tickled that it was his platoon that had thought it up and not somebody else's. Martin wangled an interview with Major Ambrose, and convinced him that it was 'ver' 'por' '. Platoon morale, don't you know. By some miracle, Jack even won the approval of Regimental Sergeant-Major Brown. God knows what argument he used for that; RSM Brown frowned on everything. Must have been his genes.

Permission materialised for us to use some dilapidated pre-fab or other for rehearsals. Martin and Jack buttonholed everyone in sight for favours, items of importance for certain sketches, and general assistance. Blind eyes were encouraged among our training staff over mysterious failures to turn up to lessons. If either Private Forrest or Private Gatewood was missing, it was explained that he had permission to be absent on an errand of paramount importance connected with 'the show'. Curiously, Martin found it unavoidable that he should miss a five-mile training run in full battle order. Much regretted, of course, but there it was; the show had to go on.

Word got about. Gossip spreads as fast in an army depot as it does in a City office or a boarding school tuck-shop. Before long the impending performance was as talked about as if it were an imminent eclipse of the sun or a coming millennium. Members of the Permanent Staff looked at us curiously as if we had suddenly grown an extra ear. Members of other platoons pulled our legs about it – pure jealousy, naturally. It sucked in more members of our own platoon. Irving Bryce said he knew a bit about make-up, and offered his services. Somebody else had had some training in commercial art, and was recruited for the publicity. Taffy's choral rehearsals attracted a more regular attendance.

In due course, posters began to appear in the most frequented parts of the barracks – the guardroom, the cookhouse, and the NAAFI. Copies found their way into the Sergeants' Mess and the Officers' Mess. Legend had it that one appeared in the 'IN' tray of the Regimental Sergeant-Major. What we should have done, to make sure that absolutely everyone found out, was to put copies on the insides of the lavatory doors. I have always thought that within such confined accommodation sat the biggest captive audience on the face of the earth. If, after three or four days of such exposure to news about the show, anyone remained ignorant, he was either acutely myopic or chronically constipated, and in neither case fit to enjoy it. But we didn't. Pity.

However, judging from the comments we attracted from all quarters, it seemed that the vast majority of the Depot intended to come and see, if only out of curiosity, or, as I hinted earlier, boredom. Perhaps it was due to the fact that our posters gave a copper-bottomed assurance that, for the trivial cost of a shilling (5p.), every member of the audience would be treated to a feast of music, drama, and wit the like of which had not been seen in an Army establishment since the celebrations of Mafeking.

Pot Luck. That's what we called it. I still have a yellowing copy of the programme. *Pot Luck*. That's what you took. The programme was being just a little – what was it the gentleman said? – 'economical with the truth'. For a start, there was no music. Apart from Jack Gatewood's guitar. We had no orchestra. Ha – orchestra! We didn't even have the use of a piano. All our singing (another misnomer) had to be unaccompanied. I don't recall any scenery either, apart from two curtains. There were one or two pretty basic props, but that was about all. Making a virtue out of necessity, general opinion decided that perhaps it was a good thing that the scenery would leave a lot to the audience's imagination, because many of the lines in the script wouldn't.

How we found time for rehearsals in between training and bulling and going to the pictures with our painful arms and disappearing on weekend leave I don't know. My memory of those rehearsals is faded now, but they must have been ramshackle in the extreme; Martin's professional aspirations must have been put under colossal strain. He had to inculcate a minimum of dramatic discipline into a company of inexperienced young men who regarded the whole exercise as a gigantic wheeze. Everyone wanted to get his pet idea into the show. Everyone had jokes and outlines of sketches that would absolutely kill them. Martin and Jack listened, said 'Yes, fine', and went about their business. They got their own way in the end.

Like every show in similar situations, it was under-talented, under-funded, and under-rehearsed – and we were a sensation. They loved us. Well, they laughed and clapped a lot, so I presume they did.

There were two halves – described as the *First Twinge* and the *Second Spasm*. Programme notes credited Martin and Jack with the script and direction. Costumes were attributed to the generosity of the Company Quartermaster-Sergeant. Regimental Sergeant-Major Brown was mentioned in despatches for the 'Choreography'. About ten of our platoon must carry the blame for the actual performance. Another half-dozen or so fell about in hysterics behind the curtains doing 'Stage Management', and the rest of the platoon were given thanks for 'Moral Support'.

Without any warning, Sergeant Flynn turned up, and insisted on taking over the duties of commissionaire – welcoming VIP's at the door, showing people to their seats, and so on. He had dressed himself in blues – number one uniform – and looked magnificent. He put his hands behind his back, flexed his knees, threw out his chest, and, uniquely, beamed on everyone – as proud as a nun at her first Nativity play. We took back everything we had said about his parentage.

I don't think many of the witticisms in our so-called scripts would have reached an anthology of British humour. I'll show you what I mean. One of our sketches involved four or five of us coming up in front of the footlights (yes, we had some lights), right underneath the bottom of the curtains. We lay on the floor wearing full battle order.

Martin lifted his head and peered into an obviously dim distance. After several seconds of uncertainty, recognition dawned on his camouflaged face. He lowered himself flat to the ground again, turned to Taffy next to him, and said in an urgent whisper, 'Enemy in sight. Pass it on.'

Taffy duly passed it on, and so did everyone else, right down to the other end of the line. Albert Pegg at the other end, having received this startling piece of military intelligence, also lifted himself up to peer into the murk. He frowned formidably, then turned to the man next to him.

'How many?' he muttered. 'Pass it on.'

It was passed on, all the way back to Martin. Martin raised himself to peer again. He too frowned fiercely.

'About five. Pass it on.'

All the way back to Albert. Another gimlet-eyed gaze into the far yonder.

'How far away?'

'How far away – how far away – ' and so on.

Martin squinted and calculated.

'About a mile.'

This got back to Albert, who was suddenly struck by a thought.

'What are we whispering for?'

'What are we whispering for – what are we whispering for – '

It was left to Martin to apply the *coup de grâce*.

'It's me asthma.'

Yes, I know, but we got a laugh.

We got laughs too with a sketch about the lady soldiers who served in the canteen day in, day out. There was a sort of chorus to start it: 'We're WRAC'S serving in the Mess' (WRAC – Women's Royal Army Corps). There was a popular radio programme at the time called *Much Binding in the Marsh*, which used this song to wind up proceedings each week. Jack shamelessly cribbed the tune and wrote his own words. If anyone had found out, we could have been prosecuted for it, I suppose, because we were charging for admission.

We dressed up in the obligatory white turbans which all cooks and hotplate servers used to wear in those days, we blacked out a tooth or two, and we upholstered ourselves with pillows and foam-filled bras and things. Perhaps they felt sorry for us. But perhaps not; there's something about drag before an all-male audience that brings out the – well, I don't know exactly what it brings out, but it brings out something. I'm sure the psychologists would have a field day explaining. Whatever it was, they lapped it up.

Taffy finally got his vocal quartet on to the boards. There was a well-known close-harmony group at the time called the 'Inkspots'. We pinched the idea, we stole the barber-shop style, we copied two tunes, and we called ourselves the 'Soupstains'. Three of us were awful, but thanks to Taffy's baritone, we got away with it.

Glancing at the programme again, I see that there was an item called *Magic Moments*, so we must have had a conjuror. Alas, I don't remember him.

Jack played his guitar and warbled a tune or two, and Martin used material that he had clearly resurrected from previous college revues. One creaking rhyme I recall was:

'We've done symbolic plays by Peter Ustinov,
And some doubtful plays for which we were abused-inov.
We've toured the evening classes
Bringing culture to the maasses,
But we feel our audiences have not enthused-inov.'

Somebody took some tumbles, somebody else got a custard pie in the face (you can see how original we were), and we made topical jokes about every Depot dignitary we could cram into a rhyme. And they loved that too.

We really couldn't go wrong. As the evening developed, we began to get the idea that we were quite good at this sort of thing. By the time the last sketch ended, with, naturally, 'the Company' belting out some discordant topical chorus with more of Martin's aching rhymes, we were convinced that we were only a step away from going on tour with ENSA. We took our final bows in a bath of sweat and bemusement. The audience had been incidental; we would have enjoyed ourselves just as much in an empty hall.

Every member of our platoon, at that moment, saw the whole evening as further evidence, if further evidence were needed, that we were the smartest, cleverest, most talented, and most versatile platoon in the whole bloody Army.

Pardonable overstatement. Perhaps not even pardonable. But I like to think that, on that one evening at least, Sergeant Paddy Flynn might have stopped pursing his lips, and might even have allowed something resembling a twinkle to appear in a baleful eye.

16   Closer to the pips

THE COMPANY SERGEANT-MAJOR AT OUR first Depot was in the habit – well, we only knew him for a week, but he seemed to do it several times – of lecturing us on the subject of leave. His peroration was always the same: 'Leave, for a soldier, is a privilege, not an entitlement.'

We were due for a week's leave at the end of our basic ten weeks' training. After what we'd been through, we felt we deserved it. 'Privilege' – 'entitlement' – we didn't care what the Army called it so long as we got it.

Luckily for us, circumstances were on our side. Nobody knew what to do with a squad of recruits who had just completed their first ten weeks. Decisions had to be made about who should be sent out to their regimental battalions (mostly in Germany). People had to be selected for various courses. There were tests and interviews. Postings took time. Nobody wanted a superfluous couple of dozen young men about the place who, having just survived everything the Army could throw at them for ten weeks, thought they knew everything. I have no doubt that our NCO's, after all that time, were just as pleased to see the back of us as we were to see the back of them. Since we had been kept going by the thought of that week of leave, to have denied it to us on a sudden whim would have been asking for trouble. We were a big enough pain in the neck when we were kept busy; idle, we would have brought the place to a state of chaos. And, finally, to cap it all, it was getting on for Christmas, when everyone wanted to go home – even NCO's. (We often doubted whether they had parents, but we were ready to concede that they might have families – if only long-suffering ones.)

There was the small matter of the passing-out parade. Paddy drilled us right into the ground, but I think we acquitted ourselves well enough on the day. The great show was over, and we had had our liquid celebrations the night before. Paddy turned up to that too – by our earnest invitation. He was wearing civilian clothes this time – and bless him, he had pressed the sleeves of his sports jacket.

So we were suffering from a touch of the anticlimaxes after the show, and many members were no doubt nursing a hangover or two, but we got through. Paddy pursed his lips, but at least he did not say this time that we resembled a 'bunch of quearhs'. By midday, it was all over, and by half-past, none of us was on the premises. We spared no backward glance for buildings, officers, sergeants, even each other. We were off. (We never saw Paddy again.) We knew we would be back soon enough. We knew too that our fate had not been sealed. Well, not yet anyway.

Remember what we were called? 'Potential Leaders'. Officer material – that's what we were. Yes. Well, potential officer material. We understood that there would be a series of searching tests to determine the actual extent of our potential.

This brings me to a point about military commissions that I have often heard referred to and have never understood. Have you ever had a conversation with someone who mentioned a bloke he knew in the Armed Forces (usually the Army), and who at some point in his account of this person said, 'Of course, he was offered a commission, but he turned it down.' Sometimes a man tells it of himself.

There are two aspects to this anecdote. Firstly, I have never understood why, when someone is offered a rise in rank, a rise in pay, a rise in status, a rise in standards of physical comfort, and a rise in general self-importance, he turns it down. It seems to me a bit like the man who says, if he were selected as the subject of *This is Your Life*, he would not appear on the stage. But I have heard of only one man who actually refused when the time came.

And the story is often told as if this deserving soldier is far too wily to be caught by the beguiling offers of the military hierarchy, as if the Queen's Commission were some kind of trap. As if there were thousands of these poisoned chalices to be given away, and the only way the War Office can find recipients is to deceive them.

Now, I know what you might say: 'What about the Western Front?' Yes, I agree. The life expectancy of junior officers in the Flanders trenches was about two or three weeks, if that. But the life expectancy of everyone else was not exactly lengthy. And you must agree that the Flanders trenches were something of a special case. None of us had to look forward to Armageddon like that. True, there was Korea, and Cyprus, and Kenya, and Malaya, but we would have been just as reluctant to be posted there as privates, never mind as officers.

So what are you saying? Don't you believe these chaps when they say they were offered commissions and turned them down? Well – frankly – no.

And there's another point. The Army doesn't *offer* commissions. Not just like that. (Again, the Western Front is different. Common sense – if you're up there in the blood-soaked trenches, and every subaltern has been killed and half the sergeants too, and you're the colonel, you have to pin the pips on the shoulders of somebody, and pretty damn quick. But the circumstances are special, and they hardly constitute an offer.)

I repeat, the Army does not offer commissions. Well, not in my experience anyway. It may be suggested to a talented man that he might care to consider applying to be considered for officer training, but that is a long way from having the pips presented on a plate, with watercress round the edge (as P.G. Wodehouse would have said). Anybody I have known who has made it to officer rank has had to work for it. The only exceptions I would allow are those specialist trades like Medical Officer or Intelligence Officer or Paymaster – things like that – where the resident sawbones or egghead or accountant has to be awarded some special status so that he can pursue his calling. But line officers, the ones who actually do the soldiering, have to work for it.

Curiously, I have generally heard this story in connection only with the Army, rarely if ever with the Navy or the RAF. This could imply all sorts of interpretations. Firstly, that the Navy and the RAF are much more stingy in making their favours available. Secondly, that because it is much more difficult to obtain commissions in the normal way in those two arms of the Services, the men who tell tall stories decide therefore to confine such claims to the Army on the grounds that more people are likely to believe them. Thirdly, that the tellers of tall stories are thicker on the ground in the Army than they are up in the air or at sea. One could speculate endlessly.

The fact was that we knew we had been designated 'Potential Leaders'. A second fact was that we knew that we would have a long trail ahead of us before we would be allowed to sport a peaked cap and a cane. A third fact was the mystery that surrounded this special status.

'Potential Leader'. It sounded somehow more dashing than 'Potential Officer'. What was exciting about Biggles and Allan Quartermain and the Red Baron was not that they were brave officers; it was that they were intrepid leaders. Most of us quite liked the idea; it was flattering. It meant moreover that we had been picked out as having special merit even before we had walked into our first barracks. And none of us had wanted to be there. So how had they – the Army – done it?

Had they pulled in calligraphy experts to assess our handwriting on our deferment forms? 'See here? Where it says "beg leave to be deferred from military service in order to complete university studies"? Note the forward-sloping long consonants – clear sign of bravery. And the flourish on the tails of the "g's" and the "y's" – plenty of dash and imagination. Note the squarish "o's" and "a's" – dependability and loyalty. Unmistakable officer material.'

Had those doctors noticed something during our pre-service medicals? 'Ah – dry palms – doesn't sweat under stress. Good chap.'

We had often pondered this problem over the blanco and boot polish, and speculations flowed fast and useless, like spilt wine on a polished table.

One of our number offered the theory that the distinction was a social one: if you had been to public school, you were classified 'Potential Leader'; if you had not, you weren't. That didn't hold up. There were indeed a lot of public school products among us, as I have already explained, but there were a lot of exports from grammar schools as well. And from others too. We were a truly Heinz mixture.

Which led on to yet another hypothesis. This suggested that it was a question of academic achievement: if you had two or more 'O' Levels, you were a P.L.; if you hadn't, you weren't. But we could disprove that too. We knew everything about everybody in the platoon. You couldn't live for ten weeks, night and day, seven days a week, with twenty-odd people, and not know absolutely everything about them. We knew who had what.

There were other lines of thought – mostly frivolous admittedly. That it was a question of Christian names: if you had two or more, you were a PL; if you only had one, you weren't. Then there was the business of choice of service. It came out in general gossip that many of us had not put down the Army as our first choice. This therefore 'proved' that anyone who had the sense to put down the Army second, or, better, third, must be shrewd and perceptive, and thus deserved to be considered as officer potential, while those who had been daft enough to *ask* to go into the Army didn't deserve to lead anything.

Oh – and the intelligence tests. We had been provided with little booklets covered with dots and squares and things, and had been required to join them up or put circles round them or whatever. The more cynical among us were of the opinion that, as a means of separating chimpanzees from orang-utans, they might have limited use, but that their value as a means of determining a young man's capacity for leading men in battle was decidedly limited. And it was out of court in any case, because we did these tests *after* we had come into the Army, by which time our 'Potential Leader' nomenclature had been established.

We had discussed all this before our interviews with the PSO, and we had discussed it many times since. We didn't get very far.

This uncertainty about our status was not confined to ourselves; it seemed that the Army was a bit in the dark too. It was not entirely confident about the validity of its selections, because it submitted us to no fewer than three more sets of tests, to reassure itself that it had got it right the first time.

So the Christian names and the 'O' Levels and the jolly old school and the handwriting were not going to see us through. Well, not quite (more of that later).

We had interviews. After only six days – that was the first. With the PSO, as I have described. That nasty captain who asked in a weasely way why we wanted to become officers, and why we thought we had what it took.

Then had come the questions about our school record – being vice-captain, first eleven colours, and so on. I don't think he was very impressed when I offered the titbit that I had been the School Librarian.

Just to complete the destruction of our self-confidence, he asked us remote questions about various current affairs, and showed not a glimmer of gratification on the few occasions when we got them right.

That process, if you recall, resulted in every member of the squad bar one being allowed to continue with the 'Potential Leader' platoon. Not especially efficacious, then, as a means of weeding out the tares from the corn.

For a while, we forgot about the selection process, as we moved on to our new barracks, and came under the benign care of Sergeant-Major Jefferson, and graduated to the scalding disapproval of Paddy Flynn. We were too busy surviving – proving our heterosexuality.

Round about the half-way mark in our ten weeks' 'basic' that we were told we were due for 'USBY'.

Yes, it baffled us too. Those in the know got so used to talking in acronyms that they forgot that it amounted to a foreign language to those not in the know. Or, more darkly, they jolly well knew that it amounted to a foreign language, and so used the technique in order to keep several jumps ahead. A form of one-upmanship – a 'life skill' that had recently become popular thanks to the books of Stephen Potter.

If you can remember being at a new school where every old hand used to refer to members of staff by their nickname, you will recall the difficulty of trying to find out their real names.

We tumbled to it in the end, by a sort of osmotic gossip. The letters stood for 'Unit Selection Board' – U.S.B. The last 'Y' was added through a felicitous touch of euphony, and through the reali-sation – even by the Army – that the three letters, as they stood, could not be pronounced.

It was a captain who had been designated to conduct our first interviews – the by-now infamous PSO. These new USBY inter-views were to be run by a Major. Just to let us know that the Army took them that much more seriously. Since we had had our first interviews only five weeks before – if that – either the Army was monitoring, and monitoring very closely indeed, the possible leakage of our leadership potential, or it was still uncertain as to whether the PSO had got it right – or indeed as to whether they had got it right when they had marked us as 'Potential Leaders' in the first place.

What had five weeks square-bashing and bulling told them? They surely weren't going to weed us out on the basis of our foot drill or our marksmanship; on our ability to climb a rope twice without dropping; on our stamina in completing a mile in eight minutes in full battle order. That made for good soldiers; it didn't make for good officers. All right, so you needed to be able to do all these things, but that was not the whole story – was it? If it were, all you had to do was mark these tests and hand out the pips to the recruits who came top of the class. So there had to be something else. What was it? What was this mysterious quality they were looking for?

It was decided, presumably, that the Brigade Major would detect it. Why 'Brigade' Major I'm not sure. Some Headquarter staff job, I suppose. Pen-pusher. Clipped moustache, well-laundered fingertips, and highly-polished boots. It certainly sounded impressive – probably intended to be. We had never heard of him before.

We braced ourselves for a searching analysis and general grilling reminiscent of the Inquisition. Barked questions and gimlet glances; hesitant answers scribbled on clipboards by fleshless, hatchet-faced clerks with knobbly knuckles. Everything taken down and used in evidence. By the end of it we would lie, psychologically stripped and dissected – the truth about our officer potential – or lack of it – mercilessly laid open for all the world to see – even ourselves.

The Major asked each one of us – we compared notes later – where we had gone to school, how many games we played, whether we had been a prefect, why we wanted to be officers, and who was the Russian delegate at the United Nations.

Nobody was weeded out. We were all still there in the platoon photograph that was taken towards the end of our ten weeks.

So much for the Inquisition.

We carried on our basic training. We sweated in the gym and dangled from ropes under the impassive gaze of Corporal Duke; we writhed under the tongue of Staff Sergeant Barron. We puffed and swore on the square, and frequently doubled up with laughter, under the pursed lips and deadpan denunciation of Paddy Flynn. We lounged and tried to stay awake during the lectures on military law by Major Ambrose – he always did his training with us in centrally-heated huts, as often as not just after lunch. Enough to send a nervous hind to sleep.

Once in a while we were caught for fatigues. The sort of work the Raj reserved for Untouchables – cleaning out the fat in cold baking tins in the cookhouse, or polishing whatever brass objects presented themselves to the inventive gaze of the Orderly Sergeant. Never, incidentally, peeling potatoes or whitewashing the coal, despite all the old jokes. Two of our squad were detailed to sweep up in the Orderly Room after all the clerks had gone off duty.

For those who think the Orderly Room refers to its state of tidiness, I must point out that it was, in effect, the Depot's office quarter, the red tape repository, the bumf factory. Records were kept there. Records.

Our two intrepid recruit sweepers noticed, half way through their charring, three things. One, that they were standing right next to a filing cabinet the labels on which proclaimed it to contain confidential personal records; two, that the cabinet was unlocked; and three, that they were alone.

So they did what any loyal, steadfast soldier would have done under the circumstances – they had a quick butcher's. Within an hour they were back in the barrack room telling us what Major Ambrose thought about every one of us, especially about our officer potential.

It wasn't quite as world-shaking as one might have expected. It seemed that the democratic Major had given it as his considered opinion that every recruit who had been to public school was fit to become an officer; those who had not, weren't.

Well, that dished me, for a start. Mind you, I don't suppose my rejection of his pestiferous hockey match had done me much good. Not a good team man, you see. Interestingly, I don't remember anybody being especially depressed by this information. It shows either that the Army, after only eight weeks or so, had turned us into hardened fatalists, or that we had little regard for Major Ambrose's judgment.

With some reason. Why else was the Army devising so many other selection processes? It seemed that they didn't trust him either.

For our biggest test was yet to come. News of this arrived in time, not to spoil our Christmas, but certainly in time to ruin our New Year celebrations. We were all to report to some remote Army station in the middle of nowhere in the southern counties, for a series of tests and interviews under the auspices – very portentously – of the 'War Office Selection Board'. I think it was the first time we had come across the word 'war' in the whole of our military service hitherto.

210

I expect you are ahead of me. Yes – 'WOSBY'. The acronymisation – if there is such a word – served the very useful purpose of trimming its dignity. Rather like the NAAFI. I mean, the 'Navy, Army, and Air Force Institutes' sounds pretty important and dignified, but 'NAAFI' doesn't. Similarly, even if you are not a born-again Christian, you are prepared to accord respect and tolerance to the 'Cambridge Inter-Collegiate Christian Union', but it is harder to do the same to 'CICCU' – pronounced, unfortunately if predictably, as 'Kick-you'. We were given to understand that the Birmingham University Music Society had similar problems.

However, to WOSBY. It is easy to make jokes at this distance of time, but the tests loomed pretty large when they were in front of us rather than comfortably behind us. It is perhaps appropriate to confess at this point that, until quite recently, I used to have a recurring dream (admittedly not very often), in which I had to do my National Service all over again. It didn't frighten me, but it made the heart sink to depths of Stygian dimensions. The relief on waking was as great as if I had been scared out of my wits.

I don't know quite what that indicates, but I would hazard a fair guess that, if nothing else, it showed that we were not fond of the Army. It was a pointer to the fact that Army life was a roller-coaster of ups and downs – of elation at successes, of depression at failures, of bafflement over the more enigmatic military decisions, of moments of great physical well-being, of other moments of unbelievable fatigue, of exasperation at small annoyances, of ground-rolling laughter, of gnawing worry about coming challenges, of vulnerability to rumour, of aching desire for an armchair at home, for an uninterrupted hot bath, for privacy, for a moment of peace, for anything that didn't have corporals or khaki in it.

I have no doubt that our learning to cope with these huge and frequent swings of mood and circumstance was in itself a form of training, and it didn't do us any harm in the long run. But that did not save us from suffering at the time.

We suffered now at the prospect of WOSBY. True, we had survived the PSO and the USBY Brigade Major, but that was in the past. That was lightweight stuff. Surely that couldn't be all that the Army had to throw at us. Was WOSBY going to be just another USBY? Was there nothing more searching? Had they thought of nothing else more demanding, or more subtle, to inflict upon us in order to detect the presence of this mysterious, and hitherto hidden quality (well, hidden to us anyway) called 'Officer Potential'?

We were told that the tests were to last three days. That looked significant. USBY had lasted less than half an hour, if that, and the PSO had disposed of each of us in less than fifteen minutes. So that was promising and sinister at one and the same time.

There were to be two types of test – outdoor and indoor. We were divided up into groups of about five or six. These might contain some of our old squad, and equally, could contain complete strangers from distant regiments based all over the country.

For the outdoor tests, we wore denims, over which we were told to tie something like a waist-length cotton pinafore or sleeveless jerkin, in a bright colour, rather in the manner of speedway riders. These bore a number fore and aft, which accentuated the similarity to speedway riders. The idea of the numbers, you would have thought, was to ensure anonymity, and hence to assist the examiners to be more impartial.

However, all the examiners carried lists, on which was written every candidate's name. Moreover, on the occasions when they were called upon to address a candidate, they used his name, not his number. Yet another of those features of military life, which, like the Almighty, was totally inscrutable.

And talking of inscrutable, the examiners – three expressionless majors and a po-faced lieutenant-colonel – followed the candidates everywhere, carrying clipboards and notepads – with barely a flicker of an eyelid. They said few words to the candidates, and even fewer, it appeared, to each other. Bit like having an interview before the selection board of a Trappist monastery. Unnerving.

The candidates were called upon to engage in tasks designed to test at the same time their team spirit and their initiative. As the one involved the submerging of the individual personality and the other the emphasising of it, we were understandably baffled as to what was required of us. The problems themselves were ghastly things – mysterious affairs to do with streams and planks and ropes and barrels. We had to take turns to devise a solution, and then to help the next poor uninventive wretch when he put forward *his* brilliant idea. If any of us, by luck or military alchemy, showed signs of coming near a solution, he was told that he had run out of time. Our ignoble, debris-strewn failures were predictable, frequent, and regular. Grim glances flew between the spectating officers, and names were ticked off on notepads with flourishes of sickening finality.

There were stories of eager, or despairing, candidates being found, at night, in their pyjamas, clambering all over these planks and fences and poles, actually trying to practise in advance.

Indoors, it was a little more comfortable, and comforting. We wore battledress. We sat round tables and talked. Discussions. We were invited to hold forth on the situation in Cyprus, the Mau Mau terrorists in Kenya, the problem of over-population in India, and so on. Another dilemma. Stiff-upper-lip, school-ingrained modesty inclined us to be reticent on subjects on which we did not feel qualified to speak (nearly everything). On the other hand, we knew that the faceless field officers with the clipboards were sitting behind us, and were expecting to be given some material on which to judge us. They wouldn't keep their pencils poised in the air for ever. So we had to say something. On the other hand again, if we hogged the conversation merely in order to make an impression, we were in the alternative danger of appearing as a show-off, a loudmouth, a know-all.

Problem – how to ingratiate ourselves with the inquisitors at the back, without appearing either as a wan, tongue-tied ignoramus, or as a loquacious poseur. We frowned in concentration, we nodded vigorously at what we thought was a telling point made by someone else, and we hoped that, by our portentous, if silent, demeanour, we would convey the fact we were just the sort of learned, balanced, disciplined, fair-minded, undemonstrative young men that the Army wanted to lead its troops into battle.

We also had to give a lecture – on any subject of our choosing. About ten minutes. Quite an ordeal for many. I had the common sense to talk about something I knew about rather than something I fancied the Army would want to hear. Being keen on history, I talked about Richard III and the Princes in the Tower. Yes, I know – not exactly the sort of riveting stuff to appeal to an examining board of military stuffshirts, but I had recently read a book about it. And, because of its relative obscurity, I had good reason to believe that nobody else in the room had. I could launch myself on to the saddle of my subject and gallop away, without the danger of being unseated by sudden awkward questions; my lecture, if nothing else, would have the virtue of fluency, though it might be a touch short on comprehensibility.

Anyway, I got away with it. There was a loud silence when I had finished. It was quite some time before one of the majors cleared his throat and said, 'Yes, thank you, Coates. You may sit down.' By that I don't mean that my talk was in any way impressive; it was simply that nobody could think of anything to say when I had finished. I would have achieved the same effect if I had done a striptease.

I heard later that Bill Glover, with his bulging portfolio of degrees and diplomas, gave a lecture on 'The Limits of Human Aspiration'. I bet the silence after that lasted for ages. They failed him, by the way.

We did some more intelligence tests, with the dots and the squares. So you can see that the Army had stretched every psychological muscle in order to provide us with fresh and stimulating challenges. It was so vital to determine the presence, and the level, of this mysterious human element known as 'Officer Potential'.

Finally, we each had to go before each of the four officers,

214

for one last searching interview (that is, four all told) that would get right to the bottom of our personality. The hounds of their questions would sniff out whatever secrets and murky mysteries of our characters and potential that had hitherto remained hidden.

All three majors and the half-colonel asked us where we had gone to school, whether we had been prefects, how many games we played, why we wanted to become officers, and the details of the latest Cabinet reshuffle.

Then, and only then, the Army felt that its file of information on each of us was comprehensive enough for it to be able to inform us whether we were to be selected for four months of officer training.

I should have stressed at the outset that, throughout our three-day stay at this WOSBY camp, every effort had been made to keep the atmosphere friendly and informal. Well, that's what they had told us.

In keeping with this worthy intention, when the selections were finally made, nobody told us to our face what the results were. Instead, half an hour before we were due to leave – I think we were actually waiting out in the road for the lorry to take us to the railway station – a disinterested lance-corporal clerk handed each of us a cheap white envelope.

We tore them open. This is what mine said:

'No. 67 RANK Coates [sic] NAME Coates BM
YOU ARE NOTIFIED THAT THE DECISION OF THIS BOARD REGARDING YOUR APPLICATION FOR A COMMISSION IN HER MAJESTY'S FORCES IS: -
A RECOMMENDED FOR OCS TRAINING.
~~B NOT RECOMMENDED AT PRESENT, BUT YOUR CO WILL BE CALLED UPON FOR A REPORT IN THREE MONTHS' TIME OR IF IN THE MEANWHILE YOU HAVE BEEN POSTED TO A SERVICE UNIT, THREE MONTHS AFTER SUCH POSTING.~~
~~C NOT RECOMMENDED.~~'

There followed the date and the signature of Lieutenant-Colonel Clipboard.

To my gratification, and surprise, all the lettering in 'B' and 'C' had been carefully ruled out.

One in the eye for Major Ambrose.

17   Not a pip, but a stripe

IT WAS ONE THING TO be told that you had been recommended for a four-month course at Officer Cadet School; it was quite another actually to get there. Those of us who had been successful at WOSBY, and who had looked forward to congratulations from the Commanding Officer on our triumphant return to the Regimental Depot, suffered a stark disappointment. Those of us who had hoped for a speedy posting to Officer Cadet School suffered another.

When we returned from our passage through fire at WOSBY, eager to demonstrate to everybody that we really were proper, proven 'Potential Leaders', nobody took the slightest notice of us. All the training company NCO's were now engaged with a new squad of recruits; the Permanent Staff treated us like lepers, as they had done before – as indeed they treated everyone else. Our previous source of information, low-down, and entertainment – Eddie – had been posted to the battalion in Germany. No officer came near us, and we had learned enough sense by now not to go ambling aimlessly about the Depot with no weapon, tool, or document in the hand, and so run the risk of bumping into the Regimental Sergeant-Major with no visible reason for our existence.

For the best part of a month, then, our daily round consisted of trips to the cookhouse during the day (by as circuitous a route as we could devise, one that did not take us past an important person's open office door), trips to the NAAFI in the evening, and long sessions in the barrack room in between, playing cards.

We found out what had happened to those who had failed WOSBY. Some were posted to the battalion in Germany. A couple applied, and were accepted, for a course to become physical training instructors. One university graduate, not exactly devastated by his failure to qualify himself for a four-month spell of allegedly inhuman privation at Officer Cadet School, offered himself as a candidate for the Army's famous Russian course, and soon found himself back at his beloved university for the next twenty months.

I say 'famous', because it was much talked about at the time – talked about among young men faced with National Service anyway. Now that the Soviet Union has been been defunct for a whole generation, it is not so easy to recall the atmosphere of tension that existed between East and West. It was bad enough in the eighties, when President Reagan referred to that 'evil empire'. It was far, far worse in the fifties. We were only a few years away from the eyeball confrontation of the Berlin Air Lift and the open hostilities of the Korean War. It was Cold War and Hot War at one and the same time.

Atom spies and defections to the Kremlin were the scare stories of the age. Accounts of Senator Joe McCarthy and his witch-hunts for Communists under every American bed were regular reading fare. Secretary John Foster Dulles' paranoid suspicion of the Russians was as notorious as Mr. Vyshinsky's invariable use of the veto on behalf of Stalin in the Security Council a few years before.

NATO was so much a part of the life of Western Europe that I venture to claim that a majority of the population could have told you who the NATO Supreme Commander was. How many people could do that today? In 1955 we had every confidence that NATO could give a good account of itself in the event of a Russian invasion. How many of us could provide ten connected, fact-based, relevant sentences abut NATO today? Yet a lot of 'those who know' felt some heat under the collar when Mr. Trump said it was irrelevant.

I am not saying that these assertions are true; I am merely illustrating what I think was the climate of opinion of the time.

One of the ways in which our political masters decided to prepare themselves to deal with whatever devious schemes the Russians might dream up in their impenetrable Slavonic fastnesses (and they were credited with cunning of Machiavellian, almost

Satanic, subtlety) was to train a legion of bright young men to become experts in the Russian language. To monitor the non-stop propaganda of *Pravda*? To equip themselves to become spies in a dry dock on Lake Baikal or a steel works in Dnieperpetrovsk? To live in earphones and decipher Russian radio signals? To interrogate the hosts of defectors who were expected to besiege Checkpoint Charlie in Berlin in order to divine how many of those defectors were *really* defectors and how many were actually underhand, shifty, fork-tongued double agents?

We were never told. But the implication was conveyed, unmistakably, that the Russian Course was 'a good thing'.

It was also perceived as 'a good thing' by a host of well-educated young men who were considering how best to spend their two years in khaki (or blue – I presume the Navy had a Russian Course too – I never heard of an RAF one; perhaps pilots over Lake Ladoga had to take their chance). Those who had no pretensions to leadership, Sam Browne belts, revolvers on lanyards, Military Crosses, and dashing peaked caps with the sides pulled down, or who had every reason to try and avoid the danger of a front-line trench on the one hand and the boredom of an Orderly Room typewriter on the other, saw the Army Russian Course as an excellent alternative. Academic work, congenial surroundings (it took place in Cambridge University), and near-total absence of any reminders of Army life – uniforms, sergeant-majors, fatigues, rifle drill, and so on.

I did hear, incidentally, that there was a Greek course too, though perhaps not quite so congenial. There is a story attached to this.

We had a chap at my college who was very clever. Yes, I know we were all supposed to have a few brains, but this chap was, as I said, *very* clever. Won no end of prizes. Valuable prizes too. It was customary to set the monetary value of these prizes against the money owed to the college on our termly college bills. Well, the story went that this chap – we'll call him John – won so many prizes during one term that, when they came to present him with his college bill, it was found that *they* owed *him* money.

Anyway, the time came for John to do his National Service. He was a classicist, by the way. Could do Latin and Greek in his sleep, quote Virgil *ad infinitum,* swear in iambic pentameters. So much so that it was rumoured that John was not very worldly – *too* bookish, in fact. Didn't play games. Not especially athletic. We shook our heads; poor John might be in for a bad time in the Army.

Well, he got through his basic training. No great achievement, you may say; after all, we had. He then showed his first sign of enterprise by getting himself a cushy posting in some orderly room or other, where he had to stamp envelopes for four or five hours each day, keep his battledress blouse pockets free from biro inkstains, and make sure he got his weekend leave pass each Friday. Each weekday evening he could curl up with his beloved classical authors – naughty plays by Aristophanes and the rude bits from Ovid; read the papers from cover to cover – spot of bother with that jumped-up colonel, Nasser, and the Suez Canal; trouble in Persia about oil (the title 'Shah of Persia' used to add a nice touch of oriental decadence and mystery to the news bulletins); confounded terrorists in Cyprus; Commies in Malaya, and so on – and count the hours to the following Friday.

Then he was summoned one day to London – to a lofty set of premises connected with the War Office. There he met another young man similar to himself – ex-classicist from university. After an appropriate wait in an anteroom, John was called in to meet a board of stern-looking officers plastered with red tabs, and given a Greek newspaper.

'Can you read that?' he was asked.

John frowned over the headlines. Then he turned to the inside pages, his frown deepening.

His interrogators waited impatiently.

'Well?'

John shook his head.

'This is a modern Greek newspaper. I read Ancient Greek.'

'Isn't it much the same?'

John made a face.

'Not really. Same alphabet. But the grammar's changed out of all recognition. And what about all the new words – after two and a half thousand years? And the slang and the idiom. I don't know. . . . '

He bowed his head again over the close print, and grimaced in bafflement.

The officers admitted defeat.

'Very well, Private – Er – that will be all.'

John was told to wait in the anteroom while the second young man was being questioned.

After about twenty minutes he came out.

'What did they say to you?' he asked John.

'They tried to get me to read a Greek newspaper.'

The young man's face lit up.

'They did with me too. How did you get on?'

John went through his bafflement procedure again.

'Didn't make much of it.'

The young man looked surprised.

'Really? Oh, I had no trouble at all. Fluent, I was. They were very impressed.'

'Ah,' said John.

A week later, this young man was posted to a bomb-strewn, ambush-plagued, terrorist-swarming Cyprus, and John went back quietly to his envelope-stamping, his newspapers, and his enjoyment of the latest translation of Thucydides.

All of which is a long way from WOSBY.

What happened to us after WOSBY? Well, as I say, some were posted to the battalion. Some got on courses of one kind or another. There were a few who had not passed WOSBY, but who had not failed either. Remember there were three classifications on that little form we were given before we left – 'Recommended', 'Not Recommended', or 'Deferred' – meaning they could have another shot at it in three months' time. To fill in these three months, they were usually promoted acting lance-corporal (unpaid, naturally), and attached to training platoons, or sent off on a weapon-training course.

That left us. The ones with all that officer potential. While one group of our recent basic training squad learnt a useful skill, trade, or craft on a course, and another joined the forces of NATO to strengthen the Western European shield against the teeming red millions of the Russian Army, we sat around wondering whether the Depot authorities were even aware of our existence.

They must have been really, but they gave little evidence of it to us.

We did get put on fatigues from time to time. It was January; we spent chilly hours delivering coal in rusty buckets to the houses in the Married Quarters. Bit like old council houses really. Totally undistinguished. The one thing I remember about them is the Army name for them, or rather for the people who lived in them. They were known as the 'Married Families'. Yes – Married Families. Did that mean that the Army, by implication, recognised the existence of unmarried families? If so, it was very modern of them. And totally out of character; their official morality came straight out of the pages of Jane Austen and Louisa May Alcott.

One might be disposed to wonder what the authorities responsible for arranging accommodation these days might make of common law wives and partners and live-in lovers, and legions of step-children. It must make the official nomenclature a nightmare. Imagine – 'Flats, NCO's, Common Law Wives, Extended Families, for the use of', as opposed to 'Houses, Officers, Partners, Children, for the use of' or 'Accommodation, Other Ranks, Lovers, Bastards, for the use of' – with all the awful class-ridden implications built in.

We spent one day in the Orderly Room. Someone had discovered several boxes of training pamphlets under the bed. They had been lying there collecting the dust for so long that they had become out of date – particularly with regard to nomenclature. The Army has a passion for nomenclature; it doesn't matter whether you look after a thing properly, or whether you can use it properly, or whether you can even find it, so long as it appears on the ledgers correctly named. So we spent an entire day, sitting at desks, with hundreds of these training pamphlets in front of us, going through them, crossing out the word 'jeep' and inserting 'quarter-ton truck'.

The Army, incidentally, has another passion – or had in my day. That is for making things feel, sound, and look 'smart'. If it had had its way, it would probably have made them smell and taste smart too. The classic example of this, in my experience, was rifles. I hope I have been successful in conveying to even the most casual reader that we spent a good deal of our time in drill – both foot drill and rifle drill. That casual reader will have observed the curious irony that we spent – oooh, getting on for thirty hours learning how to carry the rifle at the correct angle over the shoulder, how to port it, slope it, present it, secure it, change it from one shoulder to the other (both at the halt and on the march), and only about two hours actually firing it. But no matter; that is not my point.

Nor is my point the difficulty of having to learn how to swing a nine-pound nightmare of knobs, nuts, and projecting corners from one side of the body to another, without moving one's feet, legs, body, or head, and without ever shifting one's gaze from its fixed forward direction.

My point concerns this business of smartness. The Army equated it so often with noise. It arranged as many movements as it could to coincide with slapping the rifle with the flat of the hand, or sometimes with the base of the hand. If you got it wrong, this could be very painful. So, naturally, we, like generations of soldiers before, turned to devious ways of making the business easier. We discovered that the more screws you loosened, the more the thing rattled. Fine. We produced the required noise. But we also produced the situation in which the amount of noise that could be made by hitting it varied in inverse proportion to its accuracy as a weapon, the logical conclusion of which was a perfect drill instrument that was a completely useless firearm. But it was crisp, and smart, and soldierly.

Then we were put on weekend guard. Two hours on and four hours off – from Saturday lunchtime to Monday morning. Can you imagine!

The Army loves guarding things. So much so that the practice has entered the national consciousness. Sentry duty is one of the best-known activities of a soldier's life. Civilians don't know about Staff Sergeants or Orderly Rooms or Call Signs or Part One Orders, but they all know about sentries. Millions of grown men remember with misty eye the sentry box in their toy soldier set. We have all seen the sentries outside Buckingham Palace.

We all have a mental picture of the solitary, greatcoated, alert soldier silhouetted against the night sky, with rifle and bayonet at the ready. Must have the bayonet fixed. As if the sentry, presented with a challenge, is going to charge – instead of simply shooting.

We spent quite a lot of time learning how to fix bayonets in our rifle drill – to the accompaniment, as I have told you, of much lurid sarcasm from Paddy Flynn. Even in our first week, at the Depot, the Company Sergeant-Major had reverently informed us that any regiment which had been given the freedom of the city was entitled to march through its streets with bayonets fixed, drums beating, and colours flying. Knowing what we already did about the propensity of members of our Permanent Staff for taking liberties with the local female population, we could not help thinking that such a contingency was rather remote.

Sergeant Lugg had told us several times about the vital importance of sentry duty. He stressed the blackness of the crime if a sentry went to sleep on his watch and 'endangered the lives of his comrades'. (His sense of awe managed an 'h' for that.) The phrase stuck out so far from the usual earthiness and simplicity of his vocabulary that it lost validity. No matter how many times he repeated it, and he did – often – and despite its obvious truth, it always carried with it a ring of empty rhetoric.

However, freedom of the city or no freedom of the city, dead comrades or no dead comrades, we knew that one day we would be caught for guard duty. In our case it meant spending forty-two hours in the Depot Guardroom, apart from the times when we were actually patrolling.

The Guardroom was the first place seen by any visitor to the Depot. Naturally, therefore, it had to look smart. Every tap in the adjoining washroom would sparkle (where the rust hadn't eaten away the chromium, that is). There was not a single brass radiator fitment that did not glitter. The telephone receiver was lifted and reverently dusted every day. The water in the fire buckets would be regularly, and frequently, changed. The buckets themselves would be arranged against the wall with an artistic symmetry that would have brought tears of aesthetic joy to the eyes of a sergeant-major. Not a single dust-pan was unpolished, and of course the broom handles were a spotless, virginal white. When it came to making a favourable impression on a visitor by showing him a pleasant, airy, well-maintained guardroom, you had to hand it to the Depot guard commanders; they certainly knew how to go about it.

Mind you, the visitor had to make a few allowances for the roughness of military life. This was an establishment to house men who might be called upon at a moment's notice to go to war.

There was only one light bulb, for instance, and it hung naked from a grimy ceiling on a long piece of scruffy flex. The flaking distemper on the walls made it difficult to determine whether the more recent application had been in dysenteric yellow or gangrenous green. The furnishings consisted only of a trestle table bristling with splinters for the unwary, a few chairs, and some rusting iron folding beds. Iron bars and cobwebs vied to obscure the one lofty, inaccessible window.

Still, we were there to protect our surroundings, not moan about them. Our first surprise was that our bayonets were not considered necessary. Nobody told us to fix them; indeed nobody made any reference to them at all. A bigger surprise was the discovery that our rifles were not going to be needed either. Since our duties were to involve guarding not only the barrack rooms, offices, and

Married Families' quarters, but the arms stores and magazines, it was obvious to the dullest student of military affairs that rifles were quite unnecessary.

We were issued with pick-axe handles ('Helves Pick', to be precise) from the gaily-painted rack in the corner. As the Guard Commander on the other hand had the relatively dangerous job of keeping an eye on the un-issued Helves Pick and of procuring the midnight pot of tea, he was provided with a loaded Sten gun.

The guard personnel – us – were divided into two groups. The first – split again into twos – had to stand at the main gate, open it for the cars of tardy, convivial officers, escort all unidentifiable or incoherent arrivals to the Guardroom, and demand to inspect the identity cards of one and all. The second group was dignified by the somewhat sinister title of 'Prowler Guard'. It was their job to patrol the entire barracks, try all the door-handles, tug all the padlocks, keep the Officers' Mess boiler going, and inform the Guard Commander every half-hour that they were still alive. Everyone did two hours on and four hours off. So – work it out for yourself – it needed a dozen of us all told.

Meantime, the Guard Commander, and his deputy, spent the whole time from midday Saturday to dawn on Monday in the Guardroom, taking turns to make the tea and watch the Helves Pick in the corner. If they felt like relieving the monotony, they tried to cadge cigarettes off each other, or they let a couple of prisoners out of the cells for an hour or two to make up a four at solo. Finally, at five on Monday morning, they turned the rest of the guard out of bed to polish the taps, dust the telephone, and scrape the broom-handles.

We had to bring to the Guardroom everything we would need for forty-odd hours – everything – including our mattresses and bedding – not forgetting our Mug, Knife, Fork, and Spoon. We were to live in our full uniform – even sleep in it. Constant vigilance, you see. No chance of 'endangering the lives of our comrades' with us. Dear me, no.

Those of us on gate guard could liven things up a bit by insisting on seeing everyone's identity card – even those belonging to officers who told us that it was 'quite all right, but they had just left it in the Officers' Mess'. We could draw ourselves up stiffly like the Spartans at Thermopylae and say, 'Terribly sorry, sir. Orders, sir. Hope you will understand, sir.' We could throw our weight around with private soldiers, especially diminutive sanitary orderlies and batmen, not only demanding to see their identity cards but asking them to quote their Army numbers to us. Well, there were two of us, and only one of them. And we had our invaluable Helves Pick. But it was crushingly, stupefyingly boring.

Not much better for the Prowler Guard. The Guard Commander, an evilly-disposed, pinch-faced corporal with acne, showed us a plan of the barracks, pointed out to us with a nicotine-stained finger the position of every important door and padlock, and told us how often to stoke the Officers' Mess boiler. There was not much scope for the imagination with that. We devised a primitive form of golf, using a pick helve and a pebble. The barracks was the links. A lost pebble counted two strokes. Down a drain counted three.

Forty-two hours of it. In my time off I was able to read over 350 pages of *War and Peace*. I remember the fact of reading that much. I recall little of the actual characters of Pierre or Natasha or Count Rostov. What one recalls is the seediness, the grime, the chewiness in the mouth; the bundled-up, fitful sleep; bare boards and rusting iron; the clock-watching; the bad temper and small-mindedness of the Guard Commander; the depression of the small hours; the endless periods of absolutely nothing happening. One of the longest weekends of one's life.

We actually turned up for one parade – pay parade. Gave the game away, really. But £1.40 was £1.40.

Then, right out of the blue, we were summoned to appear before the Commanding Officer. It was like being given an audience with the Pope. We thought, with that propensity of the young for assuming that the world revolves around them, that our Officer

Cadet School postings had come through, and that the Commanding Officer wanted to inform us in person. We prepared ourselves for 'CO's Orders' with zest.

'CO's Orders' were neither orders nor interviews in the strict sense of the word. It was the term applied to the, shall we say, meetings conducted by the Commanding Officer about once a week, or as circumstances dictated. There were usually three occasions for these meetings.

The first was a loud, brief, summary trial. The defendant was marched into the CO's office at an impossibly rapid pace, in absurdly small steps because of the smallness of the space available. The Regimental Sergeant-Major bawled the commands at the top of his voice.

'67891234 Private Grubb – QUICK MARCH – LEF'- RIGH'- LEF' – RIGH' – LEF' – RIGH' – LEF' TURN – LEF ' – RIGH' – LEF' – RIGH' – HALT!!!'

These commands had transferred the hapless defendant from a position of stiff attention outside the office to a position of even stiffer attention in front of the CO's desk – all of seven yards. If the office had floorboards, the stamping of boots would cause the paper clips to jump.

The Regimental Sergeant-Major then introduced the defendant to his Commanding Officer – '67891234 Private Grubb – SAHH!!!' – just in case the Commanding Officer had not been able to read the charge sheet on the desk in front of him, or had not been listening when the Orderly Room Chief Clerk had told him half an hour before.

The charge was then read out to the wilting defendant. The Regimental Sergeant-Major gave the evidence for the prosecution, with due deference to the Commanding Officer's tender feelings and sensibilities. The circumlocution would have done credit to a Chancery lawyer from *Bleak House*. 'On the evening of the fourteenth last, at approximately twenty-three hundred hours' and 'the accused was detected by the Night Orderly Sergeant' – that sort of thing. How was he behaving? 'In an inebriated condition.' Where was he? 'In unauthorised premises – to wit the rear of the recreational area appertaining to the accommodation of Corporal Smithers in the Married Families Quarters.' What was he doing? 'He was discovered committing urination against the wooden structure at the bottom of the said recreational accommodation – SAH!!!'

In other words, poor old Grubb, who was never very good at holding his liquor, had shipped a drop too much on board, had been taken short on his way back from the local, and had had a quiet pee against Corporal Smithers' back garden shed.

Military law dictated that the over-indulging Grubb should have an opportunity to give his side of the story – 'do you have anything to say in your defence?' What could he say, poor devil? That he hadn't had a pee? The RSM would have been ready for him. 'The Night Orderly Sergeant examined the slats of the aforementioned wooden structure and found that they were wet, sir. And they smelt of urination, SAH!!!'

Private Grubb – 67891234 – who was an old hand at this – remained painfully at attention – perhaps wincing slightly at the force of the RSM's voice in his right ear – and informed the CO that no, he had nothing to say in his own defence.

He was reminded that his offence fell under the section of the Army Act connected with 'conduct to the prejudice of good order and military discipline', and was awarded so many days' fatigues, so many days in the Guardhouse, or so many days' stoppage of pay.

'Yes, sir. Thank you, sir.'

'67891234 Private Grubb – Salute! Aybooouut – TURN! LEF' – RIGH' – LEF' – RIGH' – LEF' – RIGH' – ' until he was out of the office, where he was handed over to the wooden-faced Lance-Corporals of the Provost Guard in their white belts and bandoliers, and marched off to the Guardroom.

The second occasion would be at the instigation of the soldier himself. Never let it be supposed that the ordinary soldier did not have access to his Commanding Officer on any matter of legitimate concern to him. The matter which normally concerned most soldiers was leave, so many a hopeful Regular ran the gauntlet of the RSM in order to beg, plead, cajole, or appeal to the better nature of anyone who happened to be listening, so that he could go on compassionate leave to visit a dying mother – a dying mother who, according to Orderly Room records already lying in the CO's desk, had already 'died' four times. Repeated failure to convince, and repeated punishment, did not dim the optimism of these dutiful sons.

Finally, there was the occasion when Depot personnel were called before the CO to receive public praise for some recent exhibition of soldierly skill or virtue.

Whatever the agenda – condemnation, commiseration, or congratulation – no soldier was permitted to come near the Commanding Officer unless he was wearing his best uniform and best boots, with every crease, button, strap, and brass in a state of perfection normally associated with the Almighty. Indeed the most dreaded part of the whole procedure was not the CO's sentence for indecently assaulting a local barmaid, or his acid comments on the biological rarity of a man with four mothers (when the RSM was pretty sure he had never had any – not married, anyway), but the inspection beforehand.

No chance of the poor man hiding somewhere in the rear rank of a platoon. There were normally only a few on CO's Orders at any one time; the RSM had them all to himself. He could take his time. He could always find something if he were so disposed. It was not unknown for a harmless private presenting himself for official congratulation on passing a proficiency test to be promptly slapped on a charge for being improperly dressed and being marched straight in for summary sentence.

'Do you have anything to say in your defence. . . . '

We prepared ourselves with a will nevertheless. It was worth the sweat of the RSM's inspection to be told about our postings to Officer Cadet School. Even if we were put on a charge, it would break the monotony.

'Ten private soldiers – QUICK MARCH! LEF' – RIGH' – LEF' – RIGH'. . . .'

The CO leaned earnestly forward, and clasped his hands.

'We're going to put you chaps to some useful work while you're here. We're going to attach you to the training platoons when they go on the range. You are to assist the platoon sergeants with the instruction and coaching of individual recruits while actually on the firing point. You will be known as Firing Point Assistants.'

It didn't seem worth observing that this would occupy about one day a week, if that. But more was to come.

'To facilitate this, I am going to promote you all to Lance-Corporal – acting, unpaid, of course – until your postings come through.'

He unclasped his hands, and clasped them again. He adopted the manner of a monarch conferring a dukedom. 'I want you to realise the importance of your new rank. You have a new responsibility which will stop you from behaving as you have up to now. You have a new dignity to maintain, a new standard and a new example to set. From now on I want you to make your friends among the lance-corporals and the corporals. Congratulations, and good luck.'

'Ten lance-corporals – Salute! LEEEFF – TURN! QUICK MARCH! LEF' – RIGH' – LEF' – RIGH' – LEF ' – RIGH'. . . . '

On the way back to the barrack room, John Sly sidled up to Jack Gatewood.

'I say, Corporal Gatewood.'

Jack turned to him very seriously.

'What is it, Corporal Sly?'

John twiddled his beret nervously in his hands.

'I've got to make my friends among the corporals now, not with those nasty privates. Will you be friends with me, please?'

* * * * * *

I don't think we were much use to the recruits on the firing range. It meant that, instead of having people muttering in one ear while they fumbled with unfamiliar knobs and springs, it meant that they now had them muttering in two – the sergeants on one side and us on the other.

The rest of the time, in between coal to the Married Families and cookhouse baking tins and quarter-ton trucks in the Orderly Room – and the weekly pay parade – we did nothing I can remember except play cards. One of our number taught us the basics of bridge. We became near-devotees.

Then the CO had another go.

We were summoned to a 'talk'. Well, a 'chat', actually. No parade, no RSM, no CO's Orders. What on earth could it be? We looked at each other; it *had* to be our postings this time. It had to be.

We received the full treatment – take off your berets – sit down – smoke if you wish. Good God! Was it bad news? Was he trying to tell us that we were *not* going to get our postings?

No. Nothing like that at all.

'We've called you chaps here to talk about your future with us. The fact is – while you're waiting for your posting – we're finding it difficult to keep you properly occupied. To be perfectly honest – ' a modest shrug ' – we don't know what to do with you. I was wondering whether any of you had any ideas. You know – what you would like to – what we could do with you – do with you.'

There was a long, long pause. We simply dared not look at each other, because the expressions on our faces would all have been the same. It was the classic 'emperor's-new-clothes' situation. The point was, who was going to say it? If anybody.

I can claim here, modestly or otherwise, a modicum of merit for being willing, or foolish enough, to grasp the nettle.

My reasoning went like this: we had been waiting so long for our Officer Cadet School postings that the prospect of officer training was fading into the mists of near-impossibility. The Army is like that. It surrounds you so completely that the present is all that matters – the past has ceased to exist, and the future is a limbo of rumour and gloomy prognostication. Our postings would never come. I'm told that prisoners in wartime camps often felt like this about the end of the War; it would never come.

So, if I were to jeopardise it with what I was about to say – you know, insubordination, conduct to the prejudice of good order and military discipline, CO's Orders, LEF'- RIGH' – LEF' – RIGH' , sanitary orderly for the next twenty months – well, I wasn't losing very much when all was said and done.

And anything – anything – seemed preferable to the blank boredom to which we were currently being subjected.

In short, what did I have to lose? And what might we all gain?

I cleared my throat.

'Well, sir, you could always send us on leave until our postings are due.'

And he did.

THE END